TEN CENTURIES OF SPANISH POETRY

Ten Centuries of SPANISH POETRY

AN ANTHOLOGY IN ENGLISH VERSE
WITH ORIGINAL TEXTS

From the XIth Century to the Generation of 1898

EDITED BY
Eleanor L. Turnbull

WITH INTRODUCTIONS BY
Pedro Salinas

BALTIMORE: THE JOHNS HOPKINS PRESS

Copyright 1955 by The Johns Hopkins Press, Baltimore, Maryland 21218
Printed in the U. S. A.
Library of Congress Catalog Card Number 55-8424.

Originally Published, 1955
Second Printing, 1956
Third Printing, 1962
Fourth Printing, 1966

IN MEMORIAM

Pedro Salinas

FOREWORD

In the summer of 1951, Pedro Salinas, poet, critic and professor of Spanish Literature at The Johns Hopkins University, asked me to collaborate with him in editing an anthology of Spanish poetry in English translation, from its beginnings up to his generation. Poems of his own generation had already been represented in my volume *Contemporary Spanish Poetry, Selections from Ten Poets* (The Johns Hopkins Press, 1945).

Don Pedro made the selections of the poets who were to be included in the anthology, and he indicated the poems for which I was to choose the best translations that had already been made, or if none were available that adequately rendered the original text, I was to make the translations. He had expected to write an introduction to each poet, but unfortunately he was too ill to do this. His untimely death came in December, 1951. The introductions have been supplied by condensing extracts from his book *Reality and the Poet in Spanish Poetry* (English text by Edith F. Helman, The Johns Hopkins Press, 1940) and from his manuscripts; also from notes taken by students at his lecture courses.

To make known to the people of this country who do not read Spanish the fine poetry of his native land was a project very dear to the heart of Don Pedro. He lived to see only the beginning of the anthology, but since his death I have carried on the work as a memorial to him.

I have been very fortunate in having the wise counsel of Don Pedro's friend, the eminent scholar and critic, as well as poet, Don Dámaso Alonso, member of the Royal Academy and professor at the University of Madrid. He has also written several of the introductions.

It is hoped that this volume may fill a real need and contribute to the understanding and friendship between the two countries.

Eleanor L. Turnbull

ACKNOWLEDGMENTS

I wish to express my deep appreciation to those who have helped to make this anthology possible: to Edith H. Helman for permission to use extracts from her translation, *Reality and the Poet in Spanish Poetry* from the Spanish of Pedro Salinas, and to students who have lent me their notes on Don Pedro's lecture courses; to Ethel Standish Woods for criticizing my translation from the Spanish texts; to Juan Marichal for many useful suggestions; and to all those others to whom I have gone for advice.

And to the following editors and publishers for permission to use translations from books or magazines to which they hold the copyright:

The Hispanic Society of America, publisher of *Translations from Hispanic Poets*, for two translations by Jessie Read Wendell, two by Jean Rogers Longland, six by Alice Jane McVan, and one each by Ruth Matilda Anderson, Beatrice Gilman Proske, Anna Pursche, Elizabeth du Gué Trapier, Jean Willard Burnham, and Ada Marshall Johnson.

The Clarendon Press, Oxford, publisher of the book *Luis de León*, for five translations by Aubrey F. G. Bell, for the translations by Ida Farnell from her book *Spanish Prose and Poetry*, and for the translation "King Don Sancho" by William J. Entwistle from his *European Balladry*.

Basil Blackwell, Publisher, Oxford, for Aubrey F. G. Bell's translation of Gil Vicente's poem "Flerida and Don Duardos."

The Macmillan Company, New York, publisher of *Poems* by John Masefield, for his translation of a sonnet by Quevedo.

The Society of Authors, London, for overseas permission to reprint the same sonnet.

The Newman Press, Westminister, publisher of the *Complete Works of St. John of the Cross*, for four translations by E. Allison Peers.

Mr. Donald D. Walsh, editor of *Hispania*, for two translations of Gustavo Adolfo Bécquer: Rima XI by Muna Lee and Rima LIII by Mrs. W. S. Hendrix.

The Editor of *Poet Lore* for two translations of Bécquer's Rimas: nos. XII and LII by Ina D. Singleton.

And to the following translators for permission to use their translations:

R. Selden Rose for translations (by him and Leonard Bacon) of the *Cantar de mio Cid*.

Edward Meryon Wilson for his translations of *Las Soledades* by Góngora.

Gerald Brenan for his translation of " Habla la muerte " by Calderón de la Barca.

Caroline B. Bourland and James Cleugh each for translation of a sonnet by Garcilaso, and Roy Campbell for a sonnet by Quevedo.

John Dos Passos and Philip Warnock Silver, each for translation of a poem by Antonio Machado.

Elisha K. Kane for translation of a poem by Juan Ruiz.

The translations by Henry W. Longfellow, Lord Byron, John Bowring, Felicia D. Hemans and John Gibson Lockhart are taken from *Poets and Poetry of Europe* edited by Longfellow.

Translations by Jeremiah H. Wiffen are taken from his book, *Garcilaso de la Vega*.

The translations by James Young Gibson are from his book, *The Cid Ballads and Other Poems and Translations*.

The translations by Richard C. Trench are from his book, *Calderón, his Life and Times*.

The translations by George Ticknor are from his *History of Spanish Literature*.

E. L. T.

CONTENTS

PRIMITIVE EPOCH

XVth CENTURY

RENAISSANCE

xi

xii

xiii

NEO-CLASSICISM

ROMANTICISM

GENERATION OF 1898

Primitive Epoch

Mozarabic Songs

Until a very few years ago poetry and with it all Spanish literature, began in the xiith century with the *Cantar de mio Cid*. And European lyric poetry began at the very end of the xith century with Guillaume de Poitiers, born in 1071.

Very recent discoveries, since 1948, have come to enlighten us, and now we know that the earliest works of Spanish literature are some very simple little songs of popular type in the Spanish dialect spoken by Christians under Arabic rule. Among these Christians, called Mozarabs, these little songs were sung from at least the middle of the xith century, and probably earlier, through the xiith century; they are therefore, without any doubt, the earliest lyric poetry of European countries preserved today.

The preservation of these songs was made possible because of the fact that three races, Spaniards, Moors and Jews, were living together on the

2

XIth CENTURY

Iberian peninsula. The Arabs of Spain wrote some lyric poems in Arabic called *Muwashshahas*, the last stanza of which, called *jarcha*, had to be in a vulgar tongue; the Jews of Spain, imitating the Arabs, also wrote *Muwashshahas*. The coincidence that the cultured Arabic and Hebrew poets who wrote these poems used the Spanish language for the last stanza of these little songs, was the wonderful fact that made the preservation of these recently discovered songs possible: the Arab or Hebrew poems have served as flasks of alcohol that have kept for us, what up to now are the most ancient evidence of European lyric poetry.

These beautiful little songs, in which now and then a Hebrew or Arabic word is like a relic of the life in common of the three races, are very simple and moving. They are sung by love-sick maidens, and have the passionate intensity that often can only be expressed by means of the greatest simplicity.

D. A.

JARCHAS

1

Vayse, meu corachón de mib,
¿ya, Rab,* si se me tornarád?
¡Tan mal meu dolor li-l-habib!
Enfermo yed, ¿cuándo sanrad?

2

¿Qué faré, mamma?
Meu-l-habib est' ad yana.

3

¿Qué farayu o qué serád de mibi?
Habibi,*
non te tolgas de mibi.

4

Venid la Pasca, e yo aún sin elu.
Lazrando meu corachón por elu.

5

Tant' amáre, tant' amáre,
habib, tant' amáre?
enfermaron uelios gaios,
e dolen tan male.

* *Rab,* Hebrew word meaning Lord. *Habibi,* an Arabic word meaning
beloved. There are some doubts about two words in the third song, but the
general meaning is clear.

MOZARABIC SONGS

My heart, my heart goes from me, Lord,   1
will it ever come back to me?
So great my grief for my beloved!
He is ill, when will he be well?

E. L. T.

What shall I do, my mother?   2
My beloved is at the door!

E. L. T.

What shall I do, what will become of me?   3
Beloved,
do not depart from me.

E. L. T.

Easter is coming, and I without him!   4
My heart is cruelly grieving for him.

E. L. T.

So much loving, so much loving,   5
dear one, so much loving,
eyes that once were gay are saddened,
and cruelly aching.

E. L. T.

The Lay of the Cid

The Mozarabic songs (see page 2) were written not in Castilian, but in a Spanish dialect spoken by the Christians who were under the Moorish rule in the south of the peninsula. The first Castilian literary work is the *Cantar de mio Cid*, whose author is unknown. That first work seemed to give Castilian medieval literature its character. For three centuries the most important poetic production in Spain is narrative poetry in its various forms, and this heritage has left its impress on all Spanish literature. The first poets do not interpret, ask questions, idealize, but they simply relate the historical realities closest to them. Their subject matter is drawn from historical feats, as is the case in a large part of medieval poetry. Everywhere as in Spain, medieval poetry is heroic poetry. But what is essentially distinctive of Spanish heroic poetry is its agreement with history. Spain's national hero, Rodrigo Diaz de Vivar,*

---

* Rodrigo Diaz de Vivar was born about 1030 and died in 1099. The *Cantar de mio Cid* was written during the XII century. The first page of the manuscript is lacking. This lack has been supplied from page 8 of the Chronicles of Twenty Kings (Crónica de Veinte Reyes). " King Alfonso sent the Cid to collect the tribute money from the Moorish king of Seville. The latter is

XIIth CENTURY

the Cid, is a man of flesh and bone, whose deeds are known with relative historical exactness. The poem, founded on the existence of a real man, is, as it were, a poetic biography. The Cid, unlike other heroes of fiction or legend, has no mistress, no lady of his thoughts to whom to dedicate his sword. He is married and has two daughters. A group of faithful warriors serves him on his heroic exploits. The poem recounts the main part of the Castilian hero's life. The Cid was sent into exile by the king of Castile as a result of the calumny and slander of his enemies. The poem begins when the warrior leaves his home, Vivar, with a handful of men and takes the road to Burgos.

Poetry and reality are the merit of the poem, which is primitive on account of its theme, its epoch and enterprise, but eternal and of the present time, as Spanish today as it is Castilian of the xiith century.

P. S.

attacked by the Castilian count, García Ordóñez. The Cid, protecting the vassal of the king of Castile, overcomes García Ordóñez at Cabra, and captures him ignominiously. The Cid returns to Castile with the tribute money, but his enemies prejudice the king against him and he is exiled." Here begins our first selection, which is also the beginning of the mutilated poem.–Ed.

CANTAR DE MIO CID

6   *Destierro del Cid*

De los sos ojos   tan fuertemientre llorando,
tornava la cabeça   e estávalos catando.
Vío puertas abiertas   e uços sin cañados,
alcándaras vázias   sin pielles e sin mantos
e sin falcones   e sin adtores mudados.
Sospiró mio Çid,   ca mucho avié grandes cuidados.
Fabló mio Çid   bien e tan mesurado:
" ¡grado a ti señor padre,   que estás en alto!
" Esto me an buolto   mios enemigos malos."

Allí pienssan de aguijar,   allí sueltan las riendas.
A la exida de Bivar   ovieron la corneja diestra,
e entrando a Burgos   oviéronla siniestra.
Meçió mio Çid los ombros   y engrameó la tiesta:
" albricia, Álvar Fáñez,   ca echados somos de tierra!
" mas a grand ondra   tornaremos a Castiella."

Mio Çid Roy Díaz,   por Burgos entróve,
en sue conpaña   sessaenta pendones;
exien lo veer   mugieres e varones,
burgeses e burgesas,   por las finiestras sone,
plorando de los ojos,   tanto avien el dolore.
De las sus bocas   todos dizían una razóne:
" Dios, qué buen vassallo,   si oviesse buen señore! "

Conbidar le ien de grado,   mas ninguno non osava:
el rey don Alfonsso   tanto avie le grand saña.
Antes de la noche   en Burgos dél entró su carta,
con grand recabdo   e fuertemientre seellada:
que a mio Çid Roy Díaz   que nadi nol diessen posada,
e aquel que gela diesse   sopiesse vera palabra
que perderie los averes   e más los ojos de la cara,
e aun demás   los cuerpos e las almas.
Grande duelo avien   las yentes cristianas;
ascóndense de mio Çid   ca nol osan dezir nada.

8

THE LAY OF THE CID

The Banishment of the Cid 6

He turned and looked upon them, and he wept very sore
As he saw the yawning gateway and the hasps wrenched off
      the door,
And the pegs whereon no mantle nor coat of vair there hung.
There perched no moulting goshawk, and there no falcon swung.
My lord the Cid sighed deeply such grief was in his heart
And he spake well and wisely:
              "Oh Thou, in Heaven that art
Our Father and our Master, now I give thanks to Thee.
Of their wickedness my foemen have done this thing to me."

Then they shook out the bridle rein further to ride afar.
They had the crow on their right hand as they issued from Bivar;
And as they entered Burgos upon their left it sped.
And the Cid shrugged his shoulders, and the Cid shook his head:
"Good tidings Alvar Fañez! We are banished from our weal,
But on a day with honor shall we come unto Castile."

Roy Diaz entered Burgos with sixty pennons strong,
And forth to look upon him did the men and women throng,
And with their wives the townsmen at the windows stood
      hard by,
And they wept in lamentation, their grief was risen so high.
As with one mouth, together they spake with one accord:
"God, what a noble vassal, an he had a worthy lord."

Fain had they made him welcome, but none dared to do
      the thing
For fear of Don Alfonso, and the fury of the King.
His mandate unto Burgos came ere the evening fell.
With utmost care they brought it, and it was sealéd well:
'That no man to Roy Diaz give shelter now, take heed.
And if one give him shelter, let him know in very deed
He shall lose his whole possession, nay! the eyes within his head
Nor shall his soul and body be found in better stead.'
Great sorrow had the Christians, and from his face they hid.
Was none dared aught to utter unto my lord the Cid.

El Campeador   adeliñó a su posada;
así commo llegó a la puorta,   fallóla bien çerrada,
por miedo del rey Alfons,   que assí la pararan:
que si non la quebrantás,   que non gela abriessen por nada.
Los de mio Çid,   a altas vozes llaman,
los de dentro   non les querién tornar palabra.
Aguijó mio Çid   a la puerta se llegava,
sacó el pie del estribera,   una ferídal dava;
non se abre la puerta,   ca bien era çerrada.
   Una niña de nuef años   a ojo se parava:
"Ya Campeador,   en buena çinxiestes espada!
"El rey lo ha vedado,   anoch dél entró su carta,
"con grant recabdo   e fuertemientre seellada.
"Non vos osariemos   abrir nin coger por nada;
"si non, perderiemos   los averes e las casas,
"e aun demás   los ojos de las caras.
"Çid, en el nuestro mal   vos non ganades nada;
"mas el Criador vos vala   con todas sus vertudes santas."
Esto la niña dixo   e tornós pora su casa.
Ya lo vede el Çid   que del rey non avie gracia.

. . .

7
Oración del Cid

   Estas palabras dichas,   la tienda es cogida.
Mio Çid e sus conpañas,   cavalgan tan aína.
La cara del cavallo   tornó a Santa María,
alçó su mano diestra,   la cara se santigua:
"A tí lo gradesco, Dios,   que çielo e tierra guías;
"válanme tus vertudes,   gloriosa santa María!
"D'aquí quito Castiella,   pues que el rey he en ira;
"non sé si entraré y más   en todos los mios días.
"Vuestra vertud me vala,   Gloriosa, en mi exida
"e me ayude e me acorra   de noch e de día!
Si vos assí lo fiziéredes   e la ventura me fore complida
"mando al vuestro altar   buenas donas e ricas;
"esto he yo en debdo   que faga i cantar mill missas."

Then the Campeador departed unto his lodging straight.
But when he was come thither, they had locked and barred the
      gate.
In their fear of King Alfonso had they done even so.
An the Cid forced not his entrance, neither for weal nor woe
Durst they open it unto him. Loudly his men did call.
Nothing thereto in answer said the folk within the hall.
My lord the Cid spurred onward, to the doorway did he go.
He drew his foot from the stirrup, he smote the door one blow.
Yet the door would not open, for they had barred it fast.
But a maiden of nine summers came unto him at last:
"Campeador in happy hour thou girdest on the sword.
'Tis the King's will. Yestereven came the mandate of our lord.
With utmost care they brought it, and it was sealed with care:
None to ope to you or greet you for any cause shall dare.
And if we do, we forfeit houses and lands instead.
Nay we shall lose moreover, the eyes within the head.
And, Cid, with our misfortune, naught whatever dost thou gain.
But may God with all his power support thee in thy pain."
So spake the child and turned away. Unto her home went she.
That he lacked the King's favor now well the Cid might see.

· · · ·

The Cid's Prayer

They spake these words and straightway the tent upgathered
      then,
My lord the Cid rode swiftly with all his host of men.
And forth unto Saint Mary's the horse's head turned he,
And with his right hand crossed himself:
                        "God, I give thanks to Thee
Heaven and Earth that rulest. And thy favor be my weal
Holy Saint Mary, for forthright must I now quit Castile.
For I look on the King with anger, and I know not if once more
I shall dwell there in my life-days. But may thy grace watch o'er
My parting, Blessed Virgin, and guard me night and day.
If thou do so and good fortune come once more in my way,
I will offer rich oblations at thine altar, and I swear
Most solemnly that I will chant a thousand masses there."

8   *Ximena y sus hijas llegan ante el desterrado*

Afevos doña Ximena   con sus fijas do va llegando;
señas dueñas las traen   e adúzenlas en los braços.
Ant el Campeador doña Ximena   fincó los inojos amos.
Llorava de los ojos,   quísol besar las manos:
"Merçed, Canpeador,   en ora buena fostes nado!
"Por malos mestureros   de tierra sodes echado.

"Merçed, ya Çid,   barba tan complida!
"Fem ante vos   yo e vuestra ffijas:
"iffantes son   e de días chicas,
"con aquestas mis dueñas   de quien so yo servida.
"Yo lo veo   que estades vos en ida
"e nos de vos   partir nos hemos en vida.
"Dadnos consejo   por amor de santa María!"
Enclinó las manos   la barba vellida,
a las sues fijas   en braço las prendía,
llególas al coraçón   ca mucho las quería.
Llora de los ojos,   tan fuerte mientre sospira:
"Ya doña Ximena,   la mi mugier tan complida,
"commo a la mie alma   yo tanto vos quería.
"Ya lo veedes   que partir nos emos en vida,
"yo iré y vos   fincaredes remanida.
Plega a Dios   e a santa María,
"que aun con mis manos   case estas mis fijas,
"e quede ventura   y algunos días vida,
"e vos, mugier ondrada,   de mí seades servida!"

9   *La despedida*

La oraçión fecha,   la missa acabada la an,
salieron de la eglesia,   ya quieren cavalgar.
El Çid a doña Ximena   ívala abraçar;
doña Ximena al Çid   la manol va besar,
llorando de los ojos,   que non sabe qué se far.

His Wife and Daughters Come to the Exiled One   8

And lo! the Dame Xiména came with her daughters twain.
Each had her dame-in-waiting who the little maiden bore.
And Dame Xiména bent the knee before the Campeador.
And fain she was to kiss his hand, and, oh, she wept forlorn!
    "A boon! A boon! my Campeador. In good hour wast thou
            born.
And because of wicked slanderers art thou banished from
            the land.

    "Oh Campeador fair-bearded a favor at thy hand!
Behold I kneel before thee, and thy daughters are here with me,
That have seen of days not many, for children yet they be,
And these who are my ladies to serve my need that know.
Now well do I behold it, thou art about to go.
Now from thee our lives a season must sunder and remove,
But unto us give succor for sweet Saint Mary's love."
    The Cid the nobly-bearded, reached down unto the twain,
And in his arms his daughters has lifted up again,
And to his heart he pressed them, so great his love was grown,
And his tears fell fast and bitter, and sorely did he moan:
"Xiména as mine own spirit I loved thee, gentle wife;
But o'er well dost thou behold it, we must sunder in our life.
I must flee and thou behind me here in the land must stay.
Please God and sweet Saint Mary that yet upon a day
I shall give my girls in marriage with mine own hand rich
            and well,
And thereafter in good fortune be suffered yet to dwell,
May they grant me, wife, much honored, to serve thee then
            once more."

The Farewell   9

And now the prayer is over and the mass in its due course.
From church they came, and already were about to get to horse.
And the Cid clasped Xiména, but she, his hand she kissed.
Sore wept the Dame, in no way the deed to do she wist.
He turned unto his daughters and he looked upon the two:

E él a las niñas   tornólas a catar:
"a Dios vos acomiendo   e al Padre spirital;
"agora nos partimos,   Dios sabe el ajuntar."
Llorando de los ojos,   que non vidiestes atal,
assís parten unos d'otros   commo la uña de la carne.
   Myo Çid con los sos vassallos   penssó de cavalgar,
a todos esperando,   la cabeça tornanda va,
A tan grand sabor   fabló Minaya Álbar Fáñez:
"Çid, do son vuestros esfuerços?   en buena nasquiestes
          de madre:
"pensemos de ir nuestra vía,   esto sea de vagar.
"Aun todos estos duelos   en gozo se tornarán;
"Dios que nos dió las almas,   consejo nos dará."

                 .   .   .

10   *Amanecer en el pueblo*

Ya crieban los albores   e vinie la mañana,
ixie el sol,   Dios, qué fermoso apuntava!
En Castejón   todos se levantavan,
abren las puertas,   de fuera salto davan,
por ver sus lavores   e todas sus heredanças.
Todos son exidos,   las puertas abiertas an dexadas
con pocas de gentes   que en Castejón fincaran.

                 .   .   .

11   *Llegada de la familia a Valencia*

En cabo del cosso   mio Çid descavalgava,
adeliñó a su mugier   e a sues fijas amas;
quando lo vió doña Ximena,   a piedes se le echava:
"Merçed, Campeador,   en buen ora çinxiestes espada!
"Sacada me avedes   de muchas vergüenças malas;
"afeme aquí, señor,   yo e vuestras fijas amas,
"con Dios e convusco   buenas son e criadas."

"To the Spiritual Father, have I commended you.
We must depart. God knoweth when we shall meet again."
Weeping most sore—for never hast thou beheld such pain—
As the nail from the flesh parteth, from each other did they part.
   And the Cid with all his vassals disposed himself to start,
And as he waited for them anew he turned his head,
Minaya Alvar Fañez then in good season said:
   "Cid! Where is now thy courage? Upon a happy day
Wast thou born. Let us bethink us of the road and haste away.
A truce to this. Rejoicing out of these griefs shall grow.
The God who gave us spirits shall give us aid also."

Dawn in the Town   10

   And now the dawn was breaking and morning coming on,
And the sun rising. Very God! how beautifully it shone!
All men arose in Castejón, and wide they threw the gates;
And forth they went to oversee their farmlands and estates.
All were gone forth, and the gates stand open as they were
         thrown.
And but a little remnant were left in Castejón.

Arrival of the Family at Valencia   11

When that career was ended, from the steed the Cid got down,
And hastened forth his lady and daughters twain to greet.
When Dame Xiména saw him she cast her at his feet:
"Brand thou girdest in good season. Thy favor, Campeador!
Thou hast brought me forth from insults that were exceeding
         sore.
Look on me, lord! Look also on my daughters as on me.
By God's help and thine they are noble, and gently reared
         they be."

A la madre e a las fijas   bien las abraçava,
del gozo que avién   de los sos ojos lloravan.
   Todas las sus mesnadas   en grant deleyt estavan,
armas teníen   e tablados crebantavan.
Oíd lo que dixo   el que buena çinxo espada:
"vos doña Ximena,   querida mugier e ondrada,
"e amas mis fijas   mio coraçón e mi alma,
"entrad conmigo   en Valençia la casa,
"en esta heredad   que vos yo he ganada."
Madre e fijas   las manos le besavan.
A tan grand ondra   ellas a Valençia entravan.

   Adeliño mio Çid   con ellas al alcáçer,
allá las subie   en el más alto logar.
Ojos vellidos   catan a todas partes,
miran Valençia   cómmo yaze la çibdad,
e del otra parte   a ojo han el mar,
miran la huerta,   espessa es e grand,
e todas las otras cosas   que eran de solaz;
alçan las manos   pora Dios rogar,
desta ganançia   cómmo es buena e grand.

.   .   .

And the Cid straightway embraced them, mother and daughters
        twain.
Such joy they had that from their eyes the tears began to rain.
His men rejoiced. The quintains, they pierced them with spear,
He who girt sword in a good time, hark what he said and hear.
  "Oh thou my Dame Xiména, beloved and honored wife,
And ye two both my daughters that are my heart and life,
To the city of Valencia now do ye enter in,
The fair estate that for you it was my lot to win."
  His hands they have kissed straightway, the daughters and
        their dame.
So with exceeding honor to Valencia they came.

  With them the lord Cid hastened to the citadel apace,
He has ta'en the ladies straightway up to the highest place.
And forth in all directions they turn their lovely eyes,
And they behold Valencia and how the city lies,
And in another quarter they might perceive the sea.
They look on fertile meadows close sown and great that be,
And on all things whatever that were of fair estate.
God they praised with hands uplifted for that good prize and
        great.

        .   .   .

R. Selden Rose
and
Leonard Bacon

Gonzalo de Berceo

It is well-known that in the Middle Ages monasteries, besides performing their strictly religious function, acted as centres of culture and storehouses of learning, and were somewhat like student boarding houses where the tradition of intellectual work was preserved. The intellectuals, educated in the monasteries, and almost always living in them, possessed a high degree of culture. Their language was the clerical Latin. Gonzalo de Berceo was one of these learned scholars of the convent. Born at the end of the xiith century, he received all his education at the Monastery of San Millan de la Cogolla, to which he belonged, if not as a monk, as a secular cleric.

Berceo read many lives of saints and stories of miracles in the Latin books of the monastery, but around him were people who neither spoke Latin nor knew how to read or write; these edifying and wonderful stories were closed to them. He had the happy idea of writing in the new Castilian language, just coming into literary usage, those stories of saints and miracles. His books are popularized versions in which the scholar wishes to give to the illiterate, on hearing these stories in the new Castilian language, the same spiritual pleasure that he experienced on reading them in Latin. Therefore Berceo is not original, if we consider

END OF XIIth
TO MIDDLE OF XIIIth CENTURY

originality consists in the invention of subjects and plots. But could any-
thing be more original than introducing poetic expression into the Cas-
tilian language, daring to make verses, and to raise humble words, with
which the good folk speak, to the dignity of a literary language?

Berceo wrote nine poems; three of them tell of the lives of saints,
Vida de Santo Domingo de Silos, Vida de San Millan de la Cogolla,
and *Vida de Santa Oria,* each of them based on a Latin book. *Los
Milagros de Nuestra Señora,* one of the many literary works that was
scattered over Europe in the form of poetic worship of Mary, is a com-
pilation of tales of miraculous happenings caused by the intervention of
the Virgin.

Berceo used a new poetic form (*la cuaderna vía*), stanzas of four
lines having the same rhyme, each line of fourteen syllables, the Alex-
andrine. In his time this form was a great innovation. Berceo, with the
ingenuous courage of his spirit, was breaking into that uncultivated field
of the Spanish language like a farmer who opens ground with his plow-
share, without dreaming of the future seeding, while he traces in the
virgin soil the line of the furrow or of the new poetic form.

P. S.

INTRODUCCIÓN

de los *Milagros de Nuestro Señora*

Yo maestro Gonçalvo de Verçeo nomnado
Iendo en romería caeçí en un prado
Verde e bien sençido, de flores bien poblado,
Logar cobdiçiaduero pora omne cansado.

Daban olor sovejo las flores bien olientes,
Refrescavan en omne las caras e las mientes,
Manavan cada canto fuentes claras corrientes,
En verano bien frías, en ivierno calientes.

Avie hi grand abondo de buenas arboledas,
Milgranos e figueras, peros e manzanedas,
E muchas otras fructas de diversas monedas;
Mas non avie ningunas podridas ni azedas.

La verdura del prado, la olor de las flores,
Las sombras de los árbores de temprados sabores
Refrescáronme todo, e perdí los sudores;
Podrie vevir el omne con aquellos olores.

Nunqua trobé en sieglo logar tan deleitoso,
Nin sombra tan temprada, ni olor tan sabroso
Descargué mi ropiella por iazer más viçioso,
Póseme a la sombra de un árbor fermoso.

Yaziendo a la sombra perdí todos cuidados,
Odí sonos de aves dulces e modulados:
Nunqua udieron omnes órganos más temprados,
Nin que formar pudiessen sones más acordados.

THE PRAISE OF SPRING   **12**

from *The Miracles of our Lady*

I, Gonzalo de Berceo, in the gentle summertide,
Wending upon a pilgrimage, came to a meadow's side;
All green was it and beautiful, with flowers far and wide.—
A pleasant spot, I ween, wherein the traveller might abide.

Flowers with the sweetest odors filled all the sunny air,
And not alone refreshed the sense, but stole the mind from care;
On every side a fountain gushed, whose waters pure and fair,
Ice-cold beneath the summer sun, but warm in winter were.

There on the thick and shadowy trees, amid the foliage green,
Were the fig and the pomegranate, the pear and apple seen;
And other fruits of various kinds, the tufted leaves between,
None were unpleasant to the taste and none decayed, I ween.

The verdure of the meadow green, the odor of the flowers.
The grateful shadows of the trees, tempered with fragrant showers,
Refreshed me in the burning heat of the sultry noontide hours;
Oh, one might live upon the balm and fragrance of those bowers!

Ne'er had I found on earth a spot that had such power to please.
Such shadows from the summer sun, such odors on the breeze;
I threw my mantle on the ground, that I might rest at ease,
And stretched upon the greensward lay in the shadow of the trees.

There soft reclining in the shade, all cares beside me flung,
I heard the soft and mellow notes that through the woodland rung;
Ear never listened to a strain, for instrument or tongue,
So mellow and harmonious as the songs above me sung.

Henry W. Longfellow

13   *SANT MIGAEL DE LA TUNBA*

de los *Milagros de Nuestra Señora*

Sant Migael de la Tunba es un grand monesterio,
El mar lo cerca todo, elli iaze en medio:
El logar perigloso, do sufren grand lazerio
Los monges que hi viven en essi cimiterio.

En esti monesterio que avemos nomnado,
Avie de buenos monges buen convento provado,
Altar de la Gloriosa rico e mui onrrado,
En él rica imagen de precio mui granado,

Estava la imagen en su trono posada,
So fijo en sus brazos, cosa es costumnada
Los reis redor ella, sedie bien compannada,
Como rica reina de Dios santificada.

.   .   .

Colgava delant ella un buen aventadero,
En el seglar lenguage dízenli moscadero:
De alas de pavones lo fizo el obrero,
Luzie como estrellas semejant de luzero.

Cadió rayo del çielo por los graves peccados,
Ençendió la eglesia de todos quatro cabos,
Quemó todos los libros e los pannos sagrados,
Por pocco que los monges que non foron quemados.

.   .   .

Maguer que fué el fuego tan fuert e tan quemant,
Nin plegó a la duenna, nin plegó al ifant,
Nin plegó al flabello que colgava delant,
Nin li fizo de danno un dinero pesant.

Nin ardió la imagen, nin ardió el flabello,
Nin prisieron de danno quanto val un cabello,
Solamiente el fumo non se llegó a ello,
Nin nuçió mas que nuzo io al obispo don Tello.

SAN MIGUEL DE LA TUMBA 13

from *The Miracles of our Lady*

San Miguel de la Tumba is a convent vast and wide;
The sea encircles it around, and groans on every side;
It is a wild and dangerous place, and many woes betide
The monks that in that burial place in penitence abide.

Within those dark monastic walls amid the ocean flood,
Of pious fasting monks there dwelt a holy brotherhood;
To the Madonna's glory there an altar high was placed,
And a rich and costly image the sacred altar graced.

Exalted high upon a throne, the Virgin Mother smiled,
And as the custom is, she held within her arms the Child;
The kings and wisemen of the East were kneeling by her side;
Attended was she like a queen whom God had sanctified.

.   .   .

Descending low before her face a screen of feathers hung,—
A *moscador* or fan for flies, 'tis called in vulgar tongue;
From the feathers of the peacock's wing 'twas fashioned bright
    and fair,
And glistened like the heavens above when all its stars are there.

It chanced that for the people's sins, fell lightning's blasting
    stroke;
Forth from all four sacred walls the flames consuming broke;
The sacred robes were all consumed, missal and holy book;
And hardly with their lives the monks their crumbling walls
    forsook.

.   .   .

But though the desolating flame raged fearfully and wild,
It did not reach the Virgin Queen, it did not reach the Child;
It did not reach the feathery screen before her face that shone,
Nor injured in a farthing's worth the image or the throne.

The image it did not consume, it did not burn the screen;
Even in the value of a hair they were not hurt, I ween;
Not even the smoke did reach them, nor injure more the shrine
Than the bishop, hight Don Tello, has been hurt by hand of mine.

Continens e contentum, fue todo astragado,
Tornó todo carbones, fo todo asolado:
Mas redor de la imagen quanto es un estado,
Non fizo mal el fuego, ca non era osado.

Esto tovieron todos por fiera maravella,
Que nin fumo nin fuego non se llegó a ella,
Que sedie el flabello más claro que estrella,
El ninno mui fermoso, fermosa la ponzella.

La Virgo benedicta reina general,
Como libró su toca de esti fuego tal,
Asín libra sus siervos del fuego perennal,
Liévalos a la gloria do nunqua vean mal.

14   *LA BATALLA DE SIMANCAS*

de la *Vida de San Millán*

Quando estaban en campo los reis, azes paradas,
Mezclaban las feridas, las lanzas abaxadas,
Temiense los christianos de las otras mesnadas,
Ca eran ellos poccos, e ellas muy granadas.

Mientre en esta dubda sedien las buenas yentes,
Asuso contral çielo fueron parando mientes:
Vieron dues personas fermosas e luçientes,
Mucho eran más blancas que las nieves reçientes.

Vienen en dos caballos plus blancos que cristal,
Armas quales non vió nunqua omne mortal.
El uno tenie croza, mitra pontifical,
El otro una cruz, omne non vió tal.

Continens et contentum,—all was in ruins laid;
A heap of smouldering embers that holy pile was made:
But where the sacred image sat, a fathom's length around,
The raging flame dared not approach the consecrated ground.

It was a wondrous miracle to those that thither came,
That the image of the Virgin was safe from smoke and flame,—
That brighter than the brightest star appeared the feathery screen,—
And seated there the Child still fair, and fair the Virgin Queen.

.   .   .

The Virgin Queen, the sanctified, who from an earthly flame
Preserved the robes that pious hands had hung around her frame,
Thus from an ever-burning fire her servants shall deliver,
And lead them to that high abode where the good are blessed
        forever.

Henry W. Longfellow

THE BATTLE OF SIMANCAS   14

from *The Life of San Millán*

And when the kings were in the field,—their squadrons in array,—
With lance in rest they onward pressed to mingle in the fray;
But soon upon the Christians fell a terror of their foes,—
These were a numerous army,—a little handful those.

And whilst the Christian people stood in this uncertainty,
Upward to heaven they turned their eyes, and fixed their thoughts
        on high;
And there two figures they beheld, all beautiful and bright,
Even than the pure new-fallen snow their garments were more
        white.

They rode upon two horses more white than crystal sheen,
And arms they bore such as before no mortal man had seen.
The one, he held a crozier,—a pontiff's mitre wore;
The other held a crucifix,—such man ne'er saw before.

Avien caras angélicas, çelestial figura.
Desçendien por el aer a una grant pressura,
Catando a los moros con turva catadura,
Espadas sobre mano, un signo de pavura.

Los christianos con esto foron más esforzados,
Fincaron los inojos en tierra apeados,
Ferien todos los pechos con punnos çerrados,
Prometiendo emienda a Dios de sus peccados.

Quando çerca de tierra fueron los caballeros,
Dieron entre los moros dando golpes çerteros
Fiçieron tal domage en los más delanteros,
Que plegó el espanto a los más postremeros.

A vuelta destos ambos que del çielo vinieron,
Aforzaron christianos, al ferir se metieron,
Juraban los moriellos por la ley que prisieron,
Que nunqua en sos días tal priesa non ovieron.

Caien a muy grant priessa los moros descreidos,
Los unos desmembrados, los otros desmedridos,
Repisos eran mucho que hi eran venidos,
Ca entendien del pleyto que serien mal exidos.

Cuntiólis otra cosa que ellos non sonnaban,
Essas saetas mismas que los moros tiraban,
Tornaban contra ellos, en ellos se fincaban
La fonta que fiçieron cara-ment la compraban.

.   .   .

El que tenie la mitra e la croza en mano,
Essi fué el apostol de Sant Juan ermano,
El que la cruz tenie e el capiello plano,
Esse fué Sant Millán el varón cogollano.

Their faces were angelical, celestial form had they,—
And downward through the fields of air they urged their rapid way;
They looked upon the Moorish host with fierce and angry look,
And in their hands with dire portent their naked sabres shook.

The Christian host beholding this, straightway take heart again;
They fall upon their bended knees, all resting on the plain,
And each one with his clenchéd fist to smite his breast begins,
And promises to God on high he will forsake his sins.

And when the heavenly knights drew near unto the battle
  ground,
They dashed among the Moors and dealt unerring blows around;
Such deadly havoc there they made the foremost ranks among,
A panic terror spread unto the hindmost of the throng.

Together with these two good knights, the champions of the sky,
The Christians rallied and began to smite full sore and high;
The Moors raised up their voices and by the Koran swore
That in their lives such deadly fray they ne'er had seen before.

Down went the misbelievers,—fast sped the bloody fight,—
Some ghastly and dismembered lay, and some half dead with
  fright;
Full sorely they repented that to the field they came,
For they saw that from the battle they should retreat with shame.

Another thing befell them,—they dreamed not of such woes,—
The very arrows that the Moors shot from their twanging bows
Turned back against them in their flight and wounded them
  full sore,
And every blow they dealt the foe was paid in drops of gore.

. . .

Now he that bore the crozier, and the papal crown had on,
Was the glorified Apostle, the brother of Saint John;
And he that held the crucifix, and wore the monkish hood
Was the holy San Millán of Cogolla's neighborhood.

Henry W. Longfellow

Juan Ruiz, Archpriest of Hita

We have very little biographical data on Juan Ruiz. He was an arch-priest in the town of Hita and it is thought that he was in prison towards the end of his life, by order of Cardinal Gil de Albornoz.

His work, preserved in three manuscripts, has always circulated under the name of *Libro de Buen Amor*, Book of Good Love, a name taken from the text itself. It is presented as a long poem written for the most part in *cuaderna vía* (see page 19), but it is in reality a collection of all the author had written in the course of his life. It may be said with some reason that the book is a whole literature in a nutshell, a microcosm of literary conceptions of the age. If any sentiment predominates in it, it is the sentiment of love. The title does not deceive us in qualifying the poem as erotic, for it is always just that, either directly or indirectly. At intervals, the author in the name of morals, which he represents as a priest, lashes at that lawless passion, but a little further on he relates how he gives himself up as a willing victim on its altar, simply because of his human state. Without doubt there is discussion, after the medieval fashion, for and against love, but the archpriest defends both sides.

c. 1283–c. 1350

Juan Ruiz's themes, for the most part, stem from that fund of Latin literature that in the Middle Ages was a treasury for all the countries of Western Europe. But what is original in Juan Ruiz is the only thing that is important: his interpretation of that life of which he was a part. The preceding ages had introduced the heroic spirit as the basis for earthly existence, as in the *Cid*, or aspiration for the heavenly world beyond, as exemplified in Berceo. Juan Ruiz passes from these spheres to a new conception in which life is neither brave nor contemplative, but simply to be enjoyed. He uses satire which, willy nilly, acts to undermine all the Castilian idealists. It is he that pushes to the footlights on the stage of the world the personage, until then hidden backstage, the mediocre individual with the usual quantity of virtues and vices. And precisely because he could communicate authentically through his own person the throbbing of that kind of life that unites us in a vast community of fellowbeings, as opposed to those lofty beings like the Cid or the Saint, is the reason why Juan Ruiz was the exceptional poet of our Middle Ages.

P. S.

15   *EL AMOR*

El amor faz sotil al omme que est rrudo,
ffázele fabrar fermoso al que antes es mudo,
al omme que es covarde fázelo muy atrevudo,
al perezoso faze ser presto e agudo.

Al mançebo mantiene mucho en mançebez
e al viejo faz perder mucho la vejez,
ffaze blanco e fermoso del negro como pez,
lo que non vale una nuez amor le da grand prez.

.   .   .

El bavieca, el torpe, el neçio, el poble
a su amiga bueno paresçe, e rrico onbre
más noble que los otros; por ende todo onbre
como un amor pierde luego otro cobre.

16   *DOÑA ENDRINA*

¡Ay Dios e quán fermosa viene doña Endrina por la plaça!
¡Qué talle, qué donaire, qué alto cuello de garça!
¡Qué cabellos, qué boquilla, qué color, qué buenandança!
Con saetas de amor fiere quando los sus ojos alça.

17   *CORAÇÓN QUEXOSO*

¡Ay coraçón quexoso! cosa desaguisada,
¿por qué matas el cuerpo do tienes tu morada?
¿por qué amas la dueña que non te preçia nada?
Coraçón, por tu culpa, bivirás vida penada.

.   .   .

IN PRAISE OF LOVE   15

Love to the foolish giveth wit by great and potent art,
Love to the dumb or slow of speech can eloquence impart,
Can make the craven, shrinking coward valiant and strong of heart,
Can by his power the sluggard spur out of his sleep to start.

Love to the young eternal youth can by his craft bestow,
The all-subduing might of eld can even overthrow;
Can make the face as swart as pitch full white and fair to grow,
And give to those not worth a doit full many a grace, I trow.

The dolt, the fool, the slow of wit, the poor man or the base
Unto his mistress seemeth rich in every goodly grace.
Then he that loseth lady fair should straightway set his face
Toward finding one that worthily may fill her vacant place.

Ida Farnell

LADY SLOE   16

Ah God, how lovely Lady Sloe looked walking through the square!
What swanlike neck and girlish waist, what grace beyond compare,
What little mouth, what color fresh, and what outshining hair,
Though mortally her beaming eyes shot missiles everywhere.

Elisha K. Kane

LAMENT OF A DESPISED LOVER   17

Say, lovelorn heart, that art condemned upon despair to feed,
Why slay the form wherein thou dwellst and make it pine and
      bleed?
Why serve a lady who of love taketh but little heed?
Alas, poor heart, thy fault, I trow, thou'lt rue in very deed!

¡Ay, ojos, los mis ojos! ¿por qué vos fustes poner
en dueña que non vos quiere nin catar, nin ver?
ojos, por vuestra vista vos quesistes perder,
penaredes, mis ojos, penar e amortesçer.

¡Ay, lengua sin ventura! ¿por qué queredes dezir,
por qué quieres fablar, por qué quieres departir
con dueña que te non quiere nin escuchar nin oír?
¡ay cuerpo tan penado, commo te vas a morir!

18   *ENDRINA Y TROTA-CONVENTOS*

"Amigo,"—diz la vieja,—"en la dueña lo veo
que vos quiere e vos ama e tiene de vos desseo;
quando de vos le fablo e a ella oteo,
todo se le demuda el color e el desseo.

Yo a las de vegadas mucho canssada callo;
ella me diz que fable e non quiera dexallo;
fago que non acuerdo, ella va començallo,
oye me dulçemente, muchas señales fallo.

En el mi cuello echa los sus braços entranbos,
ansí una grand pieça en uno nos estamos,
sienpre de vos dezimos, en ál nunca fablamos,
quando alguno viene otra rrazón mudamos.

Los labrios dela boca tienbranle un poquillo,
el color se le muda bermejo e amarillo,
el coraçón le falta ansí a menudillo,
apriétame mis dedos en sus manos quedillo."

Ye weeping eyes with beauty dimmed, unhappy was the day
When first toward a lady false ye let your glances stray.
Methinketh for such grievous fault ye will full dearly pay,
And tears will rob you of your light, and take your pride away.

Alas, thou hapless, foolish tongue, oh say, why wast thou fain
To speak with her, that ever held thy words in proud disdain?
From one thus reckless of thy woe what thoughtest thou to gain?
And thou, poor tortured body, thou art wasted with thy pain.

Ida Farnell

ENDRINA AND TROTA-CONVENTOS   18

Then spake the old dame cheerily: 'Right well I wot, perdie,
That she is all afire with love, that lady fair to see,
For when with eyes upon her face I' gin to speak of thee
I see the warm flush on her cheek, and her eyes right full of glee.

Weary of oft-told tales of thee, belike of speech I fail,
Then straight with soft, entreating words mine ears she will assail,
And when I plead forgetfulness will start herself the tale,
While with love-tokens on her face no coy denials avail.

Round me she flingeth both her arms, when pangs of love oppress,
And so in close embrace we bide with many a fond caress;
Erewhile of thee she speaketh, and must needs her love confess;
If others come, we change our talk that naught thereof they guess.

Full oft I see those ruddy lips a-trembling by my fay;
While suddenly the roses from her soft cheeks fade away;
Full oft, full oft her panting heart its burden doth betray;
And the pressure of her hand reveals Don Love's all-potent sway.'

Ida Farnell

19   *DÍA DE LA PASCUA*

Día era muy ssanto de la pascua mayor,
el sol era salido muy claro e de noble color;
los ommes e las aves e toda noble flor,
todos van rrescebir cantando al amor.

Rescíbenlo las aves, gayos e ruy señores,
calandrias, papagayos, mayores e menores,
dan cantos placenteros e dulces ssabores,
más alegría fazen los que son mas mejores.

Rrescíbenlo los árbores con rramos e con flores
de divessas maneras, de divessas collores,
rrescíbenlo ommes e dueñas con amores,
con muchos instrumentos salen los atanbores.

20   *DE LAS PROPIEDADES QUE LAS*
                   DUEÑAS CHICAS HAN

En pequeña girgonça yaze grand resplandor,
en açucar muy poco yaze mucho dulçor,
en la dueña pequeña yaze muy grand amor,
pocas palabras cunplen al buen entendedor.

Es pequeño el grano de la buena pemienta,
pero más que la nuez conorta e calienta,
así dueña pequeña, si todo amor consienta,
non hay plazer del mundo que en ella non sienta.

Como en chica rosa está mucha color,
e en oro muy poco grand preçio e grand valor,
como en poco bálsamo yaze grand buen olor,
ansí en dueña chica yaze muy grand sabor.

Como robí pequeño tiene mucha bondad,
color, virtud e preçio e noble claridad,
ansí dueña pequeña tiene mucha beldad,
fermosura, donaire, amor e lealtad.

EASTER DAY 19

The joyous festival hath dawned, the holy Easter Day,
And the great Sun all glorious hath started on his way,
And men, and birds, and bright-hued flowers in beauteous array
Come forth to welcome Love with songs and meet him on his way.

There welcome him a crowd of birds, the jay, the nightingale,
Finches and parrots, great and small, do bid their lord 'All Hail!'
And sweetest melodies are heard, and many an amorous tale,
And many a carol ye may hear, and many a madrigal.

There welcome him the trees and plants, adorned in brightest green,
And flowers of divers hues and kinds in all their pomp are seen;
And men and women welcome him with bright and gladsome mien;
While joyous music ringeth forth from many a tambourine.

Ida Farnell

PRAISE OF LITTLE WOMEN 20

In a little precious stone what splendor meets the eyes!
In a little lump of sugar how much of sweetness lies!
So in a little woman love grows and multiplies;
You recollect the proverb says,—" a word unto the Wise."

A pepper-corn is very small, but seasons every dinner
More than all other condiments, although 'tis sprinkled thinner;
Just so a little woman is, if Love will let you win her.—
There's not a joy in all the world you will not find within her.

And as within the little rose you find the richest dyes,
And in the little grain of gold much price and value lies,
As from a little balsam much odor doth arise,
So in a little woman there's a taste of paradise.

Even as a little ruby its secret worth betrays,
Color and price and virtue, in the clearness of its rays,—
Just so a little woman much excellence displays,
Beauty and grace and love and fidelity always.

Chica es la calandria e chico el ruy señor
pero más dulçe canta que otra ave mayor;
la muger por ser chica, por eso non es pior;
con doñeo es más dulçe que açúcar nin flor.

Son aves pequeñuelas papagayo e orior,
pero qualquier dellas es dulçe gritador,
adonada, fermosa, preçiada cantador:
bien atal es la dueña pequeña con amor.

De la muger pequeña non hay conparaçión,
terrenal parayso es e grand consolaçión,
solaz e alegría, plazer e bendiçión,
mejor es en la prueva que en la salutaçión.

Sienpre quis muger chica más que grande nin mayor,
non es desaguisado del grand mal ser foidor,
del mal tomar lo menos, dízelo el sabidor,
por ende de las mugeres la mejor es la menor.

21　　　　　*CÁNTICA DE LOORES DE SANTA MARÍA*

Quiero seguir a ti, flor de las flores,
sienpre dezir cantar de tus loores,
non me partir de te servir,
mejor de las mejores.

Grand fiança he yo en ti, Señora,
la mi esperança en ti es toda ora,
de tribulança sin tardança,
venme librar agora.

Virgen muy santa, yo paso atribulado,
pena atanta, con dolor atormentado,
en tu esperança coita atanta
que veo, mal pecado.

The skylark and the nightingale, though small and light of wing
Yet warble sweeter in the grove than all the birds that sing;
And so a little woman, though a very little thing,
Is sweeter far than sugar and flowers that bloom in spring.

The magpie and the golden thrush have many a thrilling note
Each as a gay musician doth strain his little throat,
A merry little songster in his green and yellow coat;
And such a little woman is, when Love doth make her dote.

There's naught can be compared to her, throughout the wide creation;
She is a paradise on earth,—our greatest consolation,—
So cheerful, gay and happy, so free from all vexation;
In fine, she's better in the proof than in anticipation.

If as her size increases are woman's charms decreased,
Then surely it is good to be from all the great released.
Now of two evils choose the less—said a wise man of the East,
By consequence, of woman-kind be sure to choose the least.

Henry W. Longfellow

HYMN TO THE VIRGIN   21

Thou Flower of flowers! I'll follow thee,
And sing thy praise unweariedly:
Best of the best! O, may I ne'er
From thy pure service flee!

Lady, to thee I turn my eyes,
On thee my trusting hope relies;
O, let thy spirit, smiling here,
Chase my anxieties!

Most Holy Virgin! tired and faint,
I pour my melancholy plaint;
Yet lift a tremulous thought to thee,
Alas, 'midst mortal taint.

Estrella del mar, puerto de folgura,
de dolor conplido e de tristura,
venme librar e conortar,
Señora del altura.

Nunca falleçe la tu merçed conplida,
sienpre guaresçes de coitas e das vida;
nunca peresçe nin entristeçe
quien a ti non olvida.

Sufro grand mal sin meresçer a tuerto,
esquivo tal por que pienso ser muerto;
más tú me val, que non veo ál
que me saque a puerto.

Thou Ocean-Star! thou Port of joy!
From pain, and sadness, and annoy,
O, rescue me, O, comfort me,
Bright Lady of the Sky!

Thy mercy is a boundless mine;
Freedom from care, and life are thine;
He recks not, faints not, fears not, who
Trusts in thy power divine.

Unjustly I do suffer wrong,
Despair and darkness guide my song;
I see no other, come, do thou
Waft my weak bark along!

Henry W. Longfellow

XVth Century

The Marquis of Santillana

Iñigo López de Mendoza, Marquis of Santillana, in the first half of the
fifteenth century is a courtly gentleman, very refined and cultured for
his time. His *serranillas* are not popular poetry. The Marquis upon one
occasion expressed disapproval of "those who fashion songs for the low
and servile." His kind of poetry on the contrary is mildly artificial and

1398-1458

aristocratic. But these qualities are turned towards the contemplation and understanding of the elemental and popular. In the *Serranilla de la Finojosa*: the refined cavalier understands and respects the charming and teasing artlessness of the maiden who tends her cows in the meadow.

D. A.

　　　　　　　SERRANILLA DE LA FINOJOSA

Moça tan fermosa
non vi en la frontera,
como una vaquera
de la Finojosa.

Faziendo la vía
del Calatraveño
a Sancta María,
vencido del sueño,
por tierra fragosa
perdí la carrera,
do vi la vaquera
de la Finojosa.

En un verde prado
de rosas e flores,
guardando ganado
con otros pastores,
la vi tan graciosa
que apenas creyera
que fuesse vaquera
de la Finojosa.

Non creo las rosas
de la primavera
sean tan fermosas
nin de tal manera
(fablando sin glosa),
si antes sopiera
de aquella vaquera
de la Finojosa.

Non tanto mirara
su mucha beldad,
porque me dexara
en mi liberdad.
Mas dixe:—"Donosa"
(por saber quién era),
"¿dónde es la vaquera
"de la Finojosa?"

Bien como riendo,
dixo:—"Bien vengades;
"que ya bien entiendo
"lo que demandades:
"non es deseosa
"de amar, nin lo espera,
"aquessa vaquera
"de la Finojosa."

SERRANILLA   **22**

From Calatrava as I took my way
At holy Mary's shrine to kneel and pray,
And sleep upon my eyelids heavy lay,
There where the ground was very rough and wild,
I lost my path and met a peasant child:
From Finojosa, with the herds around her,
There in the fields I found her.

    Upon a meadow green with tender grass,
With other rustic cowherds, lad and lass,
So sweet a thing to see I watched her pass:
My eyes could scarce believe her what they found her,
There with the herds around her.

    I do not think that roses in the Spring
Are half so lovely in their fashioning:
My heart must needs avow this secret thing,
That had I known her first as then I found her,
From Finojosa, with the herds around her,
I had not strayed so far her face to see
That it might rob me of my liberty.

    I questioned her, to know what she might say;
"Has she of Finojosa passed this way?"
She smiled and answered me: "In vain you sue,
Full well my heart discerns the hope in you:
But she of whom you speak, and have not found her.
Her heart is free, no thought of love has bound her,
Here with the herds around her."

John Pierrepont Rice

45

Jorge Manrique

In Spain during the xvth century, poetry follows two distinct and parallel courses. One is that of the popular ballad which is poetry of war and history, full of heroes and echoes of battles and great feats. But in the courts and palaces a new spirit had been diffused, which precisely because it found favor with the people of the court, was called courtly. And yet at the very core of this artificial poetry, we come upon the most profound, grave, sincere poet produced by the Spanish Middle Ages, Jorge Manrique. He came of a family of powerful Castilian nobles and was born about 1440. The Castilian nobles of that time were divided into irate factions that reflected the cupidity of the court. The national forces were exhausting their energy in fratricidal war. Jorge Manrique was involved in a net of palace intrigues and conflicts with other nobles. He participated in four campaigns, always in the service of the king, and met his death in 1479, at the age of thirty-nine, attacking the castle of the Marqués de Villena who was rebelling against the Catholic Monarchs.

He left behind him some fifty love poems, perfect expressions of the platitudes of his time. No one could perceive behind these rhymed subtleties a man or a poet. Yet Jorge Manrique was both. He was a great poet only once but in such a way that he will endure forever. His stanzas commemorating the death of his father (1476) represent without doubt the greatest height attained by the elegaic lyric in our language.

The first thing that elicits our admiration is the perfect balance between the real fact that occasioned the poem, and the profound human generality and universal significance to which the poet rises from the circumstance. We should observe that the point of view is essentially different from that of narrative poetry, limpid, innocent, direct, without questioning and doubt. The poem of Jorge Manrique is quite the contrary: life, the reality of the world have already become the object of a deeper, more penetrating, scrutinizing glance, of disquieting interrogations, by a spirit anxious over its destiny. Jorge Manrique takes in this poem the first step in our lyric toward the inner life and its anguish. He goes straight to the core, the intimate conflict of every spiritual life. Our lives are compared to rivers carried to the sea into which flow brooks and great streams alike; death is the great final sea, equalizer of human destinies. Jorge Manrique is the exception to the general rule found in the sentiment of death in the xvth century. No egoism, no attachment to earthly things. Death is not considered the worst of all evils, but a good which is joyously accepted. Death is consoling, even more, liberating, in this superb poem on death as a passage to the higher life.

P. S.

23

COPLAS POR LA MUERTE DE SU PADRE

Recuerde el alma dormida,
abive el seso y despierte,
contemplando
cómo se passa la vida,
cómo se viene la muerte
tan callando;
cuán presto se va el plazer,
cómo después de acordado,
da dolor,
cómo, a nuestro parescer,
cualquiera tiempo passado
fué mejor.

Pues si vemos lo presente
cómo en un punto se es ido
y acabado,
si juzgamos sabiamente,
daremos lo no venido
por passado.
No se engañe nadie, no,
pensando que ha de durar
lo que espera
más que duró lo que vió,
pues que todo ha de passar
por tal manera.

Nuestras vidas son los ríos
que van a dar en la mar,
que es el morir:
allí van los señoríos
derechos a se acabar
y consumir;
allí los ríos caudales,
allí los otros medianos
y más chicos,

ODE ON THE DEATH OF HIS FATHER   23

O, let the soul her slumbers break!
Let thought be quickened and awake,—
    Awake to see
How soon this life is past and gone,
And death comes softly stealing on,—
    How silently!

Swiftly our pleasures glide away:
Our hearts recall the distant day
    With many sighs;
The moments that are speeding fast
We heed not; but the past— the past—
    More highly prize.

Onward its course the present keeps,
Onward the constant current sweeps,
    Till life is done;
And did we judge of time aright,
The past and future in their flight
    Would be as one.

Let no one fondly dream again
That Hope and all her shadowy train
    Will not decay;
Fleeting as were the dreams of old,
Remembered like a tale that's told,
    They pass away.

Our lives are rivers gliding free
To that unfathomed, boundless sea,
    The silent grave:
Thither all earthly pomp and boast
Roll to be swallowed up and lost
    In one dark wave.

Thither the mighty torrents stray,
Thither the brook pursues its way,
    And tinkling rill.

allegados son iguales,
los que biven por sus manos
y los ricos.

Dexo las invocaciones
de los famosos poetas
y oradores;
no curo de sus ficciones,
que traen yervas secretas
sus sabores.
Aquel solo me encomiendo,
aquel solo invoco yo
de verdad,
que en este mundo biviendo,
el mundo no conosció
su deidad.

Este mundo es el camino
para el otro, que es morada
sin pesar;
mas cumple tener buen tino
para andar esta jornada
sin errar.
Partimos cuando nascemos,
andamos mientra bivimos,
y llegamos
al tiempo que fenescemos;
assí que cuando morimos
descansamos.

Este mundo bueno fué
si bien usássemos dél
como devemos,
porque, según nuestra fe,
es para ganar aquel
que atendemos.

There all are equal. Side by side,
The poor man and the son of pride
        Lie calm and still.

I will not here invoke the throng
Of orators and sons of song,
        The deathless few;
Fiction entices and deceives,
And sprinkling o'er her fragrant leaves
        Lies poisonous dew.

To One alone my thoughts arise,—
The Eternal Truth,— the Good and Wise:
        To Him I cry,
Who shared on earth our common lot,
But the world comprehended not
        His deity.

This world is but the rugged road
Which leads us to the bright abode
        Of peace above;
So let us choose that narrow way
Which leads no traveller's foot astray
        From realms of love.

Our cradle is the starting-place;
In life we run the onward race,
        And reach the goal;
When, in the mansions of the blest,
Death leaves to its eternal rest
        The weary soul.

Did we but use it as we ought,
This world would school each wandering thought
        To its high state.
Faith wings the soul beyond the sky,
Up to the better world on high
        For which we wait.

Y aun aquel fijo de Dios,
para sobirnos al cielo,
descendió
a nascer acá entre nos,
y a bivir en este suelo
do murió.

Ved de cuán poco valor
son las cosas tras que andamos
y corremos,
que, en este mundo traidor,
aun primero que muramos
las perdemos:
    dellas desfaze la edad,
dellas casos desastrados
que acaescen,
dellas, por su calidad,
en los más altos estados
desfallescen.

Dezidme, la fermosura,
la gentil frescura y tez
de la cara,
la color y la blancura,
cuando viene la vejez
¿cuál se para?
    Las mañas y ligereza
y la fuerça corporal
de joventud,
todo se torna graveza
cuando llega al arraval
de senectud.

Pues la sangre de los godos,
y el linage y la nobleza
tan crescida,
¡por cuántas vías y modos
se sume su grand alteza
en esta vida!

Yes,— the glad messenger of love,
To guide us to our home above,
  The Saviour came;
Born amid mortal cares and fears,
He suffered in this vale of tears
  A death of shame.

Behold of what delusive worth
The bubbles we pursue on earth,
  The shapes we chase,
Amid a world of treachery!
They vanish ere death shuts the eye,
  And leave no trace.

Time steals them from us,— chances strange,
Disastrous accidents, and change,
  That come to all:
Even in the most exalted state,
Relentless sweeps the stroke of fate;
  The strongest fall.

Tell me,— the charms that lovers seek
In the clear eye and blushing cheek,—
  The hues that play
O'er rosy lip and brow of snow,—
When hoary age approaches slow,
  Ah, where are they?

The cunning skill, the curious arts,
The glorious strength that youth imparts
  In life's first stage,—
These shall become a heavy weight,
When Time swings wide his outward gate
  To weary age.

The noble blood of Gothic name,
Heroes emblazoned high to fame
  In long array,—
How, in the onward course of time,
The landmarks of that race sublime
  Were swept away!

Unos, por poco valer,
¡por cuán baxos y abatidos
que los tienen!
Y otros, por no tener,
con oficios no devidos
se mantienen.

Los estados y riqueza,
que nos dexan a desora,
¿quién lo duda?
No les pidamos firmeza
pues que son de una señora
que se muda;
que bienes son de Fortuna
que rebuelve con su rueda
presurosa,
la cual no puede ser una
ni estar estable ni queda
en una cosa.

Pero digo que acompañen
y lleguen hasta la huessa
con su dueño:
por esso no nos engañen,
pues se va la vida apriessa
como sueño.
Y los deleites de acá
son, en que nos deleitamos,
temporales,
y los tormentos de allá,
que por ellos esperamos,
eternales.

Los plazeres y dulçores
desta vida trabajada
que tenemos,
¿qué son sino corredores,
y la muerte la celada
en que caemos?

Some, the degraded slaves of lust,
Prostrate and trampled in the dust,
      Shall rise no more;
Others by guilt and crime maintain
The scutcheon that without a stain
      Their fathers bore.

Wealth and the high estate of pride,
With what untimely speed they glide,
      How soon depart!
Bid not the shadowy phantoms stay,—
The vassals of a mistress they,
      Of fickle heart.

These gifts in Fortune's hands are found;
Her swift-revolving wheel turns round,
      And they are gone!
No rest the inconstant goddess knows,
But changing, and without repose,
      Still hurries on.

Even could the hand of avarice save
Its gilded baubles, till the grave
      Reclaimed its prey,
Let none on such poor hopes rely;
Life, like an empty dream flits by,
      And where are they?

Earthly desires and sensual lust
Are passions springing from the dust,—
      They fade and die;
But, in the life beyond the tomb,
They seal the immortal spirit's doom
      Eternally!

The pleasure and delights which mask
In treacherous smiles life's serious task,
      What are they all,
But the fleet coursers of the chase,—
And death an ambush in the race,
      Wherein we fall?

No mirando nuestro daño,
corremos a rienda suelta
sin parar;
desque vemos el engaño
y queremos dar la buelta,
no hay lugar.

Si fuesse en nuestro poder
tornar la cara fermosa
corporal,
como podemos fazer
el ánima glorïosa,
angelical,
¡qué diligencia tan biva
toviéramos toda hora,
y tan presta,
en componer la cativa,
dexándonos la señora
descompuesta!

Essos reyes poderosos
que vemos por escrituras
ya passadas,
con casos tristes, llorosos,
fueron sus buenas venturas
trastornadas:
assí que no hay cosa fuerte,
que a papas y emperadores
y perlados,
assí los trata la Muerte
como a los pobres pastores
de ganados.

Dexemos a los troyanos,
que sus males no los vimos,
ni sus glorias;
dexemos a los romanos,
aunque oímos y leímos
sus estorias,

No foe, no dangerous pass we heed,
Brook no delay,— but onward speed,
        With loosened rein;
And when the fatal snare is near,
We strive to check our mad career,
        But strive in vain.

Could we new charms to age impart,
And fashion with a cunning art
        The human face,
As we can clothe the soul with light,
And make the glorious spirit bright
        With heavenly grace,—

How busily, each passing hour,
Should we exert that magic power!
        What ardor show
To deck the sensual slave of sin,
Yet leave the freeborn soul within
        In weeds of woe!

Monarchs, the powerful and the strong,
Famous in history and in song
        Of olden time,
Saw, by the stern decrees of fate,
Their kingdoms lost, and desolate
        Their race sublime.

Who is the champion? Who the strong?
Pontiff and priest, and sceptred throng?
        On these shall fall
As heavily the hand of Death,
As when it stays the shepherd's breath
        Beside his stall.

I speak not of the Trojan name,—
Neither its glory nor its shame
        Has met our eyes;
Nor of Rome's great and glorious dead,—
Though we have heard so oft, and read,
        Their histories.

57

no curemos de saber
lo de aquel siglo passado
qué fué dello;
vengamos a lo de ayer,
que tan bien es olvidado
como aquello.

¿Qué se fizo el rey don Juan?
Los infantes de Aragón,
¿qué se fizieron?
¿Qué fué de tanto galán?
¿Qué fué de tanta invención
como truxieron?
Las justas y los torneos,
paramentos, bordaduras,
y cimeras,
¿fueron sino devaneos?
¿qué fueron sino verduras
de las eras?

¿Qué se fizieron las damas,
sus tocados, sus vestidos,
sus olores?
¿Qué se fizieron las llamas
de los fuegos encendidos
de amadores?
¿Qué se fizo aquel trobar,
las músicas acordadas
que tañían?
¿Qué se fizo aquel dançar,
aquellas ropas chapadas
que traían?

Pues el otro su heredero,
don Enrique, ¡qué poderes
alcançava!
¡Cuán blando, cuán falaguero
el mundo con sus plazeres
se le dava!

Little avails it now to know
Of ages past so long ago,
          Nor how they rolled;
Our theme shall be of yesterday
Which to oblivion sweeps away,
          Like days of old.

Where is the king Don Juan? Where
Each royal prince and noble heir
          Of Aragon?
Where are the courtly gallantries?
The deeds of love and high emprise,
          In battle done?

Tourney and joust, that charmed the eye,
And scarf, and gorgeous panoply,
          And nodding plume,—
What were they but a pageant scene?
What but the garlands, gay and green
          That deck the tomb?

Where are the high-born dames, and where
Their gay attire and jewelled hair,
          And odors sweet?
Where are the gentle knights, that came
To kneel, and breathe love's ardent flame,
          Low at their feet?

Where is the song of Troubadour?
Where are the lute and gay tambour
          They loved of yore?
Where is the mazy dance of old,—
The flowing robes, inwrought with gold,
          The dancers wore?

And he who next the sceptre swayed,
Henry, whose royal court displayed
          Such power and pride,—
O, in what winning smiles arrayed,
The world its various pleasures laid
          His throne beside!

Mas veréis cuán enemigo,
cuán contrario, cuán cruel
se le mostró,
aviéndole sido amigo,
cuán poco duró con él
lo que le dió.

Las dádivas desmedidas,
los edificios reales
llenos de oro,
las vaxillas tan febridas,
los enriques y reales
del tesoro,
los jaezes, los cavallos
de su gente, y atavíos
tan sobrados,
¿dónde iremos a buscallos?
¿qué fueron sino rocíos
de los prados?

Pues su hermano el inocente
que en su vida sucessor
se llamó,
¡qué corte tan excelente
tuvo, y cuánto grand señor
le siguió!
Mas, como fuesse mortal,
metióle la Muerte luego
en su fragua.
¡O, juizio divinal!:
cuando más ardía el fuego,
echaste agua.

Pues aquel grand condestable,
maestre que conoscimos
tan privado,
no cumple que dél se fable,
sino sólo que lo vimos
degollado.

But, O, how false and full of guile
That world, which wore so soft a smile
          But to betray!
She, that had been his friend before,
Now from the fated monarch tore
          Her charms away.

The countless gifts,— the stately walls,
The royal palaces, and halls
          All filled with gold;
Plate with armorial bearings wrought,
Chambers with ample treasures fraught
          Of wealth untold;

The noble steeds, and harness bright,
The gallant lord, and stalwart knight,
          In rich array;—
Where shall we seek them now? Alas!
Like the bright dew-drops on the grass,
          They passed away.

His brother, too, whose factious zeal
Usurped the sceptre of Castile,
          Unskilled to reign,—
What a gay, brilliant court had he,
When all the flower of chivalry
          Was in his train!

But he was mortal, and the breath
That flamed from the hot forge of Death
          Blasted his years;
Judgment of God! that flame by thee,
When raging fierce and fearfully,
          Was quenched in tears!

Spain's haughty Constable,— the true
And gallant Master,— whom we knew
          Most loved of all,—
Breathe not a whisper of his pride;
He on the gloomy scaffold died,—
          Ignoble fall!

Sus infinitos tesoros,
sus villas y sus lugares,
su mandar,
¿qué le fueron sino lloros?
¿qué fuéron sino pesares
al dexar?

Pues los otros dos hermanos,
maestres tan prosperados
como reyes,
que a los grandes y medianos
truxieron tan sojuzgados
a sus leyes;
  aquella prosperidad
que tan alta fué sobida
y ensalçada,
¿qué fué sino claridad
que estando más encendida
fué amatada?

Tantos duques excelentes,
tantos marqueses y condes
y varones
como vimos tan potentes,
di, Muerte, ¿dó los escondes
y traspones?
  Y las sus claras hazañas
que fizieron en las guerras
y en las pazes,
cuando tú, cruda, te ensañas,
con tu fuerça las atierras
y desfazes.

Las huestes innumerables,
los pendones y estandartes
y vanderas,
los castillos impunables,
los muros y baluartes
y barreras,

The countless treasures of his care,
His hamlets green and cities fair,
　　　His mighty power,—
What were they all but grief and shame,
Tears and a broken heart, when came
　　　The parting hour?

His other brothers, proud and high,—
Masters, who, in prosperity,
　　　Might rival kings,—
Who made the bravest and the best
The bondsmen of their high behest,
　　　Their underlings,—

What was their prosperous estate,
When high exalted and elate
　　　With power and pride?
What, but a transient gleam of light,—
A flame, which, glaring at its height,
　　　Grew dim and died?

So many a duke of royal name,
Marquis and count of spotless fame,
　　　And baron brave,
That might the sword of empire wield,—
All these, O Death, hast thou concealed
　　　In the dark grave!

Their deeds of mercy and of arms,
In peaceful days, or war's alarms,
　　　When thou dost show,
O Death, thy stern and angry face,
One stroke of thy all-powerful mace
　　　Can overthrow!

Unnumbered hosts, that threaten nigh,—
Pennon and standard flaunting high,
　　　And flag displayed,—
High battlements intrenched around,
Bastion, and moated wall, and mound,
　　　And palisade,

la cava honda, chapada,
o cualquier otro reparo,
¿qué aprovecha?
que si tú vienes airada,
todo lo passas de claro
con tu flecha.

¡Oh, mundo! Pues que nos matas,
fuera la vida que diste
toda vida;
mas según acá nos tratas,
lo mejor y menos triste
es la partida
de tu vida, tan cubierta
de tristezas y dolores,
despoblada;
de los bienes tan desierta,
de placeres y dulzores
despojada.

Es tu comienzo lloroso,
tu salida siempre amarga
y nunca buena,
lo de enmedio trabajoso,
y a quien das vida más larga
das más pena.
Así los bienes—muriendo
y con sudor—se procuran
y los das;
los males vienen corriendo;
después de venidos, duran
mucho más.

Aquel de buenos abrigo,
amado por virtuoso
de la gente,
el maestre don Rodrigo
Manrique, tanto famoso
y tan valiente;

And covered trench, secure and deep,—
All these cannot one victim keep,
          O Death, from thee,
When thou dost battle in thy wrath,
And thy strong shafts pursue their path
          Unerringly!

O world! so few the years we live,
Would that the life which thou dost give
          Were life indeed!
Alas! thy sorrows fall so fast,
Our happiest hour is when, at last,
          The soul is freed.

Our days are covered o'er with grief,
And sorrows neither few nor brief
          Veil all in gloom;
Left desolate of real good,
Within this cheerless solitude
          No pleasures bloom.

Thy pilgrimage begins in tears,
And ends in bitter doubts and fears,
          Or dark despair;
Midway so many toils appear,
That he who lingers longest here
          Knows most of care.

Thy goods are bought with many a groan,
By the hot sweat of toil alone,
          And weary hearts;
Fleet-footed is the approach of woe,
But with a lingering step and slow
          Its form departs.

And he, the good man's shield and shade,
To whom all hearts their homage paid,
          As Virtue's son,—
Rodrick Manrique, — he whose name
Is written on the scroll of Fame,
          Spain's champion;

sus grandes fechos y claros
no cumple que los alabe,
pues los vieron,
ni los quiero fazer caros,
pues el mundo todo sabe
cuáles fueron.

¡Qué amigo de sus amigos!
¡Qué señor para criados
y parientes!
¡Qué enemigo de enemigos!
¡Qué maestro de esforçados
y valientes!
¡Qué seso para discretos!
¡Qué gracia para donosos!
¡Qué razón!
¡Qué benigno a los subjetos!
y a los bravos y dañosos,
un léon!

En ventura Octavïano,
Julio César en vencer
y batallar;
en la virtud, Africano,
Aníbal en el saber
y trabajar;
en la bondad, un Trajano,
Tito en liberalidad
con alegría;
en su braço, Aurelïano,
Marco Atilio en la verdad
que prometía.

Antonio Pío en clemencia,
Marco Aurelio en igualdad
del semblante;
Adrïano en elocuencia,
Teodosio en umildad
y buen talante.

His signal deeds and prowess high
Demand no pompous eulogy,—
  Ye saw his deeds!
Why should their praise in verse be sung?
The name that dwells on every tongue
  No minstrel needs.

To friends a friend;—how kind to all
The vassals of this ancient hall
  And feudal fief!
To foes how stern a foe was he!
And to the valiant and the free
  How brave a chief!

What prudence with the old and wise!
What grace in youthful gayeties!
  In all how sage!
Benignant to the serf and slave,
He showed the base and falsely brave
  A lion's rage.

His was Octavian's prosperous star,
The rush of Cæsar's conquering car
  At battle's call;
His, Scipio's virtue; his, the skill
And the indomitable will
  Of Hannibal.

His was a Trajan's goodness; his
A Titus' noble charities
  And righteous laws;
The arm of Hector, and the might
Of Tully, to maintain the right
  In truth's just cause;

The clemency of Antonine;
Aurelius' countenance divine
  Firm, gentle, still;
The eloquence of Adrian;
And Theodosius' love to man,
  And generous will;

Aurelio Alexandre fué,
en diciplina y rigor
de la guerra;
un Constantino en la fe,
Camilo en el grand amor
de su tierra.

No dexó grandes tesoros,
ni alcançó muchas riquezas
ni vaxillas,
mas fizo guerra a los moros,
ganando sus fortalezas
y sus villas;
y en las lides que venció,
muchos moros y cavallos
se perdieron;
y en este oficio ganó
las rentas y los vassallos
que le dieron.

Pues por su onra y estado,
en otros tiempos passados
¿cómo se huvo?
Quedando desamparado,
con hermanos y criados
se sostuvo.
Después que fechos famosos
fizo en esta dicha guerra
que fazía,
fizo tratos tan onrosos
que le dieron aun más tierra
que tenía.

Estas sus viejas estorias
que con su braço pintó
en joventud,
con otras nuevas victorias
agora las renovó
en senectud.

In tented field and bloody fray,
An Alexander's vigorous sway
   And stern command;
The faith of Constantine; ay, more,—
The fervent love Camillus bore
   His native land.

He left no well filled treasury,
He heaped no pile of riches high,
   Nor massive plate;
He fought the Moors,— and, in their fall,
City and tower and castled wall
   Were his estate.

Upon the hard-fought battle-ground
Brave steeds and gallant riders found
   A common grave;
And there the warrior's hand did gain
The rents, and the long vassal train,
   That conquest gave.

And if, of old, his halls displayed
The honored and exalted grade
   His worth had gained,
So, in the dark, disastrous hour,
Brothers and bondsmen of his power
   His hand sustained.

After high deeds, not left untold,
In the stern warfare which of old
   'Twas his to share,
Such noble leagues he made, that more
And fairer regions than before
   His guerdon were.

These are the records, half effaced,
Which with the hand of youth, he traced
   On history's page;
But with fresh victories he drew
Each fading character anew
   In his old age.

Por su grand abilidad,
por méritos y ancianía
bien gastada,
alcançó la dignidad
de la grand cavallería
del Espada.

Y sus villas y sus tierras
ocupadas de tiranos
las falló,
mas por cercos y por guerras
y por fuerça de sus manos
las cobró.
Pues nuestro rey natural,
si de las obras que obró
fué servido,
dígalo el de Portugal
y en Castilla quien siguió
su partido.

Después de puesta la vida
tantas vezes por su ley
al tablero,
después de tan bien servida
la corona de su rey
verdadero,
después de tanta hazaña
a que non puede bastar
cuenta cierta,
en la su villa de Ocaña
vino la Muerte a llamar
a su puerta,

diziendo: "Buen cavallero,
dexad el mundo engañoso
y su halago;
vuestro coraçón de azero
muestre su esfuerço famoso
en este trago;

By his unrivalled skill, by great
And veteran service to the state,
          By worth adored,
He stood, in his high dignity,
The proudest knight of chivalry,—
          Knight of the Sword.

He found his cities and domains
Beneath a tyrant's galling chains
          And cruel power;
But, by fierce battle and blockade,
Soon his own banner was displayed
          From every tower.

By the tried valor of his hand
His monarch and his native land
          Were nobly served;—
Let Portugal repeat the story,
And proud Castile, who shared the glory
          His arms deserved.

And when so oft, for weal or woe,
His life upon the fatal throw
          Had been cast down,—
When he had served, with patriot zeal
Beneath the banner of Castile,
          His sovereign's crown,—

And done such deeds of valor strong,
That neither history nor song
          Can count them all;
Then, on Ocaña's castled rock,
Death at his portal came to knock,
          With sudden call,—

Saying, "Good Cavalier, prepare
To leave this world of toil and care
          With joyful mien;
Let thy strong heart of steel this day
Put on its armour for the fray,—
          The closing scene.

71

y pues de vida y salud
fezistes tan poca cuenta
por la fama,
esfuércese la virtud
para sofrir esta afruenta
que vos llama.

"No se os faga tan amarga
la batalla temerosa
que esperáis,
pues otra vida más larga
de la fama glorïosa
acá dexáis.
   Aunque esta vida de onor
tampoco no es eternal
ni verdadera,
mas, con todo, es muy mejor
que la otra temporal,
perescedera.

"El bivir que es perdurable
no se gana con estados
mundanales,
ni con vida deleitable
en que moran los pecados
infernales;
   mas los buenos religiosos
gánanlo con oraciones
y con lloros;
los cavalleros famosos,
con trabajos y aflicciones
contra moros.

"Y pues vos, claro varón,
tanta sangre derramastes
de paganos,
esperad el galardón
que en este mundo ganastes
por las manos;

" Since thou hast been, in battle-strife,
So prodigal of health and life,
          For earthly fame,
Let virtue nerve thy heart again;
Loud on the last stern battle-plain
          They call thy name.

" Think not the struggle that draws near
Too terrible for man, nor fear
          To meet the foe;
Nor let thy noble spirit grieve,
Its life of glorious fame to leave
          On earth below.

"A life of honor and of worth
Has no eternity on earth,—
          'Tis but a name;
And yet its glory far exceeds
That base and sensual life which leads
          To want and shame.

" The eternal life, beyond the sky,
Wealth cannot purchase, nor the high
          And proud estate;
The soul in dalliance laid,— the spirit
Corrupt with sin,— shall not inherit
          A joy so great.

" But the good monk, in cloistered cell,
Shall gain it by his book and bell,
          His prayers and tears;
And the brave knight, whose arm endures
Fierce battle, and against the Moors
          His standard rears.

"And thou, brave knight, whose hand has poured
The life-blood of the pagan horde
          O'er all the land,
In heaven shalt thou receive, at length,
The guerdon of thy earthly strength
          And dauntless hand.

73

y con esta confiança,
y con la fe tan entera
que tenéis,
partid con buena esperança
que estotra vida tercera
ganaréis."

—"No gastemos tiempo ya
en esta vida mezquina
por tal modo,
que mi voluntad está
conforme con la divina
para todo;
    y consiento en mi morir
con voluntad plazentera,
clara y pura,
que querer ombre bivir
cuando Dios quiere que muera,
es locura.

"Tú, que por nuestra maldad,
tomaste forma servil
y baxo nombre,
Tú, que a tu divinidad
juntaste cosa tan vil
como el ombre;
    Tú, que tan grandes tormentos
sofriste sin resistencia
en tu persona,
no por mis merescimientos,
mas por tu sola clemencia
me perdona."

Assí con tal entender,
todos sentidos umanos
conservados,
cercado de su muger,
de sus fijos y hermanos
y criados,

" Cheered onward by this promise sure,
Strong in the faith entire and pure
      Thou dost profess,
Depart,— thy hope is certainty;—
The third—the better life on high
      Thou shalt possess."

" O Death, no more, no more delay!
My spirit longs to flee away
      And be at rest,—
The will of Heaven my will shall be,—
I bow to the divine decree,
      To God's behest.

" My soul is ready to depart,—
No thought rebels,— the obedient heart
      Breathes forth no sigh;
The wish on earth to linger still
Were vain, when 'tis God's sovereign will
      That we shall die.

" O thou, that for our sins didst take
A human form, and humbly make
      Thy home on earth!
Thou, that to thy divinity
A human nature didst ally
      By mortal birth,—

"And in that form didst suffer here
Torment, and agony, and fear,
      So patiently!
By thy redeeming grace alone,
And not for merits of my own,
      O, pardon me! "

As thus the dying warrior prayed,
Without one gathering mist or shade
      Upon his mind,—
Encircled by his family,
Watched by affection's gentle eye,
      So soft and kind,—

dió el alma a quien gela dió,
el cual la ponga en el cielo
en su gloria,
y aunque la vida murió,
nos dexó harto consuelo
su memoria.

His soul to Him who gave it rose.
God lead it to its long repose,
        Its glorious rest!
And, though the warrior's sun has set,
Its light shall linger round us yet,
        Bright, radiant, blest.

Henry W. Longfellow

Ancient

The *Cantar de mio Cid* is the only example left of those long narrative poems called *cantares de gesta*. The other works of this type have disappeared. And the national poetic genius, the heroic spirit of the race is expressed in all its completeness two centuries later in the ballad, that form of poetry so characteristic of Spanish literature. The ballad is an epico-lyric poem, usually very short, of heroic or warlike character, and has an historical or legendary theme. It is poetry, naturally, written to be sung, anonymous, and subject to that process of elaboration, alteration, change, by the people that composed it, as it passes from mouth to mouth, from generation to generation. This treatment of the ballad, which Menéndez Pidal has called traditional, since it passes from father to son like a common poetic background, like a spiritual heritage, kept and preserved by all, is what gives Spanish ballads their peculiar physiognomy.

According to Menéndez Pidal's theory, the first ballads are fragments of the *cantares de gesta*, the most important passages, those that left the deepest impression on the audience and were sung separately until they began to be considered separate works. Consequently, the content of the

Ballads

ballads, the subject-matter, is that of the medieval epic, as for example, the ballads about the Cid.

But there is another group of ballads that does not merely remodel or make over old themes, but poetizes living history, contemporary reality. These ballads lack, naturally, the great sweep of the *cantares de gesta*, their magnificent mural painting, but they have, on the other hand, the vividness and concentration of things recently seen, of fresh and vibrant impressions of real deeds. Besides, the brief and concise form of the ballad, which seems fragmentary, adds to its special poetic force and to its essential evocative intensity. It is a poem condensed into a small space and which expands as it enters our soul.

P. S.

[Some of the ancient ballads and songs have been preserved in several different versions, and for a few of the translations the editor has not been able to trace the exact version used by the translator.]

24

EL REINO PERDIDO

Las huestes de don Rodrigo
desmayaban y huían
cuando en la octava batalla
sus enemigos vencían.
Rodrigo deja sus tiendas
y del real se salía,
solo va el desventurado
sin ninguna compañía;
el caballo de cansado
ya moverse no podía,
camina por donde quiere
sin que él le estorbe la vía.
El rey va tan desmayado
que sentido no tenía;
muerto va de sed y hambre,
de velle era gran mancilla;
iba tan tinto de sangre
que una brasa parecía.
Las armas lleva abolladas,
que eran de gran pedrería;
la espada lleva hecha sierra
de los golpes que tenía;
el almete de abollado
en la cabeza se hundía;
la cara llevaba hinchada
del trabajo que sufría.
  Subióse encima de un cerro,
el más alto que veía;
desde allí mira su gente
cómo iba de vencida;
de allí mira sus banderas
y estandartes que tenía,
cómo están todos pisados
que la tierra los cubría;
mira por los capitanes,
que ninguno parescía;

THE LAMENTATION OF DON RODRIGO   24

The hosts of Don Rodrigo
  Were scattered in dismay,
When lost was the eighth battle,
  Nor heart nor hope had they;
He, when he saw the field was lost,
  And all his hope was flown,
He turned him from his flying host,
  And took his way alone.

His horse was bleeding, blind and lame
  —He could no farther go;
Dismounted, without path or aim,
  The King stepped to and fro;
It was a sight of pity
  To look on Roderick,
For, sore athirst and hungry,
  He staggered faint and sick.

All stained and strewed with dust and blood,
  Like to some smouldering brand
Plucked from the flame, Rodrigo showed:
  His sword was in his hand,
But it was hacked into a saw
  Of dark and purple tint;
His jewelled mail had many a flaw,
  His helmet many a dint.

He climbed unto a hill-top,
  The highest he could see—
Thence all about of that wide rout
  His last long look took he;
He saw his royal banners
  Where they lay drenched and torn,
He heard the cry of victory,
  The Arab's shout of scorn.

He looked for the brave captains
  That led the hosts of Spain,

mira el campo tinto en sangre,
la cual arroyos corría.
El triste de ver aquesto
gran mancilla en sí tenía,
llorando de los sus ojos
desta manera decía:
"Ayer era rey de España,
hoy no lo soy de una villa;
ayer villas y castillos,
hoy ninguno poseía;
ayer tenía criados
y gente que me servía,
hoy no tengo ni una almena
que pueda decir que es mía.
¡Desdichada fué la hora,
desdichado fué aquel día
en que nací y heredé
la tan grande señoría,
pues lo había de perder
todo junto y en un día!
¡Oh muerte!, ¿por qué no vienes
y llevas esta alma mía
de aqueste cuerpo mezquino,
pues se te agradecería?"

25   *ROMANCE DE FONTE–FRIDA Y CON AMOR*

Fonte-frida, Fonte-frida,
Fonte-frida y con amor,
do todas las avecicas
van tomar consolación,
si no es la Tortolica,
que está viuda y con dolor.

But all were fled except the dead,
  And who could count the slain?
Where'er his eye could wander,
  All bloody was the plain,
And while thus he said, the tears he shed
  Ran down his cheeks like rain:—

"Last night I was the King of Spain—
  To-day no king am I;
Last night fair castles held my train—
  To-night where shall I lie?
Last night a hundred pages
  Did serve me on the knee,—
To-night not one I call mine own:—
  Not one pertains to me.

"Oh, luckless, luckless was the hour,
  And cursèd was the day,
When I was born to have the power
  Of this great seniory!
Unhappy me that I should see
  The sun go down to-night!
O Death, why now so slow art thou,
  Why fearest thou to smite?"

John Gibson Lockhart

COOLING FOUNTAIN

25

Cooling fountain, cooling fountain,
  Cooling fountain, full of love,*
Where the little birds of springtime
  Seek for comfort as they rove;
All except the widowed turtle—
  Widowed, sorrowing turtle-dove.

---

* I have taken the liberty of using these two lines from the translation of
George Ticknor instead of:

  "Fount of freshness, fount of freshness,
    Fount of freshness and of love."

                                   Ed.

Por allí fuera a pasar
el traidor de Ruiseñor;
las palabras que le dice
llenas son de traición:
—Si tú quisieses, señora,
yo sería tu servidor.
—Vete de ahí, enemigo,
malo, falso, engañador,
que ni poso en ramo verde
ni en prado que tenga flor;
que si el agua hallo clara
turbia la bebía yo;
que no quiero haber marido
porque hijos no haya, no;
no quiero placer con ellos,
ni menos consolación.
¡Déjame, triste enemigo,
malo, falso, ruin traidor,
que no quiero ser tu amiga
ni casar contigo, no!

26   MONTESINOS Y DURANDARTE

Muerto yace Durandarte
debajo una verde haya,
con él está Montesinos,
que en la su muerte se halla.
Haciéndole está la fosa
con una pequeña daga;
quitándole está el almete,
desciñiéndole la espada;
por el costado siniestro
el corazón le sacara;
así hablara con él,
como cuando vivo estaba:

There the nightingale, the traitor!
  Lingered on his giddy way;
And these words of hidden treachery
  To the dove I heard him say:
"I will be thy servant, lady!
  I will ne'er thy love betray."

"Off! false-hearted—vile deceiver!
  Leave me, nor insult me so!
Dwell I, there, midst gaudy flowrets?
  Perch I on the verdant bough?
Even the waters of the fountain
  Drink I dark and troubled now.
Never will I think of marriage—
  Never break the widow-vow.

"Had I children they would grieve me,
  They would wean me from my vow.
Leave me, false one! thoughtless traitor!—
  Base one!—vain one! sad one! go!
I can never, never love thee—
  I will never wed thee—no!"

John Bowring

DEATH OF DURANDARTE   26

Closed in death lies Durandarte,
  Montesinos sees him die
And, awhile in sorrow musing
  Heaves a deep distressing sigh.

When he saw him mute and lifeless,
  And the warmth his corse forsook,
From his friend his sword and helmet
  And his armour off he took.

Then with bitter anguish weeping,
  He fulfills his last request;
And, the hero's left side opening,
  Takes the heart out from his breast.

" ¡corazón del más valiente
que en Francia ceñía espada,
ahora seréis llevado
adonde Belerma estaba!"
Envolvióle en un cendal,
y consigo lo llevaba;
entierra primero al primo;
con gran llanto lamentaba
la su tan temprana muerte,
y su suerte desdichada.
Torna a subir en la yegua,
su cara en agua bañada;
pónese luego el almete,
y muy recio le enlazaba.
No quiere ser conocido
hasta hacer su embajada,
y presentarle a Belerma,
según que se le encargara
el sangriento corazón
que a Durandarte sacara.
Camina triste y penoso,
ninguna cosa le agrada;
por do quiere andar la yegua,
por allí deja que vaya;
hasta que entró por París,
no sabe en qué parte estaba.
Derecho va a los palacios
adonde Belerma estaba.

When he saw it lie before him
  Loud he raised the voice of woe:—
" Cousin, like a fountain streaming
  " O'er thy heart my tears shall flow.

" Never France a warrior boasted
  " More undaunted in the fight:
" Mild in peace, in war a lion:
  " Never liv'd a better knight.

" To the grave thy corse consigning,
  " Long thy virtues still shall live;
" But thy heart to fair Belerma
  " Will I, as thou bad'st me, give."

Deep he digs the grave, the body
  Leaving to its native clay;
Takes a parting look, and, weeping,
  Bears the hero's heart away:

From all eyes his face concealing
  Till he had Belerma seen;
Round his head his helmet fastening,
  On he rides with pensive mien;

And, the gates of Paris entering,
  To Belerma's palace goes,
To distract her gentle bosom,
  And afflict her soul with woes.

Thomas Rodd

27   ROMANCE DE DOÑA ALDA

En París está doña Alda,
la esposa de don Roldán,
trescientas damas con ella
para bien la acompañar:
todas visten un vestido,
todas calzan un calzar,
todas comen a una mesa,
todas comían de un pan,
si no era doña Alda
que era la mayoral.
Las ciento hilaban el oro
las ciento tejen cendal,
ciento tañen instrumentos
para a doña Alda alegrar.
Al son de los instrumentos
doña Alda adormido se ha;
ensoñado había un sueño,
un sueño de gran pesar.
Despertó despavorida
con un dolor sin igual,
los gritos daba tan grandes
se oían en la ciudad.
—¿Qué es aquesto, mi señora,
qué es lo que os hizo mal?
—Un sueño soñé, doncellas,
que me ha dado gran pesar:
que me veía en un monte,
en un desierto lugar,
y de so los montes altos.

LADY ALDA'S DREAM   27

In Paris dwelt the lady fair,
    Orlando's promised bride,
Three hundred dames of honour there
    Sat with her side by side,
Of all the damsels in the land
    None fairer might ye choose,
Alike they wore their silken robes,
    Alike their broidered shoes;

Around a single board they sat,
    A single meal to share,
The Lady Alda sat alone,
    The fairest of the fair;
A hundred wove the satin fine,
    A hundred spun the gold,
A hundred played the music sweet
    That cheered her heart of old.

And while they touched the tuneful chords,
    Their lady sank to sleep,
And while she slept she dreamed a dream,
    Made every nerve to creep;
With startled eyes she wakened up,
    Her limbs they quaked for fear,
And gave a cry so loud and shrill
    That all the town might hear.

"O Lady Alda what is this?
    What means this cry of fear?"
"O maidens, I have dreamed a dream
    Will wring your hearts to hear:
Methought I stood upon a hill
    Within a desert ground,
When lo! I saw a wild hawk fly
    From out the mountain round.

un azor vide volar;
tras dél viene una aguililla
que lo ahincaba muy mal.
El azor con grande cuita
metióse so mi brial;
el águila con gran ira
de allí lo iba a sacar;
con las uñas lo despluma,
con el pico lo deshace.
Allí habló su camarera,
bien oiréis lo que dirá:
—Aquese sueño, señora,
bien os lo entiendo soltar:
el azor es vuestro esposo,
que de España viene ya;
el águila sodes vos,
con la cual ha de casar,
y aquel monte era la iglesia
donde os han de velar.
—Si es así, mi camarera,
bien te lo entiendo pagar.
　Otra día de mañana
cartas de lejos le traen;
tintas venían de fuera,
de dentro escritas con sangre,
que su Roldán era muerto
en la caza de Roncesvalles.

An eagle strong was in pursuit,
  And sought to strike him down,
The panting hawk a shelter sought
  Beneath my silken gown;
The furious eagle dragged him forth,
  While loud the hawk did shriek,
And struck its claws into his plumes,
  And tore him with its beak."

" O Lady! " quoth her waiting maid,
  " This dream is plain to me;
The wild hawk is thy noble spouse
  Who comes across the sea;
The eagle it is thou thyself,
  With whom he has to wed,
The high hill is the holy Church,
  Where the blessing must be said."

" If so be it, thou maiden sweet,
  A guerdon rich thou'lt win; "
But letters came at dawn inscribed *
  With ink outside, within
All blood; they told a dismal tale,
  That rang throughout the palace,
That brave Orlando had been slain
  In the chase of Roncevalles.

James Young Gibson

* These three lines changed from:

  " But morning dawned and letters came,
   All blood without, within;
  They told a tale, a dismal tale."

Ed.

28   *MUDARRA Y RODRIGO*

A caza va don Rodrigo,
ese que dicen de Lara;
perdido había el azor,
no hallaba niguna caza;
con el gran siesta que hace
arrimado se ha a una haya,
maldiciendo a Mudarrillo,
hijo de la renegada,
que si a las manos le hubiese
que le sacaría el alma.
El señor estando en esto,
Mudarrillo que asomaba:
—Dios te salve, buen señor,
debajo de la verde haya.
—Así haga a ti, caballero;
buena sea tu llegada.
—Dígasme, señor, tu nombre,
decirte he yo la mi gracia.
—A mí llaman don Rodrigo,
y aun don Rodrigo de Lara,
cuñado de don Gonzalo,
hermano de doña Sancha;
por sobrinos me los hube
los siete infantes de Lara.
Maldigo aquí a Mudarrillo,
hijo de la renegada;
si delante lo tuviese
yo le sacaría el alma.
—Si a ti dicen don Rodrigo,
y aun don Rodrigo de Lara,
a mi Mudarra González,
hijo de la renegada,

MUDARRA AND RODRIGO

A-hunting went the noble knight,
And Don Rodrigo was he hight,
   Rodrigo, he of Lara;
The noon-day heat was very great.
Beneath a shady beech he sate,
   And cursed the young Mudarra;
"Thou son of Moorish maid," quoth he,
"If I should lay my hands on thee,
Thou bastard of a curséd race,
I'd tear thy heart from out its place."

Thus spoke the lordling in his pride;
A stranger youth came to his side,
   And due obeisance made;
"Sir knight, God's blessing rest on thee,
Beneath the green and shady tree;"
   The knight he bowed, and said:
"Good squire, thy coming it is blest,
Pray sit thee down a while and rest!"
   "Nay, good sir knight, before I go,
Thine honored name I fain would know."

Then up and spake the knight of fame:
"'Tis Don Rodrigo is my name,
   Rodrigo, I, of Lara;
My sister, Lady Sancha fair,
Wedded Gonzalo, Lara's heir;
My nephews were the youthful band,
Whose fate is known through all the land,
   The seven sons of Lara;
I wait Mudarra in this glade,
Son of the curséd Moorish maid;
If he were now before my sight,
I'd tear his heart out to the light."

"If thou hast come from Lara's stem,
And Don Rodrigo is thy name,
   Then I'm the young Mudarra,
Born of the Moorish renegade,

de Gonzalo Gustios hijo
y alnado de doña Sancha;
por hermanos me los hube
los siete infantes de Lara;
tú los vendiste traidor,
en el val del Arabiana.
Mas si Dios ahora me ayuda
aquí dejarás el alma.
—Espéresme, don Mudarra,
iré a tomar las mis armas.
—El espera que tú diste
a los infantes de Lara;
aquí morirás, traidor,
nemigo de doña Sancha.

29   *AMOR MAS PODEROSO QUE LA MUERTE*

Conde Niño por amores
es niño y pasó la mar;
va a dar agua a su caballo
la mañana de San Juan.
Mientras el caballo bebe
él canta dulce cantar;
todas las aves del cielo
se paraban a escuchar,
caminante que camina
olvida su caminar,
navegante que navega
la nave vuelve hacia allá.
La reina estaba labrando,
la hija durmiendo está:
—Levantaos, Albaniña,
de vuestro dulce folgar,
sentiréis cantar hermoso
la sirenita del mar.

Gonzalo's son by Moorish maid;
I am the Lady Sancha's heir,
And these, they were my brothers fair,
   The seven sons of Lara;
Their lives, O traitor, thou didst sell,
In dark Arabiana's dell,
May God above be in my aid,
And I will lay thee with the dead!"

"Wait here a space within this field,
Till I shall bring my sword and shield,
   I'll fight with thee, Mudarra!"
"The space thou gavest them, I'll give,
One moment more thou hast to live;
Go, traitor, to thy doom below,
My father's curse and Sancha's foe!"
   Struck home the young Mudarra.

James Young Gibson

LOVE THAN DEATH MORE STRONG   29

The Conde Niño all for love
   Has crossed the ocean wide,
And on the morn of good Saint John
   Halts by the waterside.

The while his brave steed drinks his fill
   From out the crystal spring
The little birds all pause in air
   To hear the Conde sing.

The music draws the gallant ships
   Unto the lonely shore,
While travelers their roads forget
   And never journey more.

The queen her child awakes from sleep:
   "Arise, white maid so fair,
And hear the song the siren sings
   Borne on the salt sea air."

—No es la sirenita, madre,
la de tan bello cantar,
sino es el Conde Niño
que por mí quiere finar.
¡Quién le pudiese valer
en su tan triste penar!
—Si por tus amores pena,
¡oh, malhaya su cantar!
y porque nunca los goce
yo le mandaré matar.
—Si le manda matar, madre,
juntos nos han de enterrar.
    El murió a la media noche,
ella a los gallos cantar;
a ella como hija de reyes
la entierran en el altar,
a él como hijo de conde
unos pasos más atrás.
De ella nació un rosal blanco,
dél nació un espino albar;
crece el uno, crece el otro,
los dos se van a juntar;
las ramitas que se alcanzan
fuertes abrazos se dan,
y las que no se alcanzaban
no dejan de suspirar.
La reina llena de envidia
ambos los dos mandó cortar;
el galán que los cortaba
no cesaba de llorar.
De ella naciera una garza,
de él un fuerte gavilán;
juntos vuelan por el cielo,
juntos vuelan par a par.

"That is no siren, Mother mine,
   Singing beside the sea,
It is the faithful Conde Niño
   Who'd gladly die for me.

"Who will befriend the loyal knight
   Who has grieved for me so long?"
"If he sorrows for your sake
   Accursèd be his song!

"He never shall enjoy your love
   Lying in his tomb!"
"If you kill him, cruel one,
   I will share his doom!"

The unhappy count at midnight died,
   At cock crow she expired.
Beside the altar they laid her down
   In royal robes attired.

A count's son only was the knight,
   Below her he must rest.
From out his body a pale thorn grew,
   A white rose from her breast.

The one grew and the other grew
   Till they could interlace,
And the little branches mounting up
   Strongly did embrace.

The little branches that stayed below
   Never ceased to sigh,
And envy filled the wicked queen,
   Who bade that they should die.

When a weeping courtier cut them down
   They changed their flowery guise,
She a heron and he a hawk
   Flew upward through the skies.

Elizabeth du Gué Trapier

30   *REY DON SANCHO*

—¡Guarte, guarte, rey don Sancho.
no digas que no te aviso,
que del cerco de Zamora
un traidor había salido:
Vellido Dolfos se llama,
hijo de Dolfos Vellido;
si gran traidor fué su padre,
mayor traidor es el hijo;
cuatro traiciones ha hecho,
y con ésta serán cinco!
    Gritos dan en el real:
¡A don Sancho han mal herido!
¡Muerto le ha Vellido Dolfos;
gran traición ha cometido!
    Desque le tuviera muerto
metióse por un postigo;
por las calles de Zamora
va dando voces y gritos:
—¡Tiempo era doña Urraca,
de cumplir lo prometido!

31   *EL CONDE ARNALDOS*

    ¡Quién hubiese tal ventura
sobre las aguas del mar
como hubo el conde Arnaldos
la mañana de san Juan!
Con un falcón en la mano
la caza iba a cazar,
y venir vió una galera
que a tierra quiere llegar;
las velas traía de seda,
la jarcia de un cendal.
Marinero que la manda,
diciendo viene un cantar

KING DON SANCHO   30

'King Don Sancho, King Don Sancho,
　　Never say you've not been told,
From this city of Zamora
　　Has gone forth a traitor bold;
He calls himself Vellido Dolfos,
　　Son of Dolfos, traitor old;
Four the treasons he's committed,
　　With a fifth the tale is told.
If the sire was a foul traitor,
　　Fouler is the offspring's mould.'
Shouts break out in the encampment:
　　'Sancho's hit and lying cold:
Murdered by Vellido Dolfos,
　　By the traitor overbold.'
Killed the king, he's fled for shelter
　　By a postern in the hold,
Through the streets of fair Zamora
　　Have his shouts and clamours rolled:
'Time it is to pay, Urraca,
　　If your promise you would hold.'

William J. Entwistle

COUNT ARNALDOS   31

Who was ever sped by fortune
　　O'er the ocean's waters, say,
As the happy Count Arnaldos,
　　On the morn of San Juan's day?
In his hand he held a falcon,
　　And he went to chase the game,
When a gay and splendid galley
　　To the shore advancing came.
All its fluttering sails were silken,
　　All its shrouds of flounces clear,
And the gay and clear-voiced helmsman
　　Sang a song so sweet to hear

que la mar ponía en calma,
los vientos hace amainar,
los peces que andan al hondo,
arriba los hace andar;
las aves que andan volando,
las hace al mástil posar.
      —Galera, la mi galera,
Dios te me guarde de mal.—
Allí habló el conde Arnaldos,
bien oiréis lo que dirá:
—Por Dios te ruego, marinero,
dígasme ora ese cantar.—
      Respondióle el marinero,
tal respuesta lo fué a dar:
—Yo no digo mi canción
sino a quién conmigo va.

32   *LA MISA DE AMOR*

      Mañanita de san Juan,
mañanita de primor,
cuando damas y galanes
van a oír misa mayor.
Allá va la mi señora,
entre todas la mejor;
viste saya sobre saya,
mantellín de tornasol,
camisa con oro y perlas
bordada en el cabezón.
En la su boca muy linda
lleva un poco de dulzor;
en la su cara tan blanca,
un poquito de arrebol,
v en los sus ojuelos garzos
lleva un poco de alcohol;

That the waves were calm and silent,
  And the noisy storm-wind hushed,
And the fish that live the deepest
  To the water's surface rushed;
While the restless birds were gathered
  Listening on the masts, and still.
"O, my galley!—O, my galley!
  God preserve us now from ill."
Thus he spake, the Count Arnaldos,
  Thus he spake, and thou shalt hear:
"Sing that song, by Heaven I charge thee!
  Sing that song, good mariner."
But the mariner was silent
  And he only answered—"No!
They alone must hear my music,
  They alone who with me go."

John Bowring

MASS OF LOVE   32

Dawn of a bright June morning,
  The birthday of Saint John,
When ladies and their lovers
  To hear High Mass are gone.

Yonder goes my lady,
  Among them all, the best;
In colored silk mantilla
  And many skirts she's dressed.

Embroidered is her bodice
  With gems of pearl and gold.
Her lips of beauty rare
  Beguiling sweetness hold.

Faint the touch of rouge
  On cheeks of fairest white,
Sparkling blue her eyes
  With subtle art made bright.

así entraba por la iglesia
relumbrando como sol,
Las damas mueren de envidia,
y los galanes de amor.
El que cantaba en el coro,
en el credo se perdió;
el abad que dice misa,
ha trocado la lición;
monacillos que le ayudan,
no aciertan responder, non,
por decir "amén, amén,"
decían "amor, amor."

ROMANCE DEL PRISIONERO

33

Que por mayo era, por mayo,
cuando hace la calor,
cuando los trigos encañan
y están los campos en flor,
cuando canta la calandria
y responde el ruiseñor,
cuando los enamorados
van a servir al amor;
sino yo, triste, cuitado,
que vivo en esta prisión;
que ni sé cuándo es de día
ni cuándo las noches son,
sino por una avecilla
que me cantaba al albor.
Matómela un ballestero;
déle Dios mal galardón.

Proudly church she entered
  Radiant as sun above,
Ladies died of envy
  And courtiers, of love.

A singer in the choir
  His place lost in the creed;
The priest who read the lesson
  The pages did not heed,

And acolytes beside him
  No order could restore;
Instead of Amen, Amen,
  They sang *Amor, Amor.*

Anna Pursche

THE PRISONER   33

It was May, the month of May,
  When the sun sends forth its heat,
When the meadows are in flower,
  When ripens the ear of wheat,
When the lark on high is singing
  And the nightingale replies,
When lovers attend their ladies
  In service to gain love's prize;
But I, here wretched and sad
  Who live within prison walls,
I know not when the day breaks,
  I know not when the night falls,
Save for the wee bird that sang
  At the dawn its orison,
But it was shot by an archer;
  May God send him malison!

E. L. T.

34   *ROMANCE DE ABENÁMAR Y EL REY DON JUAN* *

—¡Abenámar, Abenámar,
moro de la morería,
el día que tú naciste
grandes señales había!
Estaba la mar en calma,
la luna estaba crecida;
moro que en tal signo nace
no debe decir mentira.
—No te la diré, señor,
aunque me cueste la vida.
—Yo te agradezco, Abenámar,
aquesta tu cortesía.
¿Qué castillos son aquellos?
¡Altos son y relucían!
—El Alhambra era, señor,
y la otra la mezquita;
los otros los Alixares,
labrados a maravilla,
El moro que los labraba
cien doblas ganaba al día,
y el día que no los labra
otras tantas se perdía.
El otro es Torres Bermejas,
castillo de gran valía;
el otro Generalife,
huerta que par no tenía.

---

* King Juan II of Castile, in the year 1431, approached Granada with the
Moorish Infante Abenalmao whom he had promised to place on the throne
there. They besieged the city, it surrendered, and the Infante was recognized
as its king.

The Arabic poets often spoke of the lord of a region as its "spouse." This
image is found in no literature of the middle ages but the Castilian. Only after
the Spanish soldiers carried the *Romancero* to Germany and the Low Coun-
tries, do we find a besieged city spoken of as a "betrothed" or "bride."

ABENAMAR

34

"Abenamar, Abenamar,
  Moor of Moors, and man of worth!
On the day when thou wert cradled,
  There were signs in heaven and earth.

Hushed in slumber was the ocean,
  And the moon was at its full;
Never Moor should tell a falsehood,
  Whom the lucky planets rule."

Up and spoke the Moorish Ancient,
  Listen to the words he said:
" I will tell the truth, my lord,
  Though it cost me now my head."

"Abenamar, Abenamar,
  With thy words my heart is won!
Tell me what these castles are,
  Shining grandly in the sun! "

" That, my lord, is the Alhambra,
  This the Moorish Mosque apart,
And the rest the Alixares,
  Wrought and carved with wondrous art.

For the Moor who did the labour
  Had a hundred crowns a day;
And each day he shirked the labour
  Had a hundred crowns to pay.

Yonder stands the Generalife,
  Ne'er was garden half so grand;
And below, the tower Bermeja,
  Stronger none in all the land."

Allí hablara el rey don Juan,
bien oiréis lo que decía:
—Si tú quisieras, Granada,
contigo me casaría;
daréte en arras y dote
a Córdoba y a Sevilla,
—Casada soy, rey don Juan,
casada soy, que no viuda;
el moro que a mí tiene
muy grande bien me quería.

35   *LA PÉRDIDA DE ALHAMA*

Paseábase el rey moro
por la ciudad de Granada,
desde la puerta de Elvira
hasta la de Vivarrambla.
 " ¡Ay de mi Alhama! "

Cartas le fueron venidas
que Alhama era ganada;
las cartas echó en el fuego,
y al mensajero matara.
 " ¡Ay de mi Alhama! "

Descabalga de una mula,
y en un caballo cabalga;
por el Zacatín arriba
subido se había al Alhambra.
 " ¡Ay de mi Alhama! "

Como en el Alhambra estuvo,
al mismo punto mandaba
que se toquen sus trompetas,
sus añafiles de plata.
 " ¡Ay de mi Alhama! "

Up and spake the good King John,
  To the city he applied:
"If thou art willing, O Granada,
  I will woo thee for my bride,
Cordova shall be thy dowry,
  And Sevilla by its side."

"I'm no widow, good King John,
  I am still a wedded wife;
And the Moor, who is my husband,
  Loves me better than his life!"

James Young Gibson

A VERY MOURNFUL BALLAD ON THE SIEGE AND CONQUEST OF ALHAMA

35

The Moorish King rides up and down,
Through Granada's royal town;
From Elvira's gates to those
Of Bivarambla on he goes.
        Woe is me, Alhama!

Letters to the monarch tell
How Alhama's city fell;
In the fire the scroll he threw,
And the messenger he slew.
        Woe is me, Alhama!

He quits his mule and mounts his horse
And through the street directs his course;
Through the street of Zacatín
To the Alhambra spurring in.
        Woe is me, Alhama!

When the Alhambra's walls he gained,
On the moment he ordained
That the trumpet straight should sound
With the silver clarion round.
        Woe is me, Alhama!

Y que las cajas de guerra
apriesa toquen al arma,
porque lo oigan sus moriscos,
los de la Vega y Granada.
    "¡Ay de mi Alhama!"

Los moros que el son oyeron
que al sangriento Marte llama,
uno a uno y dos a dos
juntado se ha gran batalla.
    "¡Ay de mi Alhama!"

Allí hablo un moro viejo,
de esta manera hablara:
—¿Para qué nos llamas, rey,
para qué es esta llamada?
    "¡Ay de mi Alhama!"

—Habéis de saber, amigos,
una nueva desdichada:
que cristianos de braveza
ya nos han ganado Alhama.
    "¡Ay de mi Alhama!"

Allí habló un alfaquí
de barba cruda y cana:
—¡Bien se te emplea, buen rey,
buen rey, bien se te empleara!
    "¡Ay de mi Alhama!"

Mataste los Bencerrajes,
que eran la flor de Granada;
cogiste los tornadizos
de Córdoba la nombrada.
    "¡Ay de mi Alhama!"

Por eso mereces, rey,
una pena muy doblada:
que te pierdas tú y el reino
y aquí se pierda Granada.—
    "¡Ay de mi Alhama!"

And when the hollow drums of war
Beat the loud alarm afar,
That the Moors of town and plain
Might answer to the martial strain,
    Woe is me, Alhama!

Then the Moors, by this aware
That bloody Mars recalled them there,
One by one, and two by two,
To a mighty squadron grew.
    Woe is me, Alhama!

Out then spoke an agèd Moor
In these words the King before,
"Wherefore call on us, O King?
What may mean this gathering?"
    Woe is me, Alhama!

"Friends, ye have, alas, to know
Of a most disastrous blow;
That the Christians, stern and bold,
Have obtained Alhama's hold."
    Woe is me, Alhama!

Out then spoke old Alfaquí,
With his beard so white to see,
"Good King! thou art justly served!
Good King! this thou hast deserved.
    Woe is me, Alhama!

"By thee were slain, in evil hour,
The Abencerrage, Granada's flower;
And strangers were received by thee
Of Cordova the chivalry.
    Woe is me, Alhama!

"And for this, O King is sent
On thee a double chastisement;
Thee and thine, thy crown and realm,
One last wreck shall overwhelm.
    Woe is me, Alhama!

Lord Byron

36   *LA CONSTANCIA*

 Mis arreos son las armas,
mi descanso es pelear,
mi cama las duras peñas,
mi dormir siempre velar.
Las manidas son escuras,
los caminos por usar,
el cielo con sus mudanzas
ha por bien de me dañar,
andando de sierra en sierra
por orillas de la mar,
por probar si mi ventura
hay lugar donde avadar.
Pero por vos, mi señora,
todo se ha de comportar.

CONSTANCY

My ornaments are arms,
  My bed the flinty stone,
My rest is war's alarms,
  My sleep to watch alone.
Through gloomy paths unknown,
  Paths which untrodden be,
From rock to rock I go
  Along the dashing sea,
And seek from busy woe
  With hurrying steps to flee;
But know, fair lady! know,
  All this I bear for thee!

John Bowring

Songs of Traditional Type

If the little Mozarabic songs that we have mentioned above (see page 2)
are a revelation of the last five years, the discovery of the stock of Spanish
songs of traditional type may be said to be a find of the first half of
the xxth century. This does not mean that before that time a goodly
number of these songs was not known, but that they had not been
collected, studied and understood in all their delicate beauty.

The form of these little poems comes from the middle ages; and gen-
erally the themes and very often the refrains themselves have the same
origin. But often too, the stanzas have been written during the xvith
or the xviith centuries. The texts in which such songs appear are very
varied: works of well-known poets, as Santillana or Lope, song books,
as that of Herberay, musical works of the xvith or xviith centuries,
classical dramas, and so on. Such a dispersion explains why the critics
of the xixth century had no clear idea of what these songs as a whole
were, nor of their value.

As for their form, they all have a tendency towards one of two types:
the *zejel*, with a definite rhyme in each stanza, whose last line leads into
the refrain common to all the stanzas, as in "Three Moorish girls I
loved," (see page 115); or the parallelistic, with the stylistic repetition of
each thought, varied only by the change of rhyme, as in

from the Cancioneros

"Thou most belovèd one,
come to me at the dawn.

Thou, whom most I love, pray
come at the dawning day."   (see page 117)

The grace and simplicity of these songs, their very delicate expression of feeling and the strange esthetic effect they have upon us, make of them a treasury that, together with the *Romancero*, can be compared with all the cultured poetry of the Golden Age.

But the xixth century discoverer of the *Romancero* ignored these songs. Many romances were translated into English by well-known writers of that epoch. But the traditional songs were not included in the first editions of the Oxford Book of Spanish Verse and have only appeared in its last revision by Trend; so Miss Turnbull has had to translate herself most of the examples she gives in this anthology.

Soon, we may hope, the cultured world will know that these songs, whose original music has been in many cases preserved for us, are at least of as much worth as the *romances*, and no doubt other poets of the English language will feel tempted to render into their own tongue the airy grace, the changing rhythms and the indefinable charm of these little songs.

D. A.

37

Tres morillas me enamoran
en Jaén:
Axa y Fátima y Marién.

Tres morillas tan garridas
iban a coger olivas,
y hallábanlas cogidas
en Jaén:
Axa y Fátima y Marién.

Y hallábanlas cogidas
y tornaban desmaídas
y las colores perdidas
en Jaén:
Axa y Fátima y Marién.

Tres moricas tan lozanas,
tres moricas tan lozanas
iban a coger manzanas
en Jaén:
Axa y Fátima y Marién.

38

¿Por qué me besó Perico?
¿Por qué me besó el traidor?

Dijo que en Francia se usaba
y por eso me besaba,
y también porque sanaba
con el beso su dolor.
¿Por qué me besó Perico?
¿Por qué me besó el traidor

Three Moorish girls I loved   37
In Jaén,
Axa and Fátima and Marién.

Three Moorish girls so gay
Went olive-plucking there,
And found them plucked away
In Jaén,
Axa and Fátima and Marién.

And found them plucked away
And turned back in dismay,
And pale and sad were they
In Jaén,
Axa and Fátima and Marién.

Three Moorish girls so fair,
Three Moorish girls so fair
Went apple-plucking there
In Jaén,
Axa and Fátima and Marién.

Jean Rogers Longland

Why did Perico kiss me?   38
Why did the traitor kiss me?

He said 'twas the custom in France
and therefore to look not askance
when he kissed me, it was romance,
'twould cure his pain if he kissed me.
Why did Perico kiss me?
Why did the traitor kiss me?

E. L. T.

39
De los álamos vengo, madre,
de ver cómo los menea el aire.

De los álamos de Sevilla,
de ver a mi linda amiga.

De los álamos vengo, madre,
de ver cómo los menea el aire.

40
Al alba venid, buen amigo,
al alba venid.

Amigo el que yo más quería,
venid al alba del día.

Amigo el que yo más amaba,
venid a la luz del alba.

Venid a la luz del día,
non trayáis compañía.

Venid a la luz del alba,
non traigáis gran compaña.

41
Dentro en el vergel
moriré.
Dentro en el rosal
matarm'han.

Yo m'iba, mi madre,
las rosas coger;
hallé mis amores
dentro en el vergel.
Dentro del rosal
matarm'han.

Mother, I come from the aspen trees,   39
ah, how they tremble in the breeze!

From the aspen trees of Seville,
to see my sweet maid is my will.

Mother, I come from the aspen trees,
ah, how they tremble in the breeze!

E. L. T.

Come at dawn, my loved one,   40
come at dawn.

Thou most belovèd one,
come to me at the dawn.

Thou, whom most I love, pray
come at the dawning day.

Come at the light of dawn,
come to me all alone.

Come at the first light of day,
bring none from home away.

E. L. T.

There in the flower garden   41
I shall die.
There in the rosary
they'll kill me.

I went there, my mother,
to pluck roses red;
and I found, my mother,
I found love instead.
There in the rosary
they'll kill me.

E. L. T.

42   Que yo, mi madre, yo,
que la flor de la villa
m'era yo.

                Ibame yo, mi madre,
a vender pan a la villa,
y todos me decían:
—" ¡qué panadera garrida! "

                Garrida m'era yo,
que la flor de la villa
m'era yo.

                Luna que reluces,
toda la noche alumbres.

                Ay, luna que reluces
blanca y plateada,
toda la noche alumbres
a mi linda enamorada.
Amada que reluces,
toda la noche alumbres.

44   Gritos daba la morenica
so el olivar,
que las ramas hace temblar.

                La niña, cuerpo garrido,
morenica, cuerpo garrido,
lloraba su muerto amigo
so el olivar:
que las ramas hace temblar.

For I, my mother, I,   42
the flower of the town,
it was I.

I went, my mother, I,
to the town to sell my bread,
and wherever I went they said:
"What a handsome seller of bread!"

For so handsome was I,
the flower of the town,
it was I.

E. L. T.

Moon, thou with thy light   43
mayst illumine the night.

Ah, moon, thou with thy light,
white and silvery one,
mayst illumine all night
my beloved, my lovely one.
Belovéd, thou with thy light,
mayst illumine the night.

E. L. T.

The little brown maid wailing sore,   44
out in the olive grove,
makes tremble the branches above.

The little maid of graceful mien,
little brown maid of graceful mien,
her dead lover did moan, I ween,
out in the olive grove,
and the branches tremble above.

E. L. T.

45
  Malferida iba la garza
enamorada:
sola va y gritos daba.

  Donde la garza hace su nido,
ribericas de aquel río,
sola va y gritos daba.

46
  Quiero dormir y no puedo,
qu'el amor me quita el sueño.

  Manda pregonar el rey
por Granada y por Sevilla
que todo hombre enamorado
que se case con su amiga:
qu'el amor me quita el sueño.

  Que se case con su amiga.
¿Qué haré, triste, cuitado,
que era casada la mía?
qu'el amor me quita el sueño.

  Quiero dormir y no puedo,
qu'el amor me quita el sueño.

47
  ¡Todos duermen, corazón,
todos duermen y vos, non!

  El dolor que habéis cobrado
siempre os terná desvelado,
que él corazón lastimado
recuérdalo la pasión.
¡Todos duermen, corazón,
todos duermen y vos, non!

Sore wounded by love, the heron
is making moan:
wildly wailing, she goes alone.

Where the heron her nest doth hide,
sore wounded, by the riverside,
wildly wailing she goes alone.

E. L. T.

Ah, how I wish I could sleep,
but love from sleeping me doth keep!

The king has proclaimed this decree,
in Granada and in Seville,
that each man in love with his dear,
must marry to do the king's will:
But love from sleeping me doth keep.

With his dear must marry straightway.
Sad and wretched, what shall I do?
whose dear is married, lack-a-day!
And love from sleeping me doth keep.

Ah, how I wish I could sleep,
but love, from sleeping, me doth keep!

E. L. T.

All are sleeping, my sad heart,
all are sleeping, thou art not.

47

Night-long vigil thou dost make,
sorrow keeping thee awake,
for the suffering heart doth ache,
never its passion forgot.
All are sleeping, my sad heart,
all are sleeping, thou art not.

E. L. T.

48
   Entra mayo y sale abril:
   ¡tan garridico le ví venir!

   Entra mayo con sus flores,
   sale abril con sus amores
   y los dulces amadores
   comiezan a bien servir.

49
   Mano a mano los dos amores,
   mano a mano.

   El galán y la galana
   ambos vuelven al agua clara
   mano a mano.

50
   Que de noche le mataron
   al caballero,
   la gala de Medina,
   la flor de Olmedo.

   Sombras le avisaron
   que no saliese
   y le aconsejaron
   que no se fuese
   el caballero,
   la gala de Medina,
   la flor de Olmedo.*

* Lope de Vega, *El caballero de Olmedo.*

April goes out as May comes in,   48
how graceful I saw her come in!

May comes in with her flowers,
April goes out with her lovers
and the gentle adorers
their missions of love begin.

E. L. T.

Side by side the two lovers shy,   49
side by side.

The wooer and the wooed, his dear,
splash round and round in water clear,
side by side.

E. L. T.

For on that night they killed him,   50
in that dark hour,
the knight of Olmedo,
of Medina the flower.

The shades had warned him
not to depart,
they had forearmed him,
lest he should start
in that dark hour,
the knight of Olmedo,
of Medina the flower.

E. L. T.

Renaissance

Gil Vicente

Portuguese by birth, goldsmith, maker of that beautiful monstrance in the Monastery of Belem, musician, great poet, genial playwright, Gil Vicente belongs to Spanish literature as well as to the Portuguese, for he wrote in both languages. The poems that he published appear in his dramatic works. Of all of them, we are only certain that one is really his, *Grace and beauty has the maid* (see page 129). But it is perhaps the

c. 1465–1536?

most simply beautiful little song of all Spanish literature. We are in doubt as to the origin of many of the lyric poems inserted in the dramatic works of Gil Vicente as also of Lope de Vega. Gil Vicente, like Lope, was very sympathetic with the popular vein, and sometimes imitated it and at other times used it as a theme for amplification, in this way saving the little song from oblivion.

D. A.

51   *CANTIGA*

Muy graciosa es la doncella,
¡cómo es bella y hermosa!

Digas tú, el marinero
que en las naves vivías,
si la nave o la vela o la estrella
es tan bella.

Digas tú, el caballero
que las armas vestías,
si el caballo o las armas o la guerra
es tan bella.

Digas tú, el pastorico
que el ganadico guardas,
si el ganado o las valles o la sierra
es tan bella.

En la huerta nasce la rosa

En la huerta nasce la rosa:
quiérome ir allá
por mirar al ruiseñor
cómo cantaba.

Por las riberas del río
limones coge la virgo:
Quiérome ir allá
por mirar al ruiseñor
cómo cantaba.

SONG   51

   Grace and beauty has the maid,
Could anything more lovely be?

   Sailor, you who live on ships,
Did you ever see
Any ship or sail or star
As beautiful as she?

   Knight of war, in armour clad,
Did you ever see
Horse or arms or battle-field
As beautiful as she?

   Shepherd, you who guard your flock,
Did you ever see
Cattle, vale or mountain range
As beautiful as she?

Alice Jane McVan

In the garden blossoms the rose   52

   In the garden blossoms the rose:
Would that I could be there
To see how the nightingale sings
In that garden so fair!

   On the banks where the river flows
Picking lemons the maiden goes:
Would that I could be there
To see how the nightingale sings
In that garden so fair!

Limones cogía la virgo
para dar al su amigo:
quiérome ir allá
para ver al ruiseñor
cómo cantaba.

Para dar al su amigo
en un sombrero de sirgo:
quiérome ir allá
para ver al ruiseñor
cómo cantaba.

53   *Del rosal vengo, mi madre*

Del rosal vengo, mi madre,
vengo del rosale.

A riberas de aquel vado
viera estar rosal granado:
vengo del rosale.

A riberas de aquel río
viera estar rosal florido:
vengo del rosale.

Viera estar rosal florido
cogí rosas con sospiro:
vengo del rosale.

¡Del rosal vengo, mi madre,
vengo del rosale!

Picking lemons the maiden goes
To give to the loved one she knows:
Would that I could be there
To see how the nightingale sings
In that garden so fair!

To give to the loved one she knows
In her silken hat the fruit she stows:
Would that I could be there
To see how the nightingale sings
In that garden so fair!

E. L. T.

I come from the rose garden, Mother   53

I come from the rose garden, Mother,
from the rose garden I come.

On the banks where the streamlet flows,
there doth blossom many a rose:
from the rose garden I come.

On the banks of that flowing river
the rose garden is blooming ever:
from the rose garden I come.

Blooming ever before my eyes,
where I plucked the roses with sighs:
from the rose garden I come.

I come from the rose garden, Mother,
from the rose garden I come.

E. L. T.

ROMANCE

En el mes era de abril,
de mayo antes un día,
cuando lirïos y rosas
muestran más su alegría,
en la noche más serena
que el cielo hacer podía,
cuando la hermosa infanta
Flérida ya se partía,
en la huerta de su padre
a los árboles decía:
"Quedaos adiós, mis flores,
mi gloria que ser solía:
voyme a tierras extranjeras,
pues ventura allá me guía.
Si mi padre me buscare,
que grande bien me quería,
digan que amor me lleva,
que no fué la culpa mía:
tal tema tomó comigo
que me venció su porfía.
¡Triste no sé a dó vó,
ni nadie me lo decía!"
Allí habla Don Duardos:
"No lloréis, mi alegría,
que en los reinos de Inglaterra
más claras aguas había
y más hermosos jardines,
y vuesos, señora mía.
Ternéis trecientas doncellas
de alta genelosía;
de plata son los palacios
para vuesa señoría,
de esmeraldas y jacintos,
de oro fino de Turquía,
con letreros esmaltados
que cuentan la vida mía,
cuentan los vivos dolores
que me distes aquel día,
cuando con Primaleón

FLERIDA AND DON DUARDOS

54

It was the month of April,
One day from the month of May,
When the roses and the lilies
Don their loveliest array,
And the night so calm and tranquil
As e'er heavens might display,
When Flerida the fair Infanta
Was to start upon her way.
In the garden of her father
To the trees there she did say:
"Fare ye well now, O my flowers,
That were wont to make me gay,
For to foreign lands I travel,
Since my fortune thither lay.
To my father, if he seek me,
Since so well he loved me, say
That not mine, not mine the fault was,
Love it is bears me away;
For he spake with such insistence
That I might not say him nay.
But I know not, none hath told me,
Whither sad at heart I stray."
Then spake to her Don Duardos:
"Weep not, lady mine, I pray,
For within the realm of England
Clearer streams there are alway,
And gardens that are fairer far,
And thine, lady, are they.
Three hundred noble maidens
Shall thy behests obey;
Of silver are the palaces
That are thine, lady, this day.
Yea, of fine gold from Turkey,
Jacinths, emeralds, are they,
Adornèd with inscriptions
That all my life portray:
Even of the cruel pains they tell
Thou gavest me on that day
When I with Primaleon

fuertemente combatía.
¡Señora, vos me matastes,
que yo a él no lo temía!"
Sus lágrimas consolaba
Flérida, que esto oía.
Fuéronse a las galeras
que Don Duardos tenía:
cincuenta eran por cuenta;
todas van en compañía.
Al son de sus dulces remos
la princesa se adormía
en brazos de Don Duardos
que bien le pertenecía.
Sepan cuantos son nacidos ·
aquesta sentencia mía:
que contra la muerte y amor
nadie no tiene valía.

Was mortally at fray.
Not he, for him I feared not,
But thou didst me then slay."
These words now when Flerida heard
Her grief they did allay,
And to Don Duardos' ships they went
That there at anchor stay:
Fifty they were in number
That as one their anchors weigh.
To the soft sound of the rowing
The princess sleeping lay,
Asleep now in Don Duardos' arms,
Since she was his this day.
Now therefore to all men be known
The moral of my lay:
Against the might of Death and Love
In vain is all assay.

Aubrey F. G. Bell

Garcilaso de la Vega

At about 1530 a revolution took place in Spanish lyric poetry. It is usually called Italianism and many think it is merely the adoption into Castilian poetry of the eleven syllable line. Until then, the line used in the Castilian lyric was the eight syllable line, that of the ballad. But this transformation can hardly be reduced to that simple external element. In reality, Castilian poetry assimilated completely the Italian Renaissance conception of the lyric.

In 1526, Andrea Navegero was sent to Spain as Ambassador from the Venetian Republic. He was the perfect example of the Renaissance gentleman: humanist, historian, poet, imitator of Vergil and Catullus and of the poets of the Greek Anthology. There was at that time, in the court of the Emperor at Granada, a young Catalan poet, Boscán, of minor importance, but who was to play a very important historical role. He was advised by Navegero to write poems in the Italian manner in the Castilian language, and he began then to write in the new style. Boscán had an intimate friend, a man of genius and one of the greatest Spanish poets, Garcilaso de la Vega. He too tried the new style, and having written only a small number of poems, established the new poetry to this day.

1503-1536

Garcilaso was born in the heart of Spain, in Toledo. While still very young he entered the service of Charles V, as a member of the royal guard, and died of a wound in the French campaign in 1536 at the age of thirty-three. No one knew his poetry until after his death, for out of spiritual delicacy he concealed his poems and none were published during his life. Their success was immediate when they were published in 1543, and before 1560 sixteen more editions had appeared. It may be said that to no poet does Spanish poetry owe more than to Garcilaso. And this beautiful work was created simply and mysteriously, like a secret game outside of his external life, without any apparent effort, as completely by divine grace, by natural gift, as the flight of a bird or the issue of a crystalline stream.

Garcilaso was the greatest writer of love lyrics that Spain had had to that time, and still is without equal except perhaps for Bécquer. His most beautiful and celebrated poem, Eclogue I, in which the voice of love rises above the note of disillusionment and bitterness, is the purest and clearest love elegy that has ever resounded in the Spanish language.

P. S.

55

EGLOGA PRIMERA

El dulce lamentar de dos pastores,
Salicio juntamente y Nemoroso,
he de contar, sus quejas imitando;
cuyas ovejas al cantar sabroso
estaban muy atentas, los amores,
de pacer olvidadas, escuchando.
Tú, que ganaste obrando
un nombre en todo el mundo,
y un grado sin segundo,
agora estés atento, sólo y dado
al ínclito gobierno del Estado
albano; agora vuelto a la otra parte,
resplandeciente, armado,
representando en tierra el fiero Marte;

agora de cuidados enojosos
y de negocios libre, por ventura
andes a caza, el monte fatigando
en ardiente jinete, que apresura
el curso tras los ciervos temerosos,
que en vano su morir van dilatando;
espera, que en tornando
a ser restituído
al ocio ya perdido,
luego verás ejercitar mi pluma
por la infinita innumerable suma
de tus virtudes y famosas obras;
antes que me consuma,
faltando a ti, que a todo el mundo sobras.

En tanto que este tiempo que adivino
viene a sacarme de la deuda un día,
que se debe a tu fama y a tu gloria;
que es deuda general, no sólo mía,
mas de cualquier ingenio peregrino
que celebra lo dino de memoria;
el árbol de vitoria
que ciñe estrechamente
tu gloriösa frente

ECLOGUE 1   **55**

To Don Pedro de Toledo, Viceroy of Naples

The sweet lament of two Castilian swains,
Salicio's love and Nemoroso's tears,
In sympathy I sing, to whose loved strains
Their flocks, of food forgetful, crowding round,
Were most attentive: Pride of Spanish peers!
Who, by thy splendid deeds, has gained a name
And rank on earth unrivalled,—whether crowned
With cares, Alvano, wielding now the rod
Of empire, now the dreadful bolts that tame
Strong kings, in motion to the trumpet's sound,
Express vicegerent of the Thracian God;

Or whether, from the cumbrous burden freed
Of state affairs, thou seek'st the echoing plain,
Chasing, upon thy spirited fleet steed,
The trembling stag that bounds abroad, in vain
Lengthening out life,—though deeply now engrossed
By cares, I hope, so soon as I regain
The leisure I have lost,
To celebrate, with my recording quill,
Thy virtues and brave deeds, a starry sum,
Ere grief, or age, or silent death turn chill
My poesy's warm pulse, and I become
Nothing to thee, whose worth the nations blaze,
Failing thy sight, and songless in thy praise.

But till that day, predestined by the Muse,
Appears to cancel the memorial dues
Owed to thy glory and renown—a claim
Not only upon me, but which belongs
To all fine spirits that transmit to fame
Ennobling deeds in monumental songs,—
Let the green laurel whose victorious boughs
Clasp in endearment thine illustrious brows,
To the weak ivy give permissive place,

dé lugar a la hiedra que se planta
debajo de tu sombra, y se levanta
poco a poco, arrimada a tus loores;
y en cuanto esto se canta,
escucha tú el cantar de mis pastores.

Saliendo de las ondas encendido,
rayaba de los montes el altura
el sol, cuando Salicio, recostado
al pie de un alta haya, en la verdura,
por donde un agua clara con sonido
atravesaba el fresco y verde prado;
él, con canto acordado
al rumor que sonaba,
del agua que pasaba,
se quejaba tan dulce y blandamente
como si no estuviera de allí ausente
la que de su dolor culpa tenía;
y así, como presente,
razonando con ella, le decía.

Salicio

¡Oh más dura que mármol a mis quejas,
y al encendido fuego en que me quemo
más helada que nieve, Galatea!
Estoy muriendo, y aun la vida temo;
témola con razón, pues tú me dejas;
que no hay, sin ti, el vivir para qué sea.
Vergüenza he que me vea
ninguno en tal estado,
de ti desamparado,
y de mí mismo yo me corro agora.
¿De un alma te desdeñas ser señora,
donde siempre moraste, no pudiendo
della salir un hora?
Salid sin duelo, lágrimas, corriendo.

Which, rooted in thy shade, thou first of trees,
May hope by slow degrees
To tower aloft, supported by thy praise;
Since Time to thee sublimer strains shall bring,
Hark to my shepherds, as they sit and sing.

The sun, from rosy billows risen, had rayed
With gold the mountain tops, when at the foot
Of a tall beech romantic, whose green shade
Fell on a brook, that, sweet-voiced as a lute,
Through lively pastures wound its sparkling way,
Sad on the daisied turf Salicio lay;
And with a voice in concord to the sound
Of all the many winds, and waters round,
As o'er the mossy stones they swiftly stole,
Poured forth in melancholy song his soul
Of sorrow with a fall
So sweet, and aye so mildly musical,
None could have thought that she whose seeming guile
Had caused his anguish, absent was the while,
But that in very deed the unhappy youth
Did, face to face, upbraid her questioned truth.

Salicio

More hard than marble to my mild complaints,
And to the lively flame with which I glow,
Cold, Galatea, cold as winter snow!
I feel that I must die, my spirit faints,
And dreads continuing life; for, alienate
From thee, life sinks into a weary weight,
To be shook off with pleasure; from all eyes
I shrink, e'en from myself despised I turn,
And left by her for whom I yearn,
My cheek is tinged with crimson; heart of ice!
Dost thou the worshipped mistress scorn to be
Of one whose cherished guest thou ever art;
Not being able for one hour to free
Thine image from my heart?
This dost thou scorn? in gentleness of woe
Flow forth, my tears, 'tis meet that ye should flow!

El sol tiende los rayos de su lumbre
por montes y por valles, despertando
las aves y animales y la gente:
cuál por el aire claro va volando,
cuál por el verde valle o alta cumbre
paciendo va segura y libremente,
cuál con el sol presente
va de nuevo al oficio,
y al usado ejercicio
do su natura o menester le inclina:
siempre está en llanto esta ánima mesquina,
cuando la sombra el mundo va cubriendo
o la luz se avecina.
Salid sin duelo, lágrimas, corriendo.

¿Y tú, desta mi vida ya olvidada,
sin mostrar un pequeño sentimiento
de que por ti Salicio triste muera,
dejas llevar, desconocida, al viento
el amor y la fe que ser guardada
eternamente sólo a mí debiera?
¡Oh Dios! ¿Por qué siquiera,
pues ves desde tu altura
esta falsa perjura
causar la muerte de un estrecho amigo,
no recibe del cielo algún castigo?
Si en pago del amor yo estoy muriendo,
¿qué hará el enemigo?
Salid sin duelo, lágrimas, corriendo.

Por ti el silencio de la selva umbrosa,
por ti la esquividad y apartamiento
del solitario monte me agradaba;
por ti la verde hierba, el fresco viento,
el blanco lirio y colorada rosa
y dulce primavera deseaba.
¡Ay, cuánto me engañaba!
¡Ay, cuán diferente era
y cuán de otra manera

The sun shoots forth the arrows of his light
O'er hills and valleys, wakening to fresh birth
The birds, and animals, and tribes of earth,
That through the crystal air pursue their flight,
That o'er the verdant vale and craggy height
In perfect liberty and safety feed,
That with the present sun afresh proceed
To the due toils of life,
As their own wants or inclinations lead;
This wretched spirit is alone at strife
With peace, in tears at eve, in tears when bright
The morning breaks; in gentleness of woe,
Flow forth my tears, 'tis meet that ye should flow!

And thou, without one pensive memory
Of this my life, without the slightest sign
Of pity for my pangs, dost thou consign
To the stray winds, ungrateful, every tie
Of love and faith, which thou didst vow should be
Locked in thy soul eternally for me?
Oh righteous Gods! if from on high ye view
This false, this perjured maid
Work the destruction of a friend so true,
Why leave her crime of justice unrepaid?
Dying I am with hopeless, sharp concern;
If to tried friendship this is the return
She makes, with what will she requite her foe?
Flow forth, my tears, 'tis meet that ye should flow!

Through thee the silence of the shaded glen,
Through thee the horror of the lonely mountain
Pleased me no less than the resort of men;
The breeze, the summer wood, and lucid fountain,
The purple rose, white lily of the lake,
Were sweet for thy sweet sake;
For thee the fragrant primrose, dropt with dew,
Was wished when first it blew!
Oh how completely was I in all this
Myself deceiving! oh the different part
That thou wert acting, covering with a kiss

lo que en tu falso pecho se escondía!
Bien claro con su voz me lo decía
la siniestra corneja repitiendo
la desventura mía.
Salid sin duelo, lágrimas, corriendo.

¡Cuántas veces, durmiendo en la floresta,
reputándolo yo por desvarío,
vi mi mal entre sueños desdichado!
Soñaba que en el tiempo del estío
llevaba, por pasar allí la siesta,
a beber en el Tajo mi ganado;
y después de llegado,
sin saber de cuál arte,
por desusada parte
y por nuevo camino el agua se iba;
ardiendo ya con la calor estiva,
el curso, enajenado, iba siguiendo
del agua fugitiva.
Salid sin duelo, lágrimas, corriendo.

Tu dulce habla ¿en cúya oreja suena?
Tus claros ojos ¿a quién los volviste?
¿Por quién tan sin respeto me trocaste?
Tu quebrantada fe ¿dó la pusiste?
¿Cuál es el cuello que, como en cadena,
de tus hermosos brazos anudaste?
No hay corazón que baste,
aunque fuese de piedra,
viendo mi amada hiedra,
de mí arrancada, en otro muro asida,
y mi parra en otro olmo entretejida,
que no se esté con llanto deshaciendo
hasta acabar la vida.
Salid sin duelo, lágrimas, corriendo.

Of seeming love, the traitor in thy heart!
This my severe misfortune, long ago,
Did the soothsaying raven, sailing by
On the black storm, with hoarse sinister cry,
Clearly presage; in gentleness of woe,
Flow forth, my tears, 'tis meet that ye should flow!

How oft, when slumbering in the forest brown,
(Deeming it Fancy's mystical deceit,)
Have I beheld my fate in dreams foreshown!
One day, methought that from the noontide heat
I drove my flocks to drink of 'Tagus' flood,
And, under curtain of its bordering wood,
Took my cool siesta; but, arrived, the stream,
I know not by what magic, changed its track,
And in new channels, by an unused way,
Rolled its warped waters back;
Whilst I, scorched, melting with heat extreme,
Went ever following in their flight, astray,
The wizard waves; in gentleness of woe,
Flow forth, my tears, 'tis meet that ye should flow!

In the charmed ear of what beloved youth
Sounds thy sweet voice? on whom revolvest thou
Thy beautiful blue eyes? on whose proved truth
Anchors thy broken faith? who presses now
Thy laughing lip, and hopes thy heaven of charms,
Locked in th' embraces of thy two white arms?
Say thou, for whom hast thou so rudely left
My love, or stolen, who triumphs in the theft?
I have not yet a bosom so untrue
To feeling, nor a heart of stone, to view
My darling ivy, torn from me, take root
Against another wall or prosperous pine,
To see my virgin vine
Around another elm in marriage hang
Its curling tendrils and empurpled fruit,
Without the torture of a jealous pang,
Ev'n to the loss of life; in gentle woe,
Flow forth, my tears, 'tis meet that ye should flow!

¿Qué no se esperará de aquí adelante,
por difícil que sea y por incierto?
O ¿qué discordia no será juntada?
y juntamente ¿qué tendrá por cierto,
o qué de hoy más no temerá el amante,
siendo a todo materia por ti dada?
Cuando tú enajenada
de mi cuidado fuiste,
notable causa diste
y ejemplo a todos cuantos cubre el cielo
que el más seguro tema con recelo
perder lo que estuviere poseyendo.
Salid fuera sin duelo,
salid sin duelo, lágrimas, corriendo.

Materia diste al mundo de esperanza
de alcanzar lo imposible y no pensado,
y de hacer juntar lo diferente,
dando a quien diste el corazón malvado,
quitándolo de mí con tal mudanza,
que siempre sonará de gente en gente.
La cordera paciente
con el lobo hambriento
hará su ayuntamiento,
y con las simples aves sin ruïdo
harán las bravas sierpes ya su nido;
que mayor diferencia comprehendo
de ti al que has escogido.
Salid sin duelo, lágrimas, corriendo.

Siempre de nueva leche en el verano
y en el invierno abundo; en mi majada
la manteca y el queso está sobrado;
de mi cantar, pues, yo te vi agradada,
tanto, que no pudiera el mantuano
Titiro ser de ti más alabado.
No soy, pues, bien mirado,
tan disforme ni feo;
que aun agora me veo
en esta agua que corre clara y pura,
y cierto no trocara mi figura

What may not now be looked for to take place
In any certain or uncertain case?
What are too adverse now to join, too wild
For love to fear, too dissonant to agree?
What faith is too secure to be beguiled?
Matter for all thus being given by thee.
A signal proof didst thou, when, rude and cold
Thou left'st my bleeding heart to break, present
To all loved youths and maids
Whom heaven in its blue beauty overshades,
That ev'n the most secure have cause to fear
The loss of that which they as sweet or dear
Cherish the most; in gentleness of woe,
Flow forth, my tears, 'tis meet that ye should flow!

Thou hast giv'n room for hope that now the mind
May work impossibilities most strange,
And jarring natures in concordance bind;
Transferring thus from me to him thy hand
And fickle heart in such swift interchange,
As ever must be voiced from land to land.
Now let mild lambs in nuptial fondness range
With savage wolves from forest brake to brake;
Now let the subtle snake
In curled caresses nest with simple doves,
Harming them not, for in your ghastly loves
Difference is yet more great; in gentle woe,
Flow forth, my tears, 'tis meet that ye should flow!

My dairies always with new milk abound,
Summer and winter, all my vats run o'er
With richest creams, and my superfluous store
Of cheese and butter is afar renowned;
With as sweet songs have I amused thine ear
As could the Mantuan Tityrus of yore,
And more to be admired; nor am I, dear,
If well observed, or so uncouth or grim,
For in the watery looking-glass below
My image I can see—a shape and face
I surely never would exchange with him

con ese que de mí se está riendo;
¡trocara mi ventura!
Salid sin duelo, lágrimas, corriendo.

¿Cómo te vine en tanto menosprecio?
¿Cómo te fuí tan presto aborrecible?
¿Cómo te faltó en mí el conocimiento?
Si no tuvieras condición terrible,
siempre fuera tenido de ti en precio,
y no viera de ti este apartamiento.
¿No sabes que sin cuento
buscan en el estío
mis ovejas el frío
de la sierra de Cuenca, y el gobierno
del abrigado Estremo en el invierno?
Mas ¡qué vale el tener, si derritiendo
me estoy en llanto eterno!
Salid sin duelo, lágrimas, corriendo.

Con mi llorar las piedras enternecen
su natural dureza y la quebrantan;
los árboles parece que se inclinan;
las aves que me escuchan, cuando cantan,
con diferente voz se condolecen,
y mi morir cantando me adivinan.
Las fieras que reclinan
su cuerpo fatigado,
dejan el sosegado
sueño por escuchar mi llanto triste.
Tú sola contra mí te endureciste,
los ojos aun siquiera no volviendo
a los que tú hiciste
salid sin duelo, lágrimas, corriendo.

Mas ya que a socorrer aquí no vienes,
no dejes el lugar que tanto amaste,
que bien podrás venir de mí segura.
Yo dejaré el lugar do me dejaste;
ven, si por sólo esto te detienes.

Who joys in my disgrace:
My fate I might exchange; in gentle woe,
Flow forth, my tears, 'tis meet that ye should flow!

How have I fallen in such contempt, how grown
So suddenly detested, or in what
Attentions have I failed thee? wert thou not
Under the power of some malignant spell,
My worth and consequence were known too well;
I should be held in pleasurable esteem,
Nor left thus in divorce, alone—alone!
Hast thou not heard, when fierce the Dogstar smites
These plains with heat and drouth,
What countless flocks to Cuenca's thymy heights
Yearly I drive, and in the winter breme,
To the warm valleys of the sheltering south?
But what avails my wealth if I decay,
And in perpetual sorrow weep away
My years of youth! in gentleness of woe,
Flow forth, my tears, 'tis meet that ye should flow!

Over my griefs the mossy stones relent
Their natural durity, and break; the trees
Bend down their weeping boughs without a breeze,
And full of tenderness, the listening birds,
Warbling in different notes, with me lament,
And warbling prophesy my death; the herds
That in the green meads hang their heads at eve
Wearied and worn, and faint
The necessary sweets of slumber leave,
And low, and listen to my wild complaint.
Thou only steel'st thy bosom to my cries,
Not ev'n once rolling thine angelic eyes
On him thy harshness kills; in gentle woe,
Flow forth, my tears, 'tis meet that ye should flow!

But though thou wilt not come for my sad sake,
Leave not the landscape thou hast held so dear;
Thou may'st come freely now, without the fear
Of meeting me, for though my heart should break,
Where late forsaken I will now forsake.

Ves aquí un prado lleno de verdura,
ves aquí un espesura,
ves aquí un agua clara,
en otro tiempo cara,
a quien de ti con lágrimas me quejo.
Quizá aquí hallarás, pues yo me alejo,
al que todo mi bien quitarme puede;
que pues el bien le dejo,
no es mucho que el lugar también le quede.—

Aquí dió fin a su cantar Salicio,
y sospirando en el postrero acento
soltó de llanto una profunda vena.
Queriendo el monte al grave sentimiento
de aquel dolor en algo ser propicio,
con la pasada voz retumba y suena.
La blanca Filomena,
casi como dolida
y a compasión movida,
dulcemente responde al són lloroso.
Lo que cantó tras esto Nemoroso
decidlo vos, Piérides; que tanto
no puedo yo ni oso,
que siento enflaquecer mi débil canto.

Nemoroso

Corrientes aguas, puras, cristalinas;
árboles que os estáis mirando en ellas,
verde prado de fresca sombra lleno,
aves que aquí sembráis vuestras querellas,
hiedra que por los árboles caminas,
torciendo el paso por su verde seno;
yo me vi tan ajeno
del grave mal que siento,
que de puro contento

Come then, if this alone detains thee, here
Are meadows full of verdure, myrtles, bays,
Woodlands, and lawns, and running waters clear,
Beloved in other days,
To which, bedewed with many a bitter tear,
I sing my last of lays.
These scenes perhaps, when I am far removed,
At ease thou wilt frequent
With him who rifled me of all I loved;
Enough! my strength is spent;
And leaving thee in his desired embrace,
It is not much to leave him this sweet place.

Here ceased that youth his Doric madrigal,
And sighing, with his last laments let fall
A shower of tears; the solemn mountains round,
Indulgent of his sorrow, tossed the sound
Melodious from romantic steep to steep,
In mild responses deep;
Sweet Echo, starting from her couch of moss,
Lengthened the dirge, and tenderest Philomel,
As pierced with grief and pity at his loss,
Warbled divine reply, nor seemed to trill
Less than Jove's nectar from her mournful bill.
What Nemoroso sang in sequel, tell
Ye, sweet-voiced Sirens of the sacred hill!
Too high the strain, too weak my groveling reed,
For me to dare proceed.

Nemoroso

Smooth-sliding waters, pure and crystalline!
Trees, that reflect your image in their breast!
Green pastures, full of fountains and fresh shades!
Birds, that here scatter your sweet serenades!
Mosses, and reverend ivies serpentine,
That wreathe your verdurous arms round beech and pine,
And, climbing, crown their crest!
Can I forget, ere grief my spirit changed,
With what delicious ease and pure content

con vuestra soledad me recreaba,
donde con dulce sueño reposaba,
o con el pensamiento discurría
por donde no hallaba
sino memorias llenas de alegría;

y en este mismo valle, donde agora
me entristesco y me canso, en el reposo
estuve ya contento y descansado.
¡Oh bien caduco, vano y presuroso!
Acuérdome durmiendo aquí algún hora,
que despertando, a Elisa vi a mi lado.
¡Oh miserable hado!
¡Oh tela delicada,
antes de tiempo dada
a los agudos filos de la muerte!
Más convenible suerte
a los cansados años de mi vida,
que es más que el hierro fuerte,
pues no la ha quebrantado tu partida.

¿Dó están agora aquellos claros ojos
que llevaban tras sí, como colgada,
mi alma doquier que ellos se volvían?
¿Dó está la blanca mano delicada,
llena de vencimientos y despojos
que de mí mis sentidos le ofrecían?
Los cabellos que vían
con gran desprecio el oro,
como a menor tesoro,
¿adónde están? ¿Adónde el blando pecho?
¿Dó la coluna que el dorado techo
con presunción graciosa sostenía?
Aquesto todo agora ya se encierra,
por desventura mía,
en la fría, desierta y dura tierra.

Your peace I wooed, your solitudes I ranged,
Enchanted and refreshed where'er I went!
How many blissful noons I here have spent
In luxury of slumber, couched on flowers,
And with my own fond fancies, from a boy,
Discoursed away the hours,
Discovering nought in your delightful bowers,
But golden dreams, and memories fraught with joy!

And in this very valley where I now
Grow sad, and droop, and languish, have I lain
At ease with happy heart and placid brow;
Oh pleasure fragile, fugitive, and vain!
Here I remember, waking once at noon,
I saw Eliza standing at my side;
Oh cruel fate! oh finespun web, too soon
By Death's sharp scissors clipt! sweet suffering bride,
In womanhood's most interesting prime,
Cut off, before thy time!
How much more suited had his surly stroke
Been to the strong thread of my weary life!
Stronger than steel, since in the parting strife
From thee it has not broke.

Where are the eloquent mild eyes that drew
My heart where'er they wandered? where the hand,
White, delicate, and pure as melting dew,
Filled with the spoils that, proud of thy command,
My feelings paid in tribute? the bright hair
That paled the shining gold, that did contemn
The glorious opal as a meaner gem,
The bosom's ivory apples, where, ah where?
Where now the neck, to whiteness overwrought,
That like a column with genteelest scorn
Sustained the golden dome of virtuous thought?
Gone! ah, for ever gone
To the chill, desolate, and dreary pall,
And mine the grief—the wormwood and the gall!

¿Quién me dijera, Elisa, vida mía,
cuando en aqueste valle al fresco viento
andábamos cogiendo tiernas flores,
que había de ver con largo apartamiento
venir el triste y solitario día
que diese amargo fin a mis amores?
El cielo en mis dolores
cargó la mano tanto,
que a sempiterno llanto
y a triste soledad me ha condenado;
y lo que siento más es verme atado
a la pesada vida y enojosa,
solo, desamparado,
ciego sin lumbre en cárcel tenebrosa.

Después que nos dejaste, nunca pace
en hartura el ganado ya, ni acude
el campo al labrador con mano llena.
No hay bien que en mal no se convierta y mude:
la mala hierba al trigo ahoga, y nace
en lugar suyo la infelice avena;
la tierra, que de buena
gana nos producía
flores con que solía
quitar en sólo vellas mil enojos,
produce agora en cambio estos abrojos,
ya de rigor de espinas intratable;
yo hago con mis ojos
crecer, lloviendo, el fruto miserable.

Como al partir del sol la sombra crece,
y en cayendo su rayo se levanta
la negra escuridad que el mundo cubre,
de do viene el temor que nos espanta,
y la medrosa forma en que se ofrece
aquella que la noche nos encubre,
hasta que el sol descubre
su luz pura y hermosa;
tal es la tenebrosa

Who would have said, my love, when late through this
Romantic valley, we from bower to bower
Went gathering violets and primroses,
That I should see the melancholy hour
So soon arrive that was to end my bliss,
And of my love destroy both fruit and flower?
Heaven on my head has laid a heavy hand;
Sentencing, without hope, without appeal,
To loneliness and ever-during tears
The joyless remnant of my future years;
But that which most I feel,
Is to behold myself obliged to bear
This condemnation to a life of care;
Lone, blind, forsaken, under sorrow's spell,
A gloomy captive in a gloomy cell.

Since thou hast left us, fulness, rest, and peace
Have failed the starveling flocks; the field supplies
To toiling hind but pitiful increase;
All blessings change to ills; the clinging weed
Chokes the thin corn, and in its stead arise
Pernicious darnel, and the fruitless reed.
The enamelled earth, that from her verdant breast
Lavished spontaneously ambrosial flowers,
The very sight of which can soothe to rest
A thousand cares, and charm our sweetest hours,
That late indulgence of her bounty scorns,
And in exchange shoots forth but tangled bowers,
But brambles rough with thorns;
Whilst with the tears that falling steep their root,
My swollen eyes increase the bitter fruit.

As at the set of sun the shades extend,
And when its circle sinks, that dark obscure
Rises to shroud the world, on which attend
The images that set our hair on end,
Silence, and shapes mysterious as the grave;
Till the broad sun sheds once more from the wave
His lively lustre, beautiful and pure:
Such shapes were in the night, and such ill gloom

noche de tu partir, en que he quedado
de sombra y de temor atormentado,
hasta que muerte el tiempo determine
que a ver el deseado
sol de tu clara vista me encamine.

Cual suele el ruiseñor con triste canto
quejarse, entre las hojas escondido,
del duro labrador, que cautamente
le despojó su caro y dulce nido
de los tiernos hijuelos, entre tanto
que del amado ramo estaba ausente,
y aquel dolor que siente
con diferencia tanta
por la dulce garganta
despide, y a su canto el aire suena,
y la callada noche no refrena
su lamentable oficio y sus querellas,
trayendo de su pena
al cielo por testigo y las estrellas;

desta manera suelto ya la rienda
a mi dolor, y así me quejo en vano
de la dureza de la muerte airada.
Ella en mi corazón metió la mano,
y de allí me llevó mi dulce prenda;
que aquel era su nido y su morada.
¡Ay muerte arrebatada!
Por ti me estoy quejando
al cielo y enojando
con importuno llanto al mundo todo:
el desigual dolor no sufre modo.
No me podrán quitar el dolorido
sentir, si ya del todo
primero no me quitan el sentido.

Tengo una parte aquí de tus cabellos,
Elisa, envueltos en un blanco paño,
que nunca de mi seno se me apartan;

At thy departure; still tormenting fear
Haunts, and must haunt me, until death shall doom
The so much wished-for sun to re-appear
Of thine angelic face, my soul to cheer,
Resurgent from the tomb.

As the sad nightingale in some green wood,
Closely embowered, the cruel hind arraigns
Who from their pleasant nest her plumeless brood
Has stolen, whilst she with pains
Winged the wide forest for their food, and now
Fluttering with joy, returns to the loved bough,
The bough, where nought remains:
Dying with passion and desire, she flings
A thousand concords from her various bill,
Till the whole melancholy woodland rings
With gurglings sweet, or with philippics shrill.
Throughout the silent night she not refrains
Her piercing note, and her pathetic cry,
But calls as witness to her wrongs and pains,
The listening stars and the responding sky.

So I in mournful song pour forth my pain;
So I lament,—lament, alas, in vain—
The cruelty of death! untaught to spare,
The ruthless spoiler ravished from my breast
Each pledge of happiness and joy, that there
Had its beloved home and nuptial nest.
Swift-seizing death! through thy despite I fill
The whole world with my passionate lament,
Impórtuning the skies and valleys shrill
My tale of wrongs to echo and resent.
A grief so vast no consolation knows,
Ne'er can the agony my brain forsake,
Till suffering consciousness in frenzy close,
Or till the shattered chords of being break.

Poor, lost Eliza! of thy locks of gold,
One treasured ringlet in white silk I keep
For ever at my heart, which, when unrolled,

descójolos, y de un dolor tamaño
enternecerme siento, que sobre ellos
nunca mis ojos de llorar se hartan.
Sin que de allí se partan,
con suspiros calientes,
más que la llama ardientes,
los enjugo del llanto, y de consuno
casi los paso y cuento uno a uno;
juntándolos, con un cordón los ato.
Tras esto el importuno
dolor me deja descansar un rato.

Mas luego a la memoria se me ofrece
aquella noche tenebrosa, escura,
que tanto aflige esta ánima mesquina
con la memoria de mi desventura.
Verte presente agora me parece
en aquel duro trance de Lucina,
y aquella voz divina,
con cuyo son y acentos
a los airados vientos
pudieras amansar, que agora es muda;
me parece que oigo que a la cruda,
inesorable diosa demandabas
en aquel paso ayuda;
y tú, rústica diosa, ¿dónde estabas?

¿Íbate tanto en perseguir las fieras?
¿Íbate tanto en un pastor dormido?
¿Cosa pudo bastar a tal crueza,
que, conmovida a compasión, oído
a los votos y lágrimas no dieras
por no ver hecha tierra tal belleza,
o no ver la tristeza
en que tu Nemoroso
queda, que su reposo
era seguir tu oficio, persiguiendo
las fieras por los montes, y ofreciendo
a tus sagradas aras los despojos?
¿Y tú, ingrata, riendo
dejas morir mi bien ante los ojos?

Fresh grief and pity o'er my spirit creep;
And my insatiate eyes, for hours untold,
O'er the dear pledge will, like an infant's, weep:
With sighs more warm than fire anon I dry
The tears from off it, number one by one
The radiant hairs, and with a love-knot tie;
Mine eyes, this duty done,
Give over weeping, and with slight relief
I taste a short forgetfulness of grief.

But soon, with all its first-felt horrors fraught,
That gloomy night returns upon my brain,
Which ever wrings my spirit with the thought
Of my deep loss, and thine unaided pain;
Ev'n now, I seem to see thee pale recline
In thy most trying crisis, and to hear
The plaintive murmurs of that voice divine,
Whose tones might touch the ear
Of blustering winds, and silence their dispute;
That gentle voice (now mute)
Which to the merciless Lucina prayed,
In utter agony for aid—for aid!
Alas, for thine appeal! Discourteous power,
Where wert thou gone in that momentous hour?

Or wert thou in the grey woods hunting deer?
Or with thy shepherd boy entranced? Could aught
Palliate thy rigorous cruelty, to turn
Away thy scornful, cold, indifferent ear
From my moist prayers, by no affliction moved,
And sentence one, so beauteous and beloved,
To the funereal urn!
Oh, not to mark the throes
Thy Nemoroso suffered, whose concern
It ever was, when pale the morning rose,
To drive the mountain beasts into his toils,
And on thy holy altars heap the spoils;
And thou, ungrateful! smiling with delight,
Could'st leave my nymph to die before my sight.

Divina Elisa, pues agora el cielo
con inmortales pies pisas y mides,
y su mudanza ves, estando queda,
¿por qué de mí te olvidas, y no pides
que se apresure el tiempo en que este velo
rompa del cuerpo, y verme libre pueda,
y en la tercera rueda
contigo mano a mano
busquemos otro llano,
busquemos otros montes y otros ríos,
otros valles floridos y sombríos,
donde descanse y siempre pueda verte
ante los ojos míos,
sin miedo y sobresalto de perderte?—

Nunca pusieran fin al triste lloro
los pastores, ni fueran acabadas
las canciones que sólo el monte oía
si mirando las nubes coloradas,
al tramontar del sol bordadas de oro,
no vieran que era ya pasado el día.
La sombra se veía
venir corriendo apriesa
ya por la falda espesa
del altísimo monte, y recordando
ambos como de sueño, y acabando
el fugitivo sol, de luz escaso,
su ganado llevando,
se fueron recogiendo paso a paso.

Divine Eliza! since the sapphire sky
Thou measurest now on angel-wings, and feet
Sandalled with immortality, oh why
Of me forgetful? Wherefore not entreat
To hurry on the time when I shall see
The veil of mortal being rent in twain,
And smile that I am free?
In the third circle of that happy land,
Shall we not seek together, hand in hand,
Another lovelier landscape, a new plain,
Other romantic streams and mountains blue,
Fresh flowery vales, and a new shady shore,
Where I may rest, and ever in my view
Keep thee, without the terror and surprise
Of being sundered more!

Ne'er had the shepherds ceased these songs, to which
The hills alone gave ear, had they not seen
The sun in clouds of gold and crimson rich
Descend, and twilight sadden o'er the green;
But noting now, how rapidly the night
Rushed from the hills, admonishing to rest,
The sad musicians, by the blushful light
Of lingering Hesperus, themselves addressed
To fold their flocks, and step by step withdrew,
Through bowery lawns and pastures wet with dew.

Jeremiah H. Wiffen

56   *SONETO*

¡Oh dulces prendas, por mi mal halladas,
dulces y alegres cuando Dios quería!
Juntas estáis en la memoria mía,
y con ella en mi muerte conjuradas.
   ¿Quién me dijera, cuando en las pasadas
horas en tanto bien por vos me vía,
que me habíades de ser en algún día
con tan grave dolor representadas?
   Pues en un hora junto me llevastes
todo el bien que por términos me distes,
llevadme junto el mal que me dejastes.
   Si no, sospecharé que me pusistes
en tantos bienes, porque deseastes
verme morir entre memorias tristes.

57   *SONETO*

Hermosas ninfas, que en el río metidas,
contentas habitáis en las moradas
de relucientes piedras fabricadas
y en colunas de vidrio sostenidas;
   agora estéis labrando embebecidas
o tejiendo las telas delicadas;
agora unas con otras apartadas,
contándoos los amores y las vidas;
   dejad un rato la labor, alzando
vuestras rubias cabezas a mirarme
y no os detendréis mucho según ando;
   que o no podréis de lástima escucharme,
o convertido en agua aquí llorando,
podréis allá de espacio consolarme.

SONNET   56

Oh dear love tokens that did work me harm,
So dear and smiling too when heaven did smile,
Within my memory you are joined, the while
With it you plot to bring me death's alarm!
   Who would have said, when in those hours of charm
In happy state I saw myself erstwhile,
That I one day in desolation vile
Should find that thoughts of you my peace disarm?
   Since in one hour you did from me take this,
The joy, that for completion you did give,
Now take also the sorrow you did leave.
   If not, I shall suspect that to such bliss
You brought me then, that now you might achieve
My death amidst these mournful memories.

E. L. T.

SONNET   57

   Fair Naiads of the river, that reside
Happy in grottos of rock crystal veined
With shining gems, and loftily sustained
On columns of pure glass, if now ye glide
   On duteous errands, or weave side by side
Webs of fine net-work, or in groups remove
To hear and tell romantic tales of love,
Of genii, Fays and Tritons of the tide,—
   Awhile remit your labours, and upraise
Your rosy heads to look on me. Not long
Will it detain you. Sweet'ners of my song,
   For pity hear me, watering as I go
With tears your borders, and for such short space,
In heavenly notes sing solace to my woe!

Jeremiah H. Wiffen

58 *SONETO*

En tanto que de rosa y azucena
se muestra la color en vuestro gesto,
y que vuestro mirar ardiente, honesto,
enciende el corazón y lo refrena;
   y en tanto que el cabello, que en la vena
del oro se escogió, con vuelo presto,
por el hermoso cuello blanco, enhiesto,
el viento mueve, esparce y desordena;
   coged de vuestra alegre primavera
el dulce fruto, antes que el tiempo airado
cubra de nieve la hermosa cumbre.
   Marchitará la rosa el viento helado,
todo lo mudará la edad ligera,
por no hacer mudanza en su costumbre.

59 *SONETO*

¡Oh hado esecutivo en mis dolores,
cómo sentí tus leyes rigurosas!
Cortaste el árbol con manos dañosas,
y esparciste por tierra fruta y flores.
   En poco espacio yacen mis amores
y toda la esperanza de mis cosas,
tornadas en cenizas desdeñosas,
y sordas a mis quejas y clamores.
   Las lágrimas que en esta sepultura
se vierten hoy en día y se vertieron
recibe, aunque sin fruto allá te sean,
   hasta que aquella eterna noche escura
me cierre aquestos ojos que te vieron,
dejándome con otros que te vean.

SONNET   58

   In so much as the lily and the rose
Display their colors in thy countenance,
In so much as the burning, yet chaste, glance
Kindles the heart, then doth restraint impose;
   In that the hair, whose gold some delver chose
In a deep mine, with rapid whirling dance,
The white neck's towering beauty to enhance,
The stirring winds all scattered wild dispose,
   Cull the sweet fruit of thy delightful Spring
Ere vengeful time shall come to hide with snow
The lovely summit that ariseth there,
   Frost in the wind the fading rose shall blow,
To all its glory the swift years shall bring
Change, to change not in their accustomed care.

James Cleugh

SONNET   59

   O Fate, implacable in my pursuit,
How pitiless has been thy harsh decree:
With cruel hand thou didst cut down the tree
And on the ground didst scatter flower and fruit.
   In narrow bed today my love lies mute,
And with her, all my hopes of things to be
Are but disdainful ashes, scorning me,
Deaf to my wailing, heedless of my suit.
   Accept these new-wept tears with all of those
So often shed, though naught availing thee
Where now thou dwellest in felicity,
   Until in night eternal death shall close
These eyes that saw thee, and to me be given
New eyes to see thee when I wake in heaven.

Caroline B. Bourland

60   *SONETO*

Estoy contino en lágrimas bañado,
rompiendo el aire siempre con sospiros;
y más me duele nunca osar deciros
que he llegado por vos a tal estado,
    que viéndome do estoy y lo que he andado,
por el camino estrecho de seguiros,
si me quiero tornar para huiros,
desmayo viendo atrás lo que he dejado;
    si a subir pruebo, en la difícil cumbre,
a cada paso espántanme en la vía
ejemplos tristes de los que han caído.
    Y sobre todo, fáltame la lumbre
de la esperanza, con que andar solía
por la escura región de vuestro olvido.

61   *CANCIÓN*

Yo dejaré desde aquí
de ofenderos más hablando;
porque mi morir callando
os ha de hablar por mí.
    Gran ofensa os tengo hecha
hasta aquí en haber hablado,
pues en cosa os he enojado
que tampoco me aprovecha.
    Derramaré desde aquí
mis lágrimas no hablando;
porque quien muere callando
tiene quien hable por sí.

SONNET   60

I am for ever bathed in tears, I rend
The air with sighs, and suffer more from dread
To tell thee 'tis through thee I have been led
To such a state that, seeing where I tend,
   And the long distance I have come, sweet friend,
In following thee, if I desire to leave
The vain pursuit, my heart sinks to perceive
The way behind me lengthening without end.
   And if I wish to reach the onward height,
Sad thoughts of those who in the wilderness
Have fallen, at every step awake my fear;
   Now above all things then I need the light
Of hope, by which I have been wont to steer
Through the dim tract of thy forgetfulness.

Jeremiah H. Wiffen

SONG   61

   Now go I quietly
Nor weary you with pleading;
From my deathbed, silence speeding,
More eloquent shall be.

   An evil thing it was
That my vows your spirit troubled,
And the injury was doubled
Since they nothing helped my cause.

   Though tears my eyes may dim,
No plaint shall ease my crying;
Who speaks no word at dying,
His death shall plead for him.

Beatrice Gilman Proske

Fray Luis de León

Let us examine Spanish mystical poetry first as represented in the person and work of Fray Luis de León. Born in 1528(?), he embraced the religious life at the age of fifteen, in the order of Saint Augustine. He studied philosophy and theology and soon began to teach in the convents of his order. In 1560 he took the degrees of licentiate and master at Salamanca and was named professor at that university the following year, a position he held until his death in 1591. His was the life of a professor at the richest and most glorious Spanish university of the time. But that position afforded Fray Luis no external tranquillity. The university of Salamanca was at that time a little world, divided by personal and doctrinal discord. The religious orders were almost all represented in the faculty assemblies and each of them had a certain *esprit de corps* that caused it to regard with hostility and suspicion the members of the other orders.

To a man of delicate sensibility this continual internal discord at the University caused greater suffering than to an ordinary person. This phase of Fray Luis' existence reaches a climax when, as a result of his opinions on the interpretation of the Vulgate, hostility grows so strong against him and two other professors that the Inquisition has to intervene, and pressed by his enemies, imprisons Fray Luis for five years. During the trial and imprisonment he remained absolutely submissive to the

1 5 2 8?–1 5 9 1

authority of the Church and in the end was absolved of all guilt, being ordered only to hand over a translation of the " Song of Songs."

The curious thing is that the poetry of Fray Luis de León is the most notable in Spanish lyric poetry precisely for its serene exterior, spiritual equilibrium and vision of a calm and tranquil existence. His most famous poem is " Vida retirada " in which he extols life in the country, the withdrawal from ambition and struggles. He knew the material world and let himself be hurt by it, but not conquered.

Fray Luis is a mystic. And if there is in flight, in escape, a negative attitude, that of purely and simply denying oneself to the world, we see the great lyrical inspiration of this poet convert it into positive aspiration, that is flight toward an end or objective. How does Fray Luis flee and whither? Anyone who has read his poems closely must have noticed the mysterious sensation of flying they give. The poetry of Fray Luis soars; his stanzas have a wonderful lightness. His lines abound in words expressing soaring, ascending. And naturally the port of that escape cannot be any other for a Spanish mystic than heaven. Heaven is light. But besides that, heaven is the revelation of truth, the explanation of the universe. Fray Luis was a Platonist and for him heaven is the kingdom of ideas and spirits. In his poetry the Christian ideal and Platonic clarity form an ideal world that is unequaled in the Spanish lyric.

P. S.

VIDA RETIRADA

¡Qué descansada vida
la del que huye el mundanal ruido,
y sigue la escondida
senda por donde han ido
los pocos sabios que en el mundo han sido!

Que no le enturbia el pecho
de los soberbios grandes el estado,
ni del dorado techo
se admira, fabricado
del sabio moro, en jaspes sustentado.

No cura si la fama
canta con voz su nombre pregonera,
ni cura si encarama
la lengua lisonjera
lo que condena la verdad sincera.

¿Qué presta a mi contento
si soy del vano dedo señalado,
si en busca de este viento
ando desalentado
con ansias vivas y mortal cuidado?

¡Oh campo, oh monte, oh río!
¡Oh secreto seguro deleitoso!
roto casi el navío,
a vuestro almo reposo
huyo de aqueste mar tempestuoso.

Un no rompido sueño,
un día puro, alegre, libre quiero;
no quiero ver el ceño
vanamente severo
de quien la sangre ensalza o el dinero.

THE LIFE REMOVED   62

How tranquil is the life
Of him who, shunning the vain world's uproar,
May follow, free from strife,
The hidden path, of yore
Chosen by the few who conned true wisdom's lore!

For he, with thoughts aloof,
By proud men's great estate is not oppressed.
Nor marvels at the roof
Of gold, built to attest
The Moor's skill, that on jasper pillars rests.

He heeds not though fame raise
His name afar on wings of rumour flung,
He cares not for the praise
Of cunning flatterer's tongue,
Nor for what truth sincere would leave unsung.

What boots it my content
That the vain voice of fame should favour me,
If in its service spent
I find myself to be
Vexed by dull care and gnawing misery?

O hill, O stream, O field,
O solitary refuge of delight,
Since my bark now must yield
To storm, your solace bright
I seek and flee this sea's tempestuous might.

Sleep broken by no fear
Be mine, and a day clear, serene, and free,
Shunning the look severe,
Lofty exceedingly,
Of him whom gold exalts or ancestry.

Despiértenme las aves
con su cantar süave no aprendido,
no los cuidados graves
de que es siempre seguido
quien al ajeno arbitrio está atenido.

Vivir quiero conmigo,
gozar quiero del bien que debo al cielo
a solas, sin testigo,
libre de amor, de celo,
de odio, de esperanzas, de recelo.

Del monte en la ladera
por mi mano plantado tengo un huerto,
que con la primavera
de bella flor cubierto,
ya muestra en esperanza el fruto cierto.

Y como codiciosa
de ver y acrecentar su hermosura,
desde la cumbre airosa
una fontana pura
hasta llegar corriendo se apresura.

Y luego sosegada
el paso entre los árboles torciendo,
el suelo de pasada
de verdura vistiendo,
y con diversas flores va esparciendo.

El aire el huerto orea,
y ofrece mil olores al sentido,
los árboles menea
con un manso rüido,
que del oro y del cetro pone olvido.

Ténganse su tesoro
los que de un flaco leño se confían:
no es mío ver el lloro
de los que desconfían
cuando el cierzo y el ábrego porfían.

Me may the birds awake
With their sweet, unpremeditated song,
And those dark cares forsake
That e'er to him belong
Who lives not in his independence strong!

I to myself would live,
To enjoy the blessings that to Heaven I owe,
Alone, contemplative,
And freely love forgo,
Nor hope, fear, hatred, jealousy e'er know.

Upon the bare hillside
An orchard I have made with my own hand,
That in the sweet Springtide
All in fair flower doth stand
And promise sure of fruit shows through the land.

And, as though swift it strove
To see and to increase that loveliness,
From the clear ridge above
A stream pure, weariless
Hurrying to reach that ground doth onward press;

And straightway in repose
Its course it winds there tree and tree between,
And ever as it goes
The earth decks with new green
And with gay wealth of flowers spreads the scene.

The air in gentle breeze
A myriad scents for my delight distils,
It moves among the trees
With a soft sound that fills
The mind, and thought of gold or sceptre kills.

Treasure and gold be theirs
Who to a frail bark would entrust their life:
I envy not the cares
Of those whose fears are rife
When the north wind with south wind is at strife.

La combatida antena
cruje, y en ciega noche el claro día
se torna; al cielo suena
confusa vocería,
y la mar enriquecen a porfía.

A mí una pobrecilla
mesa, de amable paz bien abastada
me baste, y la vajilla
de fino oro labrada,
sea de quien la mar no teme airada.

Y mientras miserable-
mente se están los otros abrasando
en sed insacïable
del no durable mando,
tendido yo a la sombra esté cantando.

A la sombra tendido
de yedra y lauro eterno coronado,
puesto el atento oído
al son dulce, acordado,
del plectro sabiamente meneado.

ODA A FRANCISCO SALINAS

El aire se serena
y viste de hermosura y luz no usada,
Salinas, cuando suena
la música extremada
por vuestra sabia mano gobernada.

A cuyo son divino
mi alma que en olvido está sumida,
torna a cobrar el tino,
y memoria perdida
de su origen primera esclarecida.

In the storm's strain the mast
Groans, and clear day is turned to eyeless night,
While to the skies aghast
Rise wild cries of affright
And they enrich the sea in their despite.

But me may still suffice,
Rich only in meek peace, a humble fare;
And the wrought artifice
Be his of gold plate rare
Who dreads not o'er the raging sea to fare.

And while in misery
Others are pledged to fierce ambition's throng,
Afire insatiably
For power that stays not long,
May I in pleasant shade recite my song;

Yea, lying in the shade,
My brow with bay and ivy immortal crowned,
My ear attentive made
To the soft, tuneful sound
Of zither touched by fingers' skill profound.

Aubrey F. G. Bell

ODE TO SALINAS   63

Calm grows the air around,
Arrayed in beauty and unwonted light,
Salinas, at the sound
Of music exquisite
That thy skilled hand doth cunningly indite.

And at that sound divine
My soul that in forgetfulnes hath lain,
With a new light doth shine
And unto memory plain
Of its first splendid origin attain.

Y como se conoce,
en suerte y pensamientos se mejora,
el oro desconoce
que el vulgo ciego adora,
la belleza caduca, engañadora.

Traspasa el aire todo
hasta llegar a la más alta esfera,
y oye allí otro modo
de no perecedera
música, que es de todas la primera.

Ve como el gran maestro,
a aquesta inmensa cítara aplicado,
con movimiento diestro
produce el son sagrado,
con que este eterno templo es sustentado.

Y como está compuesta
de números concordes, luego envía
consonante respuesta,
y entrambas a porfía
mezclan una dulcísima armonía.

Aquí la alma navega
por un mar de dulzura, y finalmente
en él así se anega,
que ningún accidente
extraño o peregrino oye o siente.

¡Oh desmayo dichoso!
¡oh muerte que das vida, oh dulce olvido!
¡durase en tu reposo,
sin ser restituido
jamás a aqueste bajo y vil sentido!

A este bien os llamo,
gloria del Apolíneo sacro coro,
amigos, a quien amo
sobre todo tesoro,
que todo lo demás es triste lloro.

For this new knowledge then
Its nobler thoughts and destiny restores:
Of gold, vain lure of men,
Which the blind crowd adores,
The perishable beauty it ignores.

Up through the fields of air
It wings, till in the highest sphere it dwells,
And a new music there
It hears, music that wells
Undying and all other kinds excels.

The great Master it sees,
His hand upon the mighty lyre, with train
Of skilful cadences,
Create the holy strain
That this eternal temple doth sustain.

And since in sweet content
Those numbers flow symphonious, reply
Concordant is soon sent,
And both together vie
In a mixed power of softest harmony.

Through sea of melody
In rapture sweet the soul doth onward glide,
And sinks there finally,
Until whate'er betide
Beyond it to its senses is denied.

O heavenly ravishment!
Life-giving death, oblivion's sweet defence!
O might my life be spent
In thy calm rest, nor thence
Ever return to this vile earthly sense!

To such bliss I entreat
You, glory of Apollo's sacred choir,
O friend for whom doth beat
My heart beyond desire
Of treasures that bring tears and sorrows dire.

¡Oh suene de contino,
Salinas, vuestro son en mis oídos!
por quien al bien divino
despiertan los sentidos,
quedando a lo demás amortecidos.

64　　　　　　　　*A FELIPE RUIZ*

¿Cuándo será que pueda
libre de esta prisión volar al cielo,
Felipe, y en la rueda
que huye más del suelo,
contemplar la verdad pura sin velo?

Allí a mi vida junto
en luz resplandeciente convertido
veré distinto y junto,
lo que es, y lo que ha sido,
y su principio propio y escondido.

Entonces veré cómo
el divino poder echó el cimiento
tan a nivel y plomo,
do estable eterno asiento
posée el pesadísimo elemento.

Veré las inmortales
columnas do la tierra está fundada,
las lindes y señales
con que a la mar airada
la Providencia tiene aprisionada.

Por qué tiembla la tierra,
por qué las hondas mares se embravecen,
dó sale a mover guerra
el cierzo, y por qué crecen
las aguas del océano y descrecen.

O evermore to hear
Thy heavenly music, Salinas, be mine!
Through whom awaking clear
To holy thoughts incline
The senses, to all else dull and supine.

Aubrey F. G. Bell.

ODE TO FELIPE RUIZ   64

When from this prison drear,
Philip, may I take flight into the sky,
And in the farther sphere,
Above the Earth most high,
Pure truth without concealment may descry?

In my new life elate,
Converted into light of radiant sheen,
At one and separate,
What is and what hath been
Shall I see and its true origin unseen.

There 'twill be mine to see
How the divine power the foundations laid
With such skilled accuracy
That stable, undismayed,
Earth's heaviest element therein is stayed;

And there shall I behold
The pillars that prop Earth everlastingly,
The boundary-marks that hold
In check the angry sea,
In prison fixed for it by Heaven's decree;

Why the Earth trembles, why
The waters of the deep sea rage and swell,
Whence in grim strife to vie
The north wind comes, what spell
Causes the Ocean waves to ebb and well;

De dó manan las fuentes;
quién ceba, y quién bastece de los ríos
las perpetuas corrientes;
de los helados fríos
veré las causas, y de los estíos.

Las soberanas aguas
del aire en la región quién las sostiene;
de los rayos las fraguas;
dó los tesoros tiene
de nieve Dios, y el trueno dónde viene.

¿No ves cuando acontece
turbarse el aire todo en el verano?
el día se ennegrece,
sopla el gallego insano,
y sube hasta el cielo el polvo vano.

Y entre las nubes mueve
su carro Dios ligero y reluciente
horrible son conmueve,
relumbra fuego ardiente,
treme la tierra, humíllase la gente.

La lluvia baña el techo,
envían largos ríos los collados;
su trabajo deshecho,
los campos anegados
miran los labradores espantados.

Y de allí levantado
veré los movimientos celestiales,
así el arrebatado
como los naturales,
las causas de los hados, las señales.

Quién rige las estrellas
veré, y quién las enciende con hermosas
y eficaces centellas;
por qué están las dos osas,
de bañarse en el mar siempre medrosas.

Where rise the crystal springs,
And who to the great rivers' ceaseless flow
Their store of water brings;
Of icy cold and snow
And summer heat the causes I shall know;

Who in the air sustains
Water on high, the forge of lightning flash,
The dwelling of the rains
Shall I see, and how God's lash
Furls the treasured snow, and whence the thunders crash.

Look, on a summer day
When through the air a veil of grey is thrust,
Day's face grows dark in play
Of mad north-west wind's gust,
And lightly to the sky is whirled the dust;

God moves amid the cloud,
Guiding his aery chariot swift and bright,
With dreadful thunder loud
And flashing fire's light:
Men bow themselves, Earth trembles in affright.

The roofs are washed with rain,
And rushing streams pour down from all the hills:
At his lost labour vain
And the fields' flooded drills
The peasant's heart dismayed amazement fills.

And thence uplifted, I
The motions shall behold of lofty Heaven,
All that moves naturally
And that by force is driven,
And to the signs and fates what cause is given;

And who the stars inspires
And kindles with a beauty radiant, clear,
Their efficacious fires;
Why Great and Little Bear
To bathe themselves in Ocean ever fear.

Veré este fuego eterno
fuente de vida y luz dó se mantiene;
y por qué en el invierno
tan presuroso viene,
por qué en las noches largas se detiene.

Veré sin movimiento
en la más alta esfera las moradas
del gozo y del contento,
de oro y luz labradas,
de espíritus dichosos habitadas.

65   *NOCHE SERENA*

Cuando contemplo el cielo
de innumerables luces adornado,
y miro hacia el suelo
de noche rodeado,
en sueño y en olvido sepultado,

El amor y la pena
despiertan en mi pecho una ansia ardiente;
despiden larga vena
los ojos hechos fuente;
la lengua dice al fin con voz doliente:

Morada de grandeza,
templo de claridad y hermosura,
mi alma que a tu alteza
nació, ¿qué desventura
la tiene en esta cárcel baja, oscura?

¿Qué mortal desatino
de la verdad aleja así el sentido,
que de tu bien divino
olvidado, perdido
sigue la vana sombra, el bien fingido?

I shall see where the sun,
The light and fountain of our life, abides,
Why is so swiftly run
His course of wintertides,
And why in the long nights his ray he hides;

Yea, in the highest sphere
Those dwellings of delight shall I behold:
Motionless they appear,
Fashioned of light and gold,
The mansions that the spirits blest enfold.

Aubrey F. G. Bell

NIGHT OF STARS   65

When I behold the sky
With stars innumerable spangled bright
And then the Earth descry
Encompassèd with night
Buried in sleep, oblivion infinite,

Sorrow and love arise
And with a burning fever fill my breast,
And ever from mine eyes
The tears flow without rest,
Till my tongue speaks at length, by grief oppressed:

O dwelling of great might,
Temple of lovely light incomparable,
My soul that to thy height
At birth aspired, what spell
Doth in this dark, low prison-house compel?

What mortal folly thus
From truth's possession can remove our sense,
So that oblivious
Of thy blest gifts, it thence
Strays and seeks tinselled joys and vain pretence?

El hombre está entregado
al sueño, de su suerte no cuidando,
y con paso callado
el cielo vueltas dando
las horas del vivir le va hurtando.

¡Ay, despertad, mortales;
mirad con atención en vuestro daño!
las almas inmortales,
hechas a bien tamaño,
¿podrán vivir de sombra, y solo engaño?

¡Ay, levantad los ojos
a aquesta celestial eterna esfera!
Burlaréis los antojos
de aquesa lisonjera
vida, con cuanto teme y cuanto espera.

¿Es más que un breve punto
el bajo y torpe suelo, comparado
a aqueste gran trasunto
do vive mejorado
lo que es, lo que será, lo que ha pasado?

Quien mira el gran concierto
de aquestos resplandores eternales,
su movimiento cierto,
sus pasos desiguales,
y en proporción concorde tan iguales:

La luna cómo mueve
la plateada rueda, y va en pos de ella
la luz do el saber llueve,
y la graciosa estrella
de amor le sigue reluciente y bella:

Y cómo otro camino
prosigue el sanguinoso Marte airado,
y el Júpiter benino,
de bienes mil cercado,
serena el cielo con su rayo amado:

Man lives imprisonèd
In sleep and recks not of his destiny,
While still with silent tread,
At Heaven's swift decree,
Hour after hour his life doth from him flee.

Ah mortal men awake
And turn your thoughts intent upon your loss!
Shall souls divine forsake
Such blessings for the cross
Of life unreal and dull delusion's dross?

O skyward lift your eyes,
Unto this heavenly eternal sphere!
And you will then despise
The vain delights that here
Offers our life, its every hope and fear;

Petty, if we compare
The fleeting span of this low earthly scene
With that great region where
In noblest forms are seen
What is and what shall be and what hath been.

Who sees the eternal fires
With fixèd laws move on their heavenly way,
How each with each conspires:
Uneven their array,
Yet, varying, they one ordered scheme obey;

How in the moon's clear train,
As she her silver sphere doth onward move,
Goes light of wisdom's rain,
And, gleaming there above,
Follows, serenely fair, the star of love;

But blood-red angry Mars
Chooses unto himself another way,
While, girt with thousand stars,
Jupiter, clear alway,
Benignly calms the heavens with his loved ray;

Rodéase en el cumbre
Saturno, padre de los siglos de oro,
tras él la muchedumbre
del reluciente coro
su luz va repartiendo y su tesoro:

¿Quién es el que esto mira,
y precia la bajeza de la tierra,
y no gime y suspira
por romper lo que encierra
el alma, y de estos bienes la destierra?

Aquí vive el contento,
aquí reyna la paz; aquí, asentado
en rico y alto asiento,
está el amor sagrado,
de honra y de deleites rodeado.

Inmensa hermosura
aquí se muestra toda; y resplandece
clarísima luz pura,
que jamás anochece;
eterna primavera aquí florece.

¡Oh campos verdaderos!
¡Oh prados con verdad frescos y amenos,
riquísimos mineros!
¡Oh deleitosos senos,
repuestos valles de mil bienes llenos!

66   *MORADA DEL CIELO*

Alma región luciente,
prado de bienandanza, que ni al hielo
ni con el rayo ardiente
falleces, fértil suelo
producidor eterno de consuelo:

And yonder in the height
Whirls Saturn, father of the Age of Gold,
And after him the bright
Stars in fair choir enrolled
Their light and all their treasures still unfold;

Who may all this descry
And pleasure still in this vile Earth retain,
Who will not groan and sigh
To rive the imprisoning chain
Wherein, exiled from Heaven, his soul has lain?

Lo, here dwells sweet content,
Peace reigns, and on a rich and lofty throne
Sits holy love, and blent
Together in its zone
Delight and honour are evermore at one.

Here beauty infinite
Unveils itself, and light, quintessence pure,
Transparent gleams: no night
Its radiance may obscure,
Spring's flowered splendour here is ever sure.

O fields of truth most fair!
O meadows verily ever fresh and bright,
Mines full of riches rare!
O fountains of delight!
Deep valleys with a thousand blessings dight!

Aubrey F. G. Bell

THE HEAVENLY HOME   66

Region of light eterne,
Sweet field, whose plenteous store love's garner fills,
The which no heat may burn,
No frost untimely kills,
Whose balmy fragrance heavenly peace distils!

De púrpura y de nieve
florida la cabeza coronado,
a dulces pastos mueve,
sin honda ni cayado,
el buen Pastor en ti su hato amado.

El va, y en pos dichosas
le siguen sus ovejas, do las pace
con inmortales rosas,
con flor que siempre nace,
y cuanto más se goza más renace.

Ya dentro a la montaña
del alto bien las guía; ya en la vena
del gozo fiel las baña,
y les da mesa llena,
pastor y pasto él solo, y suerte buena.

Y de su esfera cuando
la cumbre toca altísimo subido
el sol, él sesteando,
de su hato ceñido,
con dulce son deleita el santo oído.

Toca el rabel sonoro,
y el inmortal dulzor al alma pasa,
con que envilece el oro,
y ardiendo se traspasa
y lanza en aquel bien libre de tasa.

¡Oh son, oh voz, siquiera
pequeña parte alguna descendiese
en mi sentido, y fuera
de sí el alma pusiese
y toda en ti, oh amor, la convirtiese!

Conocería dónde
sesteas, dulce Esposo, y desatada
de esta prisión a donde
padece, a tu manada
junta, no ya andará perdida, errada.

See, in those pleasant meads,
His bright locks garlanded with flowers of spring,
How the Good Shepherd leads,
And, without crook or sling,
To pastures green His well-loved flock doth bring.

And as He gently leads
Behold the happy sheep behind Him going!
These with fair flowers He feeds,
Roses for ever blowing,
And, as they gather them, for ever growing.

And now unto the mountain
Of high perfection these, His sheep, He guides,
Now bathes them in the fountain,
Wherein pure joy abides;
Pastor and pasture, He alone provides.

When, travelling towards the west,
The Sun stands midway in the heavenly sphere,
He takes His noontide rest,
His loved ones gathering near,
And with sweet song delights the holy ear.

And happiness untold
Possesses them that listen to His lyre,
And poor seems earthly gold
As, filled with sacred fire,
He lifts the enraptured spirit ever higher.

O music, that at least
But some few notes might reach me from above,
And that the Soul's pure feast
Might every stain remove,
And make her one with Thee, O God of love!

Then would she dwell in peace
With Thee, sweet Spouse, and e'en as one new-born,
Gain from the flesh release,
No more imprisoned mourn,
Nor wander far from Thee as one forlorn.

Ida Farnell

67 *EN LA ASCENSIÓN*

¿Y dejas, Pastor santo,
tu grey en este valle hondo, escuro,
con soledad y llanto,
y tú rompiendo el puro
aire, te vas al inmortal seguro?

Los antes bienhadados,
y los ahora tristes y afligidos,
a tus pechos criados,
de ti desposeídos,
¿a dó convertirán ya sus sentidos?

¿Qué mirarán los ojos
que vieron de tu rostro la hermosura,
que no les sea enojos?
quién oyó tu dulzura,
¿qué no tendrá por sordo y desventura?

Aqueste mar turbado
¿quién le pondrá ya freno? quién concierto
al viento fiero airado?
Estando tu encubierto,
¿qué norte guiará la nave al puerto?

¿Ay, nube envidiosa
aun de este breve gozo, ¿qué te aquejas?
¿dó vuelas presurosa?
¡cuán rica tú te alejas!
¡cuán pobres y cuan ciegos ay, nos dejas!

THE ASCENSION   67

O Shepherd, dost Thou leave
Thy flock in this deep vale of tears obscure
In loneliness to grieve,
While Thou to Heaven's refuge sure
Ascendest through the air serene and pure?

They who before were blest
And now are wrapped in sadness and in grief,
Who leaned upon Thy breast,
In Thee all their belief,
Where without Thee may they now seek relief?

What shall their eyes behold
Who looked upon the beauty of Thy face
That shall not leave them cold?
After Thy lips' sweet grace
What will not worthless seem to them and base?

Who now the raging sea
Shall curb or unto silent peace allay
The winds' wild revelry?
Without Thy guiding ray
What star shall steer the ship upon its way?

Even of this brief delight,
Cruel and envious cloud, dost thou complain?
Whither so swift thy flight?
How rich is now thy gain!
How poor and blind are we who here remain!

Aubrey F. G. Bell

San Juan de la Cruz

The highest and most inflamed Spanish mystical poetry was to spring from the soul of another monk, San Juan de la Cruz. Born in 1542 of a humble family, he attended a Jesuit school and became a hospital nurse. We see him from his earliest youth near the sick and suffering. He enters the Carmelite Order, that of Santa Teresa, and goes to Salamanca for four years to study at the same university in which Fray Luis de León was professor.

The year 1567 is decisive in his life; it is then that his meeting with Santa Teresa takes place, and those two exceptional souls are united by no earthly love, but by communion in the same ideal. From then on San Juan devotes himself, body and soul, to the work of reform. But this aroused tremendous opposition in the other branch of the Carmelite Order, the calced, who fought against the discalced, or barefoot. The calced had the support of the ecclesiastical authorities. For San Juan the hour of cruel suffering comes: authorities order the new reformed convents closed. San Juan is imprisoned in Toledo, in a narrow and dark cell. It was in that terrible period of solitude that he began to compose his mystical verses. After some months of imprisonment, San Juan finally made his escape from prison one night and succeeded in reaching a place of safety.

1542–1591

After the conflict with the calced Carmelites calms down, he is able to devote himself to the founding of monasteries of the new discalced rule. This is a period of tremendous external activity, and there is reason to believe that in this period we must place also his activity as writer.

The work of San Juan is in the highest degree mystical. It gives the impression of being charged with poetic potency like no other written work in this world, and that is not surprising since all of a very active and deep spiritual life went into the perfecting and illuminating of three or four poems. His poetry is essentially that of escape. And what is San Juan's way of escape? It may be reduced to the one word "night." He is the poet of night, the "dark night of the soul." A light from within, an ardor of his own, is what the poet contrasts with the darkness of others. But this darkness of night is the guide that directs him; the poet is led by obscurity itself and in this way arrives at the loved one, God, and rests in Him. San Juan renounces the world and escapes into his soul, the greatest escape man has ever accomplished on this earthly surface, so full of beauties for our human senses, toward the mine of the soul immeasurably dark and at the same time incomparably luminous, and in those depths are found beauties far higher than all these that we touch with our hands of flesh or see with our mortal eyes.

P. S.

68   *NOCHE OBSCURA DEL ALMA*

En una noche obscura,
Con ansias en amores inflamada,
¡Oh dichosa ventura!
Salí sin ser notada,
Estando ya mi casa sosegada.

A escuras, y segura,
Por la secreta escala disfrazada,
¡Oh dichosa ventura!
A escuras, y en celada,
Estando ya mi casa sosegada.

En la noche dichosa
En secreto, que nadie me veía,
Ni yo miraba cosa,
Sin otra luz y guía,
Sino la que en el corazón ardía.

Aquesta me guiaba
Más cierto que la luz del mediodía,
Adonde me esperaba,
Quien yo bien me sabía,
En parte donde nadie parecía.

¡Oh noche, que guiaste,
Oh noche amable más que el alborada:
Oh noche, que juntaste
Amado con amada,
Amada en el Amado transformada!

En mi pecho florido,
Que entero para él sólo se guardaba,
Allí quedó dormido,
Y yo le regalaba,
Y el ventalle de cedros aire daba.

DARK NIGHT OF THE SOUL   68

Upon a darksome night,
Kindling with love in flame of yearning keen
—O moment of delight!—
I went, by all unseen,
New-hush'd to rest the house where I had been.

Safe sped I through that night,
By the sacred stair, disguisèd and unseen
—O moment of delight!—
Wrapt in that night serene,
New-hush'd to rest the house where I had been.

O happy night and blest!
Secretly speeding, screen'd from mortal gaze,
Unseeing, on I prest,
Lit by no earthly rays,
Nay, only by heart's inmost fire ablaze.

'Twas that light guided me,
More surely than the noonday's brightest glare,
To the place where none would be
Save one that waited there—
Well knew I whom or ere I forth did fare.

O night that led'st me thus!
O night more winsome than the rising sun!
O night that madest us,
Lover and lov'd, as one,
Lover transform'd in lov'd, love's journey done!

Upon my flowering breast,
His only, as no man but he might prove,
There, slumbering, did he rest,
'Neath my caressing love,
Fann'd by the cedars swaying high above.

El aire de la almena,
Cuando yo sus cabellos esparcía,
Con su mano serena
En mi cuello hería,
Y todos mis sentidos suspendía.

Quedéme, y olvidéme,
El rostro recliné sobre el Amado,
Cesó todo, y dejéme,
Dejando mi cuidado
Entre las azucenas olvidado.

69

CANCIONES ENTRE
EL ALMA Y EL ESPOSO

Esposa

¿Adónde te escondiste,
Amado, y me dejaste con gemido?
Como el ciervo huiste,
Habiéndome herido;
Salí tras ti clamando, y eras ido.

Pastores, los que fuerdes
Allá por las majadas al otero,
Si por ventura vierdes
Aquel que yo más quiero,
Decidle que adolezco, peno y muero.

Buscando mis amores,
Iré por esos montes y riberas,
Ni cogeré las flores,
Ni temeré las fieras,
Y pasaré los fuertes y fronteras.

When from the turret's height,
Scattering his locks, the breezes play'd around,
With touch serene and light
He dealt me love's sweet wound,
And with the joyful pain thereof I swoon'd

Forgetful, rapt, I lay,
My face reclining on my lov'd one fair.
All things for me that day
Ceas'd, as I slumber'd there,
Amid the lilies drowning all my care.

E. Allison Peers

SPIRITUAL CANTICLE   69
BETWEEN THE SOUL AND CHRIST

Bride

Where hidest thou from me,
Beloved, and I left wounded here? As yon
Swift hart, so thou didst flee;
With grief I followed on,
I sought and called for thee, but thou wert gone.

Shepherds, who go up higher
Unto your folds, if you by chance espy
Him whom I most desire,
O let him not go by,
But tell him that I suffer, grieve, and die.

Seeking my Love's lost bower,
I go through darkling woods, by rivers clear;
Nor pluck a single flower,
Nor single wild beast fear;
I go past many a fortress and frontier.

Pregunta a las criaturas

Oh bosques y espesuras,
Plantadas por la mano del Amado,
Oh prado de verduras,
De flores esmaltado,
Decid si por vosotros ha pasado.

Respuesta de las criaturas

Mil gracias derramando,
Pasó por estos sotos con presura,
Y yéndolos mirando,
Con sola su figura
Vestidos los dejó de hermosura.

Esposa

¡Ay, quién podrá sanarme!
Acaba de entregarte ya de vero.
No quieras enviarme
De hoy más ya mensajero,
Que no saben decirme lo que quiero.

Y todos cuantos vagan,
De ti me van mil gracias refiriendo
Y todos más me llagan,
Y déjame muriendo
Un no sé qué que quedan balbuciendo.

Mas, ¿cómo perseveras,
Oh vida, no viviendo donde vives,
Y haciendo porque mueras,
Las flechas que recibes,
De lo que del Amado en ti concibes?

¿Por qué, pues has llagado
A aqueste corazón, no le sanaste?
Y pues me le has robado,
¿Por qué así le dejaste,
Y no tomas el robo que robaste?

Inquiry of the creatures

O woods and forests grand,
That once as seeds within his loved hand lay,
O verdant pasture land,
Enameled with flowers, say
If he who planted you has passed this way.

Reply of the creatures

A thousand virtues flow
From him who hastened through this wooded place;
He looked about, and lo,
The beauty of his face
Clothed every living creature with his grace!

Bride

Alas! And who can cure?
Give thyself up, thy living presence show;
Ask not that I endure
More messengers, for no
One telleth me what I desire to know.

All creatures thee adore
And constantly a thousand tributes bring,
But each one wounds me more
And slays me with the thing—
I know not what—that they are murmuring.

O life, wilt thou persist
Though thou art more like death than life to me
And hast with death a tryst,
An arrowed thought which he,
Thy dearly loved one, hath conceived in thee?

Why then, Love, since thou art
The one who woundest me, dost thou not heal?
Since thou hast robbed my heart,
Why leav'st the pain I feel?
Why keepest not the plunder thou didst steal?

Apaga mis enojos,
Pues que ninguno basta a deshacellos,
Y véante mis ojos,
Pues eres lumbre dellos,
Y sólo para ti quiero tenellos.

Descubre tu presencia,
Y máteme tu vista y hermosura;
Mira que la dolencia
De amor, que no se cura
Sino con la presencia y la figura.

¡Oh cristalina fuente,
Si en esos tus semblantes plateados,
Formases de repente
Los ojos deseados,
Que tengo en mis entrañas dibujados!

Apártalos, Amado,
Que voy de vuelo.

Esposo

Vuélvete, paloma,
Que el ciervo vulnerado
Por el otero asoma,
Al aire de tu vuelo, y fresco toma.

Esposa

Mi Amado, las montañas,
Los valles solitarios nemorosos,
Las ínsulas extrañas,
Los ríos sonorosos,
El silbo de los aires amorosos.

La noche sosegada
En par de los levantes de la aurora,
La música callada,
La soledad sonora,
La cena, que recrea y enamora.

Quench thou this grief in me
Since no one else sufficeth to requite;
And let mine eyes but see
Thy face, who art their light,
Since only for thyself I care for sight.

Disclose thy presence now,
And let me by thy loveliness be slain:
The hurt of love—see how
'Tis cruel, I would fain
Thy form and presence see to cure love's pain.

O fountain crystal clear,
What if, upon thy silvered surface, thou
Shouldst quickly form the dear
Desirèd eyes and brow,
That memory draws within my vision now!

O lovèd eyes, look away!
I am about to fly.

Bridegroom

Turn back, my dove!
The wounded deer this day
Stands in the wind above
Thy flight and takes his solace from thy love.

Bride

Belovèd One, the hills,
The wooded solitary vales as fair,
The sounding rivers, rills,
Strange islands and the rare
Beseeching whisper of the amorous air.

The calm and quiet night,
Stirring of dawn asleep within the glen,
Silent music and slight,
Sounding solitude, then
The supper, and our love renewed again.

Nuestro lecho florido,
De cuevas de leones enlazado,
En púrpura tendido,
De paz edificado,
De mil escudos de oro coronado.

A zaga de tu huella
Las jóvenes discurren al camino
Al toque de centella,
Al adobado vino,
Emisiones de bálsamo Divino.

En la interior bodega
De mi Amado bebí, y cuando salía
Por toda aquesta vega,
Ya cosa no sabía,
Y el ganado perdí, que antes seguía.

Allí me dió su pecho,
Allí me enseñó ciencia muy sabrosa,
Y yo le dí de hecho
A mí, sin dejar cosa;
Allí le prometí de ser su esposa.

Mi alma se ha empleado,
Y todo mi caudal en su servicio:
Ya no guardo ganado,
Ni ya tengo otro oficio;
Que ya sólo en amar es mi ejercicio.

Pues ya si en el ejido
De hoy más no fuere vista ni hallada,
Diréis que me he perdido,
Que andando enamorada,
Me hice perdidiza, y fuí ganada.

De flores y esmeraldas
En las frescas mañanas escogidas,
Haremos las guirnaldas,
En tu amor florecidas,
Y en un cabello mío entretejidas.

This flowery bed of ours,
Safe hidden by the caves of lions bold,
These royal purple bowers
Are built of peace untold,
And crowned with shields, a thousand shields of gold.

Within thy footprints go
The young girls roaming, seeking grace like thine,
The lightning touch, whence flow
Emissions of divine,
Love-fragrant balsam and of spicèd wine.

Within the vault I drank
Of my loved one; and when I left his door,
The open plain, the bank,
The road, I knew no more,
And lost the flock that I had driven before.

He took me to his breast,
Sweet knowledge taught me; there did I confide
Myself, and there was blest;
And holding naught aside,
There did I promise him to be his bride.

My soul I did expend,
And all my wealth his will to glorify,
No flock now do I tend,
Nor other toil have I,
But loving all my life doth occupy.

If from the green I stray,
And can no more be found when day is done,
I pray that ye will say
This lost enamoured one
Did let herself be lost and then was won.

Of flowers and emeralds bright,
First-chosen gems of morning fresh and fine,
We shall garland our delight;
Thy love the flowers divine,
And interwoven in a lock of mine.

En sólo aquel cabello,
Que en mi cuello volar consideraste,
Mirástele en mi cuello,
Y en él preso quedaste,
Y en uno de mis ojos te llagaste.

Cuando tú me mirabas,
Tu gracia en mí tus ojos imprimían:
Por eso me adamabas,
Y en eso merecían
Los míos adorar lo que en ti vían.

No quieras despreciarme,
Que si color moreno en mí hallaste,
Ya bien puedes mirarme,
Después que me miraste,
Que gracia y hermosura en mí dejaste.

Cogednos las raposas,
Que está ya florecida nuestra viña,
En tanto que de rosas
Hacemos una piña,
Y no parezca nadie en la montiña.

Detente, Cierzo muerto;
Ven, Austro, que recuerdas los amores,
Aspira por mi huerto,
Y corran sus olores,
Y pacerá el Amado entre las flores.

Esposo

Entrádose ha la Esposa
En el ameno huerto deseado,
Y a su sabor reposa,
El cuello reclinado
Sobre los dulces brazos del Amado.

Debajo del manzano,
Allí conmigo fuiste desposada,
Allí te dí la mano,
Y fuiste reparada,
Donde tu madre fuera violada.

In that one lock of hair,
That blew upon my neck when thine eyes sought
And did admire it there,
Wert thou a prisoner caught,
And by one of mine eyes wounded, distraught.

Thou didst look at me; thine
Eyes impressed on me thy grace, and therefore
Didst thou love me, and mine
Eyes then did merit more
To love what they did see, and thee adore.

Think not to scorn me, though
Before too swarthy thou didst find me, now
Thou mayst look at me, so
Thou once didst look, and thou,
With grace and beauty then didst me endow!

Catch ye for us the young
She-foxes, for our grape doth flower; while here
With roses overhung,
We weave a cluster; near
Unto our mountain let no one appear.

Forbear north wind of death;
Come south wind who rememberest love's hours,
And let thy fragrant breath
Breathe through my garden bowers,
And my Beloved shall graze among the flowers.

Bridegroom

My bride has entered in
To the desired garden, and she knows
The pleasures found therein;
Her fair throat doth repose
On the dear arm of the loved one she chose.

Where the apple tree doth stand,
We were betrothed, there soul to soul did cleave;
I gave thee there my hand
And thou didst balm receive
For evil done unto thy mother, Eve.

A las aves ligeras,
Leones, ciervos, gamos saltadores,
Montes, valles, riberas,
Aguas, aires, ardores,
Y miedos de las noches veladores:

Por las amenas liras
Y canto de sirenas os conjuro
Que cesen vuestras iras,
Y no toquéis al muro,
Porque la Esposa duerma más seguro.

Esposa

Oh ninfas de Judea,
En tanto que en las flores y rosales
El ámbar perfumea,
Morá en los arrabales,
Y no queráis tocar nuestros umbrales.

Escóndete, Carillo,
Y mira con tu haz a las montañas,
Y no quieras decillo:
Mas mira las compañas
De la que va por ínsulas extrañas.

Esposo

La blanca palomica
Al Arca con el ramo se ha tornado,
Y ya la tortolica
Al socio deseado
En las riberas verdes ha hallado.

En soledad vivía,
Y en soledad ha puesto ya su nido,
Y en soledad la guía
A solas su querido,
También en soledad de amor herido.

Ye lightly soaring wings,
Ye lions, leaping bucks and fallow deer,
Ye mountains, valleys, springs
And rivers, heats that sear,
Ye sighing winds, and night's all-watching fear:

By string of pleasant lyre
I conjure you, by song of sirens, cease
Your rage; nor e'en desire
To touch the wall; release
My bride to slumber, may she sleep in peace.

Bride

Judean nymphs, while we
Among the flowers and rose bushes abide
And amber perfumes; see
Ye do without reside,
Touch not our threshold, enter not inside.

Ah, hide thee, dearest One!
And gaze thou toward the mountain top awhile,
Speak not! But look upon
The companies that file
Along with her past strange and stranger isle.

Bridegroom

The little snow-white dove
With olive branch unto the ark returns;
And now the turtle-dove
On greening bank discerns
The dear and gentle mate for whom she yearns.

In loneliness hath she
Long dwelt, alone her nest hath built to bless
Her Love, alone e'en he
Who guides her must confess
Himself as wounded in love's loneliness.

Esposa

Gocémonos, Amado,
Y vámonos a ver en tu hermosura
Al monte u al collado,
Do mana el agua pura;
Entremos más adentro en la espesura.

Y luego a las subidas
Cavernas de la piedra nos iremos,
Que están bien escondidas,
Y allí nos entraremos,
Y el mosto de granadas gustaremos.

Allí me mostrarías
Aquello que mi alma pretendía,
Y luego me darías
Allí tú, vida mía,
Aquello que me diste el otro día:

El aspirar del aire,
El canto de la dulce Filomena,
El soto y su donaire,
En la noche serena
Con llama que consume y no da pena.

Que nadie lo miraba,
Aminadab tampoco parecía,
Y el cerco sosegaba,
Y la caballería
A vista de las aguas descendía.

Bride

Let us take pleasure, Sweet;
And let the light of thy full beauty show
Mountain and dim retreat
Where purest waters flow;
Farther into the thicket let us go.

And then shall we go high
Up to the stony caverns; there shall we
Be hid, my Love, and I
Shall enter in with thee
And drink new wine of pomegranate tree.

There, unto me, thy bride,
Wilt thou show all my soul aspired to, oh,
It may e'en be beside,
That thou wilt there bestow
What thou, my Life, didst give not long ago:

The breathing of the air,
The sound of the sweet nightingale's refrain,
The dark grove's grace: ah, fair
The lovely night doth reign
With flame that doth consume and give no pain!

None saw, nor did molest,
Neither did the Arch-enemy come nigh;
From siege there now was rest;
The cavalry rode by
Descending where they saw the waters lie.

Jessie Read Wendell

[In this poem which appeared in *Translations from Hispanic Poets,* edited
by the Hispanic Society of America, with the permission of the translator, a
few slight changes of a word or a line have been made. Also the stanza
sequence has been changed to correspond with the Spanish text, which follows
the Codex of Jaén.]

70

LLAMA DE AMOR VIVA

¡Oh llama de amor viva,
Que tiernamente hieres
De mi alma en el más profundo centro!
Pues ya no eres esquiva,
Acaba ya si quieres,
Rompe la tela deste dulce encuentro.

¡Oh cauterio suave!
¡Oh regalada llaga!
¡Oh mano blanda! ¡Oh toque delicado,
Que a vida eterna sabe,
Y a toda deuda paga!
Matando, muerte en vida la has trocado.

¡Oh lámparas de fuego,
En cuyos resplandores
Las profundas cavernas del sentido,
Que estaba obscuro y ciego,
Con extraños primores
Calor y luz dan junto a su querido!

¡Cuán manso y amoroso
Recuerdas en mi seno,
Donde secretamente solo moras:
Y en tu aspirar sabroso
De bien y gloria lleno
Cuán delicadamente me enamoras!

LIVING FLAME OF LOVE   70

O living flame of love
That, burning, dost assail
My inmost soul with tenderness untold,
Since thou dost freely move,
Deign to consume the veil
Which sunders this sweet converse that we hold.

O burn that searest never!
O wound of deep delight!
O gentle hand! O touch of love supernal
That quick'nest life for ever,
Putt'st all my woes to flight,
And, slaying, changest death to life eternal!

And O, ye lamps of fire,
In whose resplendent light
The deepest caverns where the senses meet,
Erst steep'd in darkness dire,
Blaze with new glories bright
And to the lov'd one give both light and heat!

How tender is the love
Thou wak'nest in my breast
When thou, alone and secretly, art there!
Whispering of things above,
Most glorious and most blest,
How delicate the love thou mak'st me bear!

                                    E. Allison Peers

71   *COPLAS HECHAS SOBRE UN ÉXTASIS*
                      DE ALTA CONTEMPLACIÓN

> Entréme donde no supe,
> Y quedéme no sabiendo,
> Toda sciencia trascendiendo.
>
> Yo no supe dónde entraba,
> Pero, cuando allí me ví,
> Sin saber dónde me estaba,
> Grandes cosas entendí;
> No diré lo que sentí,
> Que me quedé no sabiendo,
> Toda sciencia trascendiendo.
>
> De paz y de piedad
> Era la sciencia perfecta,
> En profunda soledad,
> Entendida vía recta;
> Era cosa tan secreta,
> Que me quedé balbuciendo,
> Toda sciencia trascendiendo.
>
> Estaba tan embebido,
> Tan absorto y ajenado,
> Que se quedó mi sentido
> De todo sentir privado;
> Y el espíritu dotado
> De un entender no entendiendo,
> Toda sciencia trascendiendo.
>
> El que allí llega de vero,
> De sí mismo desfallesce;
> Cuanto sabía primero
> Mucho bajo le paresce;
> Y su sciencia tanto cresce,
> Que se queda no sabiendo,
> Toda sciencia trascendiendo.

VERSES WRITTEN UPON AN ECSTASY   71
OF HIGH CONTEMPLATION

I enter'd in—I knew not where—
And, there remaining, knew no more,
Transcending far all human lore.

I knew not where I enter'd in.
'Twas giv'n me there myself to see,
And wondrous things I learn'd within,
Yet knew I not where I could be.
I tell not what was shown to me:
Remaining there, I knew no more,
Transcending far all human lore.

That was the lore, all else above,
Of perfect peace, devotion deep.
In that profound retreat of love
The path direct I learn'd to keep.
Such secret knowledge did I reap
That, stammering, I could speak no more,
Transcending far all human lore.

Herein so deeply was I vers'd,
Throughly absorb'd and borne so high,
So far my senses were immers'd
That destitute of them was I.
My soul was dower'd from on high
With power of thought that thought no more,
Transcending far all human lore.

He that in truth attains to this
Is lost to self upon the earth.
All that, before, he counted his
Appears to him of little worth.
His knowledge comes anew to birth,
Yet, resting there, he knows no more,
Transcending far all human lore.

Cuanto más alto se sube,
Tanto menos entendía
Qué es la tenebrosa nube
Que a la noche esclarecía;
Por eso quien la sabía
Queda siempre no sabiendo
Toda sciencia trascendiendo.

Este saber no sabiendo
Es de tan alto poder,
Que los sabios arguyendo
Jamás le pueden vencer;
Que no llega su saber
A no entender entendiendo,
Toda sciencia trascendiendo.

Y es de tan alta excelencia
Aqueste sumo saber,
Que no hay facultad ni sciencia
Que le puedan emprender;
Quien se supiere vencer
Con un no saber sabiendo,
Irá siempre trascendiendo.

Y si lo queréis oír,
Consiste esta suma sciencia
En un subido sentir
De la divinal Esencia;
Es obra de su clemencia
Hacer quedar no entendiendo
Toda sciencia trascendiendo.

The nearer I approach'd the cloud
The less I understood its light,
That, howso darksome was its shroud,
Illumin'd all the gloomy night.
Wherefore a soul that knows that sight
Can never compass knowledge more,
For this transcends all human lore.

This wond'rous knowledge knowing naught
Is of a power so sov'reign high
That wise men's reasoning and thought
Defeat it not, howe'er they try.
Ne'er can their intellect come nigh
This power of thought that thinks no more,
Transcending far all human lore.

Built on so excellent a plan
This summit of true knowledge is
That neither wit nor power of man
Can ever reach such heights of bliss.
He that can climb as high as this
Through knowledge that can know no more
Shall aye transcend all human lore.

Would ye unto this summit climb?
Then know wherein its nature lies.
'Tis an experience all-sublime,
God's Self reveal'd before our eyes.
His grace alone the means supplies
Whereby man understands no more,
Yet far transcends all human lore.

E. Allison Peers

72

LA FONTE

Que bien sé yo la fonte que mana y corre,
   Aunque es de noche.

Aquella eterna fonte está ascondida,
Que bien sé yo do tiene su manida,
   Aunque es de noche.

Su origen no lo sé, pues no le tiene,
Mas sé que todo origen de ella viene,
   Aunque es de noche.

Sé que no puede ser cosa tan bella,
Y que cielos y tierra beben de ella,
   Aunque es de noche.

Bien sé que suelo en ella no se halla,
Y que ninguno puede vadealla,
   Aunque es de noche.

Su claridad nunca es escurecida,
Y sé que toda luz de ella es venida,
   Aunque es de noche.

Sé ser tan caudalosas sus corrientes,
Que infiernos, cielos riegan, y las gentes,
   Aunque es de noche.

El corriente que nace de esta fuente,
Bien sé que es tan capaz y omnipotente,
   Aunque es de noche.

El corriente que de estas dos procede
Sé que ninguna de ellas le precede,
   Aunque es de noche.

Aquesta eterna fonte está escondida
En este vivo pan por darnos vida,
   Aunque es de noche.

THE FOUNT THAT FREELY FLOWS   72

How well I know the fount that freely flows
    Although 'tis night!

The eternal fount its source has never show'd,
But well I know wherein is its abode,
    Although 'tis night.

Its origin I know not—it has none:
All other origins are here begun,
    Although 'tis night.

I know that naught beside can be so fair,
That heav'ns and earth drink deep refreshment there,
    Although 'tis night.

Well know I that its depths can no man plumb
Nor to the ground beneath it hope to come,
    Although 'tis night.

Never was fount so clear, undimm'd and bright:
From it alone, I know, proceeds all light,
    Although 'tis night.

Rich are its streams and full—this know I well;
They water nations, heav'ns and depths of hell,
    Although 'tis night.

Yea, more I know: the stream that hence proceeds,
Omnipotent, suffices for all needs,
    Although 'tis night.

From fount and stream another stream forth flows
And this, I know, as powerful as those—
    Although 'tis night.

The eternal fount is hidden in living bread,
That we with life eternal may be fed,
    Although 'tis night.

Aquí se está llamando a las criaturas,
Y de esta agua se hartan, aunque a escuras,
Porque es de noche.

Aquesta viva fuente, que deseo
En este pan de vida yo la veo,
Aunque es de noche.

Call'd to this living fount, we creatures still
Darkly may feed hereon and take our fill,
  Although 'tis night.

This living fount which is so dear to me
Is in the bread of life, which now I see,
  Although 'tis night.

                                        E. Allison Peers

Fernando de Herrera

The themes of Herrera are epic and amorous. In his love poems he employs images of war, and that gives us the key to his poetry—an extraordinary desire for perfection which is the expression of an heroic soul. His poetry has a quality so cold that it burns. The characteristic movement of the Baroque style seen in his work is the restrained movement of Greek sculpture, as in the quadriga, the four-horse chariot.

In his epic poetry Herrera unites God and country. It is the God of battles of the Old Testament—Jehovah who is not gentleness but wrath. Herrera's world is a monumental world; all his figures, like those of Michelangelo, are superhuman, larger than life; man is joined not to the world but to destiny.

In his *Ode on the Death of Don Sebastian*, Herrera sings of a defeat in the noble, majestic strains of a funeral march. To this historic event he adapts Biblical thoughts and phrases, interweaving them with rare skill, thus making a poem of admirable freshness and inspiration.

Though known as the poet of the trumpet-tongued epic, Herrera was nevertheless a great love poet. His inspiration and great love was the Countess of Gelves, to whom he alludes frequently in his poems as

1534?–1597

Light or Doña Luz. Because of this and other characteristics, love in the poems of Herrera is notably of Provençal and Petrarchian origin. For him, love is an act of service, a fire in which the soul, like the phoenix, is in turn consumed and revived. Moreover that love is distinguished by an oscillation between two elements—fire and ice—that in spite of being opposed and contradictory, do not destroy one another but coexist, and precisely for this reason they give to that love the character of a love that has no solution or requital. The poet, however, requires that his love should be so: a love not returned, in order to convert it into a pretext for living constantly soliloquizing in a state of accepted and voluntary despair.

The form in which all this is expressed, partakes of the nature of intense radiance. Love is almost an interchange of flashes of light, in whose centre is woman, a sort of epitome of the world; a love, aside from this, whose radiant inner world has very few points of contact with the reality of the flesh, and in which the state of mind is what makes possible a new poetic attitude.

Herrera is the Prince of Sighs.

From notes

73

CANCIÓN POR LA PÉRDIDA
DEL REI DON SEBASTIÁN

Voz de dolor, i canto de gemido,
i espíritu de miedo, embuelto en ira,
hagan principio acerbo a la memoria
d' aquel día fatal aborrecido
que Lusitania mísera suspira,
desnuda de valor, falta de gloria;
i la llorosa istoria
assombre con orror funesto i triste
dend' el Africo Atlante i seno ardiente
hasta do el mar d'otro color se viste,
i do el límite roxo d' Oriënte,
i todas sus vencidas gentes fieras
vên tremolar de Cristo las vanderas.

¡Ai de los que passaron, confiados
en sus cavallos i en la muchedumbre
de sus carros, en ti, Libia desierta;
i en su vigor i fuerças engañados,
no alçaron su esperança a aquella cumbre
d' eterna luz; mas con sobervia cierta
se ofrecieron la incierta
vitoria; i sin bolver a Dios sus ojos,
con ierto cuello i coraçón ufano
sólo atendieron siempre a los despojos!
I el Santo d' Israel abrió su mano,
i los dexó, i cayó en despeñadero
el carro, i el cavallo i cavallero.

Vino el día cruel, el día lleno
d' indinación, d' ira i furor, que puso
en soledad i en un profundo llanto
de gente, i de plazer el reino ageno.
El cielo no alumbró, quedó confuso
el nuevo sol, presago de mal tanto;
i con terrible espanto
el Señor visitó sobre sus males,
para umillar los fuertes arrogantes,

ODE ON THE DEATH OF   73
DON SEBASTIAN

Isa. XIII, 9   A voice of sorrow and a sound of weeping,
A spirit of fear enveloped in wrath,
Do make a sad beginning for the memory
Of that fatal day, of that hated day,
When Lusitania, the unhappy one,
Bereft of courage, and her glory gone,
Was left lamenting, sad;
Let the sorrowful tale resound with horror,
Grief and mourning from Afric's scorching plains
To the distant boundaries of the Red Sea,
And to the limits of the conquered East,
Where its wild tribes saw floating in the wind
The waving banners of the Christian host.

Isa. xxx, 1   Woe to them that marched trusting in their
strength,
Their horses and their multitude of chariots
To conquer their foe in the Libyan desert,
For they, in their mistaken power and force,
Did not exalt their hopes unto the summit
Of eternal light; but with a proud certainty
Offered uncertain victory!
And turning not their eyes unto the Lord,
This stiff-necked people, ever in their pride,
Did set their thoughts upon the spoils of war.
But then the Holy One, the Lord of Israel,
Isa. xxxi, 1, 3   Stretched forth his hand, and into the abyss
They fell, the horse, his rider and the chariot.

Isa. xiii, 9   Then came the day, the cruel day of wrath
And indignation, when all desolate
The kingdom mourned, without people and
pleasure.
Isa. xiii, 10   The heavens gave no light, the sun was darkened
In his going forth, presage of much evil;
Isa. xiii, 11   And with terrific threat, for their iniquity,
The Lord did punish them;
He laid low the haughtiness of the arrogant,

i levantó los bárbaros no iguales,
que con osados pechos i constantes
no busquen oro, mas con crudo hierro
venguen la ofensa i cometido ierro.

Los ímpios i robustos, indinados,
las ardientes espadas desnudaron
sobre la claridad i hermosura
de tu gloria i valor, i no cansados
en tu muerte, tu onor todo afearon,
mesquina Lusitania sin ventura;
i con frente segura
rompieron sin temor con fiero estrago
tus armadas escuadras i braveza.
L' arena se tornó sangriento lago,
la llanura con muertos, aspereza;
cayó en unos vigor, cayó denuedo,
mas en otros desmayo i torpe miedo.

¿Son estos, por ventura, los famosos,
los fuertes i belígeros varones
que conturbaron con furor la tierra,
que sacudieron reinos poderosos,
que domaron las órridas naciones,
que pusieron desierto en cruda guerra
cuanto enfrena i encierra
el mar Indo, i feroces destruyeron
grandes ciudades? ¿dó la valentía?
¿cómo assí s' acabaron, i perdieron
tanto eróico valor en sólo un día;
i lexos de su patria derribados,
no fueron justamente sepultados?

Tales fueron aquestos, cual hermoso
cedro del alto Líbano, vestido
de ramos, hojas con ecelsa alteza;
las aguas lo criaron poderoso,
sobre empinados árboles subido,
i se multiplicaron en grandeza
sus ramos con belleza;
i, estendiendo su sombra, s' anidaron
las aves que sustenta el grande cielo,

The beasts of the field under it had shade,
And they did multiply and there increase.
Man too found restful shelter in its shadow:
For beauty and for height it had no equal.

Dan. IV, 10   But lo, this tree in the midst of the earth,
As its green summit high did soar aloft,
So more and more it grew puffed up with pride,
Trusting alone in its exalted height.

Dan. IV, 14   Therefore the Lord did cast it down undone,
Cut off at root and overwhelmèd quite
By infidels and strangers;
Flung down from the mountainside and lying low
Upon the ground all stripped and bare of leaves,
In terror, men who had found shelter there,
From it did flee, and strange wild birds and beasts
Of the forest dwelt midst its ruined branches.

And thou, outrageous Libya, on whose
Dry sands the vanquished Lusitania died,
With all her glory ended, rejoice not,
Nor be swelled up with pride, for that thy weak
And timid hand such an unhoped-for victory
Did win, one so unworthy of remembrance;
For if just sorrow should,
Sometime, to vengeance move the Spanish courage,
Then, torn and mangled by sharp-pointed spear,
Thou, dying shalt atone the outrage done;
And Luco's waters, terror-stained, shall pay
The debt to the great deep with blood of Africa.

E. L. T.

[The bloody defeat of Alcazarquivir took place in August 1578. It was due
to the lack of foresight in preparation, and the ignorance of tactics of the rash
king of Portugal, Don Sebastian. With or without valor, an enterprise could
not prosper which was adjudged foolish beforehand by his uncles, the Cardinal
and King Philip II of Spain, and to which the nobility and clergy of Portugal
(Lusitania) at that time part of Spain, were opposed.

[Not only did they go to battle under difficult conditions, for lack of re-
sources, but they had to deal with an army (say the chronicles) of 40,000
horsemen and an immense number of Arabs and mercenaries.

[The blind confidence of the King in his own valor made him see such a
difficult victory as certain, and wishing to conquer with his forces alone, he
refused all outside assistance.]

CANCIÓN

Suäve Sueño, tu, qu'en tardo buelo
las alas perezosas blandamente
bates, d'adormideras coronado,
por el puro, adormido i vago cielo,
ven al 'ultima parte d'Ocidente,
i de licor sagrado
baña mis ojos tristes; que, cansado,
i rendido al furor de mi tormento,
no admito algun sossiego
i el dolor desconorta 'l sufrimiento,
ven a mi umilde ruego,
ven a mi ruego umilde, ¡ô amor d'aquella
que Iuno t'ofrecio, tu Ninfa bella!

Divino Sueño, gloria de mortales,
regalo dulce al misero afligido,
Sueño amoroso, ven a quien espera
cessar d'el exercicio de sus males,
i al descanso bolver todo el sentido,
¿como sufres que muera
lexos de tu poder quien tuyo era?
¿No es dureza olvidar un solo pecho
en veladora pena,
que, sin gozar d'el bien qu'al mundo as hecho,
de tu vigor s'agena?
ven Sueño alegre, Sueño, ven, dichoso,
buelve a mi alma ya, buelve 'l reposo

Sienta yo en tal estrecho tu grandeza
baxa, i esparze liquido el rocio,
huya l'Alba, qu'en torno resplandece,
mira mi ardiente llanto i mi tristeza,
i cuanta fuerça tiene 'l pesar mio,
i mi frente umedece;
que ya de fuegos juntos el Sol crece,
torna, sabroso Sueño, i tus hermosas
alas suenen aora,
i huya con sus alas pressurosas
la dessabrida Aurora,
i, lo qu'en mi faltó la noche fria,
termíne la cercana luz d'el dia.

ODE TO SLEEP   74

Sweet Sleep, with dewy poppies crowned,
Who in slow flight, thy lazy wings
Dost softly wave, wandering sleepily
Through the clear heavens, to farthest West
Come, and with thy blessèd liquid
Bathe these my weeping eyes,
That wearied by fury of torment,
From their sorrow find no relief;
Oh come, come ease my grief
In answer to my humble prayer,
Come at my call, or for the sake,
Of that fair Nymph by Juno given thee.

Blessèd Sleep, the glory of mortals,
Sweet gift to the miserable one,
Belovèd, come to him who longs
To cease from grieving o'er his sorrows,
And all his thoughts would turn to rest.
Why dost thou leave to die,
Far from thy power, him who was thine?
Is it not cruel to forget
One waking soul in grief,
Without the good thy power doth give?
Come Sleep, glad Sleep, come happy one,
Steal o'er my soul, come rest, return!

In this extremity of grief,
Descend and shed thy healing dew,
Flee thou, oh Dawn that scatters light;
See thou my sadness, my moist brow,
And the distress of my heartache,
Hear thou mine ardent plaint;
For now with fire the Sun grows hot,
Turn thou, sweet Sleep, with beauteous wings
Soar now above my head,
Flee thou, oh bleak and swift-winged Morn,
And what I lacked in the cold night,
May it come with the light of dawn.

Una corona ¡ô Sueño! de tus flores
ofresco; tu, produze 'l blando efeto
en los desiertos cercos de mis ojos;
qu'el aire entretexido con olores
halaga, i ledo mueve en dulce afeto;
i d'estos mis enojos
destierra, manso Sueño, los despojos,
ven pues, amado Sueño, ven liviano;
que d'el rico Oriënte
despunta el tierno Febo el rayo cano,
ven ya Sueño clemente,
i acabará el dolor; ¡assi te vea
en braços de tu cara Pasitea!

SONETO

75

Roxo Sol, que, con hacha luminosa
coloras el purpúreo i alto cielo,
¿hallaste tal belleza en todo el suelo,
qu'iguale a mi serena Luz dichosa?
    Aura suäve, blanda i amorosa,
que nos halagas con tu fresco buelo,
cuando el oro descubre i rico velo
mi Luz, ¿trença tocaste más hermosa?
    Luna, onor de la noche, ilustre Coro
de los errantes astros i fixados,
¿consideraste tales dos estrellas?
    Sol puro, Aura, Luna, Luzes d'oro,
¿oistes mis dolores nunca usados?
¿vistes Luz más ingrata a mis querellas?

A wreath of thy flowers, oh Sleep,
I offer, and do thou therewith
Anoint the circles of mine eyes;
And may the fragrant air caress
And gently soothe in sweet affection;
The remnants of my sorrow
Banish, oh merciful Sleep, come
Thou loved Sleep, come fickle one ere
From the Orient dawns
The white ray of tender Apollo,
Come end my woe; thus may I see thee
In the arms of thy loved Pasithea!

E. L. T.

SONNET   75

Red sun, that with thy taper shining bright,
At high midday dost fill the heavens unfurled,
Didst find such radiance in all the world,
To equal my serene, my blessèd Light?
Thou cool and loving breeze, that in thy flight
Caresses us with gentleness untold,
Didst fan fair locks more like unto spun-gold
Than the bright veil that doth enshroud my Light?
Thou moon, glory of night, illustrious choir
Of wandering and fixed stars, could ye now find
Such stars as ye do see within her eyes?
Thou sun, and wind, and moon, and flames of fire,
Heard ye my never-ending plaints that rise,
Saw ye a Light more cruel, more unkind?

E. L. T.

76   *SONETO*

Serena Luz, en quien presente espira
divino amor, qu'enciende i junto enfrena
el noble pecho, qu'en mortal cadena
al alto Olimpo levantar s' aspira;
    ricos cercos dorados, do se mira
tesoro celestial d'eterna vena;
armonía d'angélica Sirena,
qu'entre las perlas i el coral respira,
    ¿cuál nueva maravilla, cuál exemplo
de la immortal grandeza nos descubre
aquessa sombra del hermoso velo?
    Que yo en essa belleza que contemplo
(aunqu'a mi flaca vista ofende i cubre),
la immensa busco, i voi siguiendo al cielo.

77   *SONETO*

(En la muerte de la Condesa de Gelves?)

Alma bella, qu'en este oscuro velo
cubriste un tiempo tu vigor luziente
i, en hondo i ciego olvido, gravemente
fuiste ascondida sin alçar el buelo,
    Ya, despreciando este lugar, do el cielo
t'encerró i apuró con fuerça ardiente,
i, roto el mortal nudo, vas presente
a eterna paz, dexando en guerra el suelo.
    Buelve tu luz a mi, i d'el centro tira
al ancho cerco d'immortal belleza,
como vapor terrestre levantado
    Este espiritu opresso, que suspira
en vano por huir d'esta estrecheza,
qu'impide estar contigo descansado.

IDEAL BEAUTY   76

O Light serene! present in one who breathes
That love divine, which kindles yet restrains
The high-born soul—that in its mortal chains
Heavenward aspires for love's immortal wreaths!
   Rich golden locks, within whose clustered curls
Celestial and eternal treasures lie!
A voice that breathes angelic harmony
Among bright coral and unspotted pearls!
   What marvelous beauty! Of the high estate
Of immortality, within this light
Transparent veil of flesh, a glimpse is given;
   And in the glorious form I contemplate
(Although its brightness blinds my feeble sight)
The immortal still I seek and follow on to Heaven!

Henry W. Longfellow

THE DISEMBODIED SPIRIT   77

Pure Spirit! that within a form of clay
Once veiled the brightness of thy native sky;
In dreamless slumber sealed thy burning eye,
Nor heavenward sought to wing thy flight away!
   He that chastised thee did at length unclose
Thy prison doors, and give thee sweet release,
Unloosed the mortal coil, eternal peace
Received thee to its stillness and repose.
   Look down once more from thy celestial dwelling,
Help me to rise and be immortal there—
An earthly vapor melting into air;—
   For my whole soul with secret ardor swelling,
From earth's dark mansion struggles to be free,
And longs to soar away and be at rest with thee.

Henry W. Longfellow

78

SONETO

Ya el rigor importuno i grave ielo
desnuda los esmaltes i belleza
de la pintada tierra, i con tristeza
s'ofende en niebla oscura el claro cielo.

Mas, Pacheco, este mesmo órrido suelo
reverdece, i pomposo su riqueza
muestra, i del blanco mármol la dureza
desata de Favonio el tibio buelo.

Pero el dulce color i hermosura
de nuestra umana vida cuando huye
no torna, ¡ô mortal suerte!, ¡ô breve gloria!

Mas sola la virtud nos assegura;
qu'el tiempo avaro, aunqu'esta flor destruye,
contra ella nunca osó intentar vitoria.

SONNET   78

Too soon the winter cold and heavy frost
Strip from the earth's enameled countryside
Its coloured beauty; in the sky now ride
Dark gloomy clouds in sad displeasure tossed.
  Yet, dear Pacheco, earth is reëmbossed
With green and showy riches, and the tide
Of spring and western winds, warm-breathing, glide
To free the soil with marble whiteness glossed.
  Alas, when from our human life has fled
The tender hue of beauty's transient hour,
It ne'er returns. O Fate! O short-lived Fame!
  Virtue alone can save us; time may tread
With greed, but though it should destroy the flower,
A victory it never dares to claim.

Jean Willard Burnham

Anonymous

79

A CRISTO CRUCIFICADO

No me mueve, mi Dios, para quererte,
el cielo que me tienes prometido,
ni me mueve el infierno tan temido
para dejar por eso de ofenderte.
    Tu me mueves, Señor; muéveme el verte
clavado en esa cruz, y escarnecido;
muéveme el ver tu cuerpo tan herido;
muévenme tus afrentas, y tu muerte.
    Muévesme al tu amor en tal manera,
que aunque no hubiera cielo, yo te amara;
y aunque no hubiera infierno, te temiera.
    No me tienes que dar, porque te quiera;
que aunque cuanto espero no esperara,
lo mismo que te quiero te quisiera.

XVIth OR EARLY XVIIth CENTURY

TO CHRIST CRUCIFIED 79

It moves me not, my God, to love of Thee,
That promised Paradise, so full of bliss,
Nor moves me with its fires the dread abyss,
That I, in fear thereof, from sin should flee.
Thou movst me, Lord: it moves me to behold
Upon the Cross of shame that Form Divine;
It moves me sore to count those wounds of Thine;
Move me Thy death and torments manifold;
Moves me Thy love, and I must needs adore
And serve Thee, Lord, e'en though of Heaven bereft,
And though Hell were not, fear Thee evermore.
Naught needst Thou give this my poor heart to gain,
For, though of all my hopes no hope were left,
The love I bear thee now could never wane.

Ida Farnell

Later Poems from the

At the beginning of the xviith century poets continued developing the old refrains of the songs of traditional type (see above, page 112), and this was done even by Lope de Vega as well as by less famous writers.

But about 1600, new forms had appeared in poetry of popular tendency: above all the *seguidilla*, which although not strictly new settles, or has a tendency to settle, into the form which will last until the xxth

Cancioneros

century (a line of seven syllables alternating with one of five syllables).

The greater part of the songs that follow are *seguidillas*. In several of them can be seen very clearly the influence of cultured poetry. They are nevertheless very graceful and representative of the courting songs in vogue at the decline of the Golden Age.

D. A.

80

GALERITAS DE ESPAÑA

Galeritas de España
parad los remos,
para que descanse
mi amado preso.

Galeritas nuevas
que en el mar soberbio
levantáis las olas
de mi pensamiento;
pues el viento sopla
navegad sin remos
para que descanse
mi amado preso.

En el agua fría
encendéis mi fuego,
que un fuego amoroso
arde entre los hielos;
quebrantad las olas
y volad con viento
para que descanse
mi amado preso.

Plegue a Dios que deis
en peñascos recios,
defendiendo el paso
de un lugar estrecho;
y que estéis parados
sin temer encuentro
para que descanse
mi amado preso.

Plegue a Dios que os manden
pasar el invierno,
ocupando el paso
de un lugar estrecho;
y que quebrantados
os volváis al puerto,
para que descanse
mi amado preso.

GALLEYS OF SPAIN   80

Ye galleys of our land
   Arrest your oars again,
That he, my love, may rest,
   Who drags your heavy chain.

Bright galleys! on the surge
   Ye bear with every stroke,
The surges of my thoughts,
   Which fear and love awoke.
Upon the ocean's breast
   Its fair winds move again;
So let my lover rest
   Who drags your heavy chain.

The waters of the sea
   Though cold, inflame my soul;
My love's pure light would glow
   E'en at the icy pole.
That love on whirlwind's breast
   Would fly across the main,
To let my lover rest
   Who drags your heavy chain.

O wait! bright galleys now,
   In some fair harbour wait,
Or guard the narrow pass
   Of some not-distant strait;
Or, at the maid's behest,
   In tranquil port remain,
That he, my love, may rest,
   Who drags your heavy chain.

The winter hours draw nigh;
   Come, galleys, then, and stay,
In cheerful solitude,
   Within a sheltered bay;
There ye may anchor best,
   For there no dangers reign—
So let my lover rest
   Who drags your heavy chain.

                John Bowring

81

LETRILLA

Con el viento murmuraran,
madre, las hojas,
y al sonido me duermo
bajo su sombra.

Sopla un manso viento
alegre y süave,
que mueve la nave
de mi pensamiento;
dame tal contento
que me parece,
que el cielo me ofrece
bien a deshora;
y al sonido me duermo
bajo su sombra.

Si acaso recuerdo,
me hallo entre las flores
y de mis dolores
apenas me acuerdo;
de vista los pierdo
del sueño vencida
y dame la vida
el son de las hojas,
y al sonido me duermo
bajo su sombra.

LETRILLA   81

When the wind, Mother,
Rustles the leaves,
I am cradled in sleep
Under shadowy trees.

Gently and lightly
Blows a soft wind
Moving the ship
Of my slumbering mind.
Great my content,
And scarcely I know
Why blessings like these
The heavens bestow.
I am cradled in sleep
Under shadowy trees.

And if I awake
Surrounded with flowers
I have no remembrance
Of sorrowing hours.
Vanquished in sleep
From my sight they are flown;
There's life on the breeze
Where a leaf is blown.
I am cradled in sleep
Under shadowy trees.

Ada Marshall Johnson

82

DICHOSO TORMES

Fertiliza tu vega,
dichoso Tormes,
porque viene mi niña
cogiendo flores.

De la fértil vega
y el estéril bosque
los vecinos campos
maticen y broten
lirios y claveles
de varios colores
porque viene mi niña
cogiendo flores.

Vierta el alba perlas
desde sus balcones,
que prados amenos
maticen y borden;
y el sol envidioso
pare el rubio coche;
porque viene mi niña
cogiendo flores.

El céfiro blando
sus yerbas retoce
y en las frescas ramas
claros ruiseñores
saluden el día
con sus dulces voces;
porque viene mi niña
cogiendo flores.

HAPPY VALE OF TORMES   82

Thou happy vale of Tormes,
  Grow rich with sunny showers;
For my little maiden cometh,
  She comes to gather flowers!

Let mirth be in thy forest,
  And wealth upon thy plain;
Let all thy fragrant meadows
  Burst forth to life again,
With the ruddy pink and iris,
  All fresh with summer showers;
For my little maiden cometh,
  She comes to gather flowers!

Let all the grasses glisten
  With pearly drops of dew;
Let all thy gardens sparkle
  With gems of every hue;
The sun drive forth his chariot,
  With all the rosy hours;
For my little maiden cometh,
  She comes to gather flowers!

Bend, bend your heads, ye bushes,
  Beneath the gentle gales;
Pipe forth from every thicket,
  Ye tuneful nightingales;
To greet the day that dawneth,
  And gladden all the bowers;
For my little maiden cometh,
  She comes to gather flowers!

James Young Gibson

83   *EL AMOR ESQUIVO*

Madre, la mi madre,
el amor esquivo
me ofende y agrada,
me deja y le sigo.
Viera yo unos ojos
el otro domingo,
del cielo milagro,
del suelo peligro:
lo que cuentan, madre,
de los basilicos,
por mi alma pasa
la vez que los miro.
Rogáselo, madre,
rogáselo al niño,
que no tire más
que matan sus tiros.

Vime en tierra extraña,
¡ay bienes perdidos!
templado mi pecho,
cabal mi juicio;
ahora una nube
abrásame vivo.
Locura es mi intento;
consejo no admito:
mi rebelde cuello
humilde le inclino
al yugo y al arco
del rapaz maldito.
Rogáselo, madre,
rogáselo al niño,
que no tire más
que matan sus tiros.

WILY CUPID   83

O Mother mine, 'tis Cupid,
  The boy of wiles and laughter;
He teases me and pleases me,
  He runs and I run after.
'Twas but the other Sunday
  I saw a pair of eyes,
With glance of other countries,
  With light from other skies;
For like the fabled serpents
  They fixed me with their charm;
And while I looked and wondered,
  They pierced me to my harm;
O Mother mine, entreat him,
  The little boy implore,
With his deadly bow and arrows
  To shoot at me no more!

My mind was once untroubled,
  And peaceful was my breast;
But strange things flit across them,
  And I cannot, cannot rest;
I feel a cloud of darkness
  Hang o'er me like a pall;
My brain is full of folly,
  And I cannot think at all.
My rebel neck is bending,
  Is bending very low,
Before the cruel urchin,
  His quiver and his bow.
O Mother mine, entreat him,
  The little boy implore,
With his deadly bow and arrows
  To shoot at me no more!

James Young Gibson

84   *LA NIÑA REPOSA*

Mientras duerme la niña,
flores y rosas,
azuecenas y lirios
le hacen sombra.

En el prado verde
la niña reposa
donde Manzanares
sus arroyos brota.
No se mueve el viento,
ramas ni hojas,
que azucenas y lirios
le hacen sombra.

El sol la obedece
y su paso acorta,
que son rayos bellos
sus ojos y boca.
Las aves no cantan
viendo tal gloria,
que azucenas y lirios
le hacen sombra.

AMARYLLIS   84

She sleeps;—Amaryllis
  Midst flowerets is laid;
And roses and lilies
  Make the sweet shade.

The maiden is sleeping,
  Where through the green hills,
Manzanares is creeping
  Along with his rills.

Wake not Amaryllis,
  Ye winds in the glade!
Where roses and lilies
  Make the sweet shade.

The sun, while upsoaring,
  Yet tarries awhile,
The bright rays adoring
  Which stream from her smile.

The wood-music still is
  To rouse her afraid,
Where roses and lilies
  Make the sweet shade.

John Bowring

Andrés Fernández de Andrada?

The *Epístola Moral* has been attributed to several different poets by a number of critics. Others have stubbornly persisted in considering it anonymous, in spite of the fact that a series of manuscripts of the xviith century tell us that it is written by an obscure poet, Andrés Fernández de Andrada, of whom besides this epistle, unfortunately, only a very brief fragment of another poem has been preserved. Often a poem is attributed to a famous writer on the basis of a single manuscript. We have here a whole series that attribute the *Epistle* to an obscure poet. Why should we not believe what several manuscripts tell us? Why could not an obscure poet write a masterpiece?

The *Epistle to Fabio* is just that. Never has Spanish expression attained such sententious beauty. The Seneca tradition, so long persistent in Spain, reaches its highest point here. The author certainly was writing when manneristic cultism was already making progress, though

c. 1600

the date 1626, sometimes attributed to this poem, is not necessarily the correct one. The poet uses a clear-cut Spanish, he writes simply, an enemy of ostentation and dramatic gesture, without more than an occasional rhetorical development. In his happiest moments, he has a conciseness that penetrates:

> " ¡Oh muerte! ven callada,
> Como sueles venir en la saeta."

> "Oh death! come silently,
> As by the arrow you are wont to come."

Spaniards consider that the *Epistle to Fabio* represents the most enduring, the most profound sentiments of the Spanish spirit, the most genuine, beneath the many-changing and sometimes deceptive outward appearances.

D. A.

EPÍSTOLA MORAL

Fabio, las esperanzas cortesanas
Prisiones son do el ambicioso muere
Y donde al más astuto nacen canas.

El que no las limare o las rompiere,
Ni el nombre de varón ha merecido,
Ni subir al honor que pretendiere.

El ánimo plebeyo y abatido
Elija, en sus intentos temeroso,
Primero estar suspenso que caído;

Que el corazón entero y generoso
Al caso adverso inclinará la frente
Antes que la rodilla al poderoso.

Más triunfos, más coronas dió al prudente
Que supo retirarse, la fortuna,
Que al que esperó obstinada y locamente.

Esta invasión terrible e importuna
De contrarios sucesos nos espera
Desde el primer sollozo de la cuna.

Dejémosla pasar come a la fiera
Corriente del gran Betis, cuando airado
Dilata hasta los montes su ribera.

Aquel entre los héroes es contado
Que el premio mereció, no quien le alcanza
Por vanas consecuencias del estado.

Peculio propio es ya de la privanza
Cuanto de Astrea fué, cuanto regía
Con su temida espada y su balanza.

El oro, la maldad, la tiranía
Del inícuo procede y pasa al bueno.
¿Qué espera la virtud o qué confía?

EPISTLE TO FABIO   85

My Fabio, the courtier's hopes are chains
Wherein imprisoned dies the ambitious man
And even the most clever one grows grey.

Who does not either file or break these links,
Does not deserve to bear the name of man,
Nor should he wear the honor that he claims.

The soul, plebeian and mean-spirited,
He, timorous, chooses rather to remain
In state of suspense than to fall from grace.

While the upright, the true generous heart
Unto his adverse destiny will bow
Rather than bend the knee before the great.

More triumphs and more crowns did fortune give
Unto the prudent man who did retreat
Than to the fool who stubbornly did wait.

This terrible, importunate invasion
Of adverse happenings does wait for us
At the first infant wail from out the cradle.

Oh, may we let it pass as the wild flood
Of the great river Betis when it, raging,
Extends its banks unto the mountain ridges!

He who deserved the prize is named among
The heroes, and not he who gained it through
The insubstantial power of the state.

Now, in control of favorites at court,
Is what was once ruled by Astrea, goddess
Of justice, with her scales and dreaded sword.

The gold, iniquity and tyranny
Of wicked men go on and spread unto
The good. For what does virtue hope or trust?

Ven y reposa en el materno seno
De la antigua Romúlea, cuyo clima
Te será más humano y más sereno.

Adonde por lo menos, cuando oprima
Nuestro cuerpo la tierra, dirá alguno;
"Blanda le sea," al derramarla encima;

Donde no dejarás la mesa ayuno
Cuando te falte en ella el pece raro
O cuando su pavón nos niegue Junio.

Busca pues el sosiego dulce y caro,
Como en la obscura noche del Egeo
Busca el piloto el eminente faro;

Que si acortas y ciñes tu deseo
Dirás: "Lo que desprecio he conseguido;
Que la opinión vulgar es devaneo."

Más precia el ruiseñor su pobre nido
De pluma y leves pajas, más sus quejas
En el bosque repuesto y escondido,

Que halagar lisongero las orejas
De algún príncipe insigne, aprisionado
En el metal de las doradas rejas.

Triste de aquel que vive destinado
A esa antigua colonia de los vicios,
Augur de los semblantes del privado.

Cese el ansia y la sed de los oficios;
Que acepta el don y burla del intento
El ídolo a quien haces sacrificios.

Iguala con la vida el pensamiento,
Y no le pasarás de hoy a mañana,
Ni quizá de un momento a otro momento.

Come and repose on the maternal breast
Of ancient, time-honored Seville, whose clime
To you will be more human, more serene.

Where when the earth our body does oppress,
At least someone will say, as it is strewn
Above us there: "On thee may earth be light."

There where you will not leave the table fasting
When no rare fish is served thereon, or when
Juno to us her peacock does deny.

Seek then the sweet, the loved tranquillity,
As pilot on the Ægean sea does seek
Through darkness for the lofty beacon light;

For if you check and bridle your desire,
Then you will say: "I've gained what I despise;
For popular opinion has gone mad."

The nightingale does value his poor nest
Of straw and feathers and his sad laments,
Secluded and secure within the forest,

More than he prizes the rich cage behind
Whose golden bars imprisoned he must sing
His song to flatter a famed prince's ear.

Ah, sad is he whose fate it is to live
Within that ancient colony of vice,
Where he must read the face of the court minion!

Cease then the thirst and anxious care for office,
For he accepts the gift and mocks your purpose,
The idol before whom you sacrifice;

And modify your thought to suit your life,
For then it will not haste from this day to
The morrow, nor from moment unto moment.

Casi no tienes ni una sombra vana
De nuestra antigua Itálica, y ¿esperas?
¡Oh error perpetuo de la suerte humana!

Las enseñas grecianas, las banderas
Del senado y romana monarquía
Murieron, y pasaron sus carreras.

¿Qué es nuestra vida más que un breve día
Do apena sale el sol cuando se pierde
En las tinieblas de la noche fría?

¿Qué más que el heno, a la mañana verde,
Seco a la tarde? ¡Oh ciego desvarío!
¿Será que de este sueño me recuerde?

¿Será que pueda ver que me desvío
De la vida viviendo, y que está unida
La cauta muerte al simple vivir mío?

Como los ríos, que en veloz corrida
Se llevan a la mar, tal soy llevado
Al último suspiro de mi vida.

De la pasada edad ¿qué me ha quedado?
O ¿qué tengo yo a dicha, en la que espero,
Sin ninguna noticia de mi hado?

¡Oh, si acabase, viendo cómo muero,
De aprender a morir antes que llegue
Aquel forzoso término postrero;

Antes que aquesta mies inútil siegue
De la severa muerte dura mano,
Y a la común materia se la entregue!

Pasáronse las flores del verano,
El otoño pasó con sus racimos,
Pasó el invierno con sus nieves cano;

Of our antique Italica remains
Scarcely an empty shadow, and you wait?
Oh constant error of our human state!

The Grecian standards perished and the flags
Of Roman monarchy and senate fell,
And swiftly their careers did run their course.

Our life, what is it more than one brief day
In which the sun scarce rises ere 'tis gone,
Lost in the cold and darkness of the night?

What is it more than grass at morning green,
At evening dry? Oh blind delirium!
Will I some day from such a dream awake?

Ah, will it be that I may see I stray
From life while living, and that watchful death
Is joined unto my very simple breathing?

Even as rivers reach the sea in their
Swift flowing, even so I, borne along
Reach to the very last breath of my living.,

What has remained to me of my past state,
Or what have I of joy for which I hope,
Without a clue to trace my destiny?

Oh, that at last I might learn how to die,
Seeing that I must die, before it comes,
That unavoidable, ultimate end;

Before this useless grain be harvested
By death's severe, inexorable hand,
And to the common element returned!

The flowers of summer passed, and autumn too
Passed with its clustered grapes, and afterwards,
Hoary with age, the winter also passed.

Las hojas que en las altas selvas vimos
Cayeron, ¡y nosotros a porfía
En nuestro engaño inmóviles vivimos!

Temamos al Señor que nos envía
Las espigas del año y la hartura,
Y la temprana lluvia y la tardía.

No imitemos la tierra siempre dura
A las aguas del cielo y al arado,
Ni la vid cuyo fruto no madura.

¿Piensas acaso tú que fué criado
El varón para rayo de la guerra,
Para sulcar el piélago salado,

Para medir el orbe de la tierra
Y el cerco donde el sol siempre camina?
¡Oh quien así lo entiende, cuánto yerra!

Esta nuestra porción, alta y divina,
A mayores acciones es llamada
Y en más nobles objetos se termina.

Así aquella que al hombre solo es dada,
Sacra razón y pura, me despierta,
De esplendor y de rayos coronada;

Y en la fría región dura y desierta
De aqueste pecho enciende nueva llama,
Y la luz vuelve a arder que estaba muerta.

Quiero, Fabio, seguir a quien me llama,
Y callado pasar entre la gente,
Que no afecto los nombres ni la fama.

El soberbio tirano del Oriente
Que maciza las torres de cien codos
Del cándido metal puro y luciente,

The leaves we saw on the tall forest trees
Did fall, but we ourselves, persistent still,
Go on unshaken in this our delusion.

Oh, let us fear the Lord who sends us tasseled
Corn, and the fruitful early and late rains,
And the rich harvests far beyond our need.

Let us not imitate the earth, so hard
Always to rains of heaven and to the plow,
Nor ape the vine whose fruit does not mature.

But do you think, perchance, man was created
For thunderbolt and havoc of grim war,
To plow the salty waves of the high seas,

To measure the circumference of the earth
And the path where the sun forever circles?
Oh, how he errs who understands it so!

This our high portion here, our lot divine
Is unto greater, nobler actions called
And on more lofty objects does it end.

And thus that pure and sacred reason which
With radiance and with power crowned, to man
Alone is given, does awake me now;

And in the cold, the cruel desert region
Of this my heart is kindled a new flame,
And the light burns again that once was dead.

Fabio, I wish, to follow him who calls
Me, and to pass unnoticed through the crowd,
For I aspire to neither name nor fame.

The haughty tyrant of the eastern land
Who hoards in towers of a hundred cubits
His treasured store of pure and shining metal,

Apenas puede ya comprar los modos
Del pecar; la virtud es más barata,
Ella consigo mesma ruega a todos.

¡Pobre de aquel que corre y se dilata
Por cuantos son los climas y los mares,
Perseguidor del oro y de la plata!

Un ángulo me basta entre mis lares,
Un libro y un amigo, un sueño breve,
Que no perturben deudas ni pesares.

Esto tan solamente es cuanto debe
Naturaleza al simple y al discreto,
Y algún manjar común, honesto y leve.

No, porque así te ascribo, hagas conceto
Que pongo la virtud en ejercicio:
Que aun esto fué difícil a Epiteto.

Basta al que empieza aborrecer el vicio,
Y el ánimo enseñar a ser modesto;
Después le será el cielo más propicio.

Despreciar el deleite no es supuesto
De sólida virtud; que aun el vicioso
En sí propio le nota de molesto.

Mas no podrás negarme cuán forzoso
Este camino sea al alto asiento,
Morada de la paz y del reposo.

No sazona la fruta en un momento
Aquella inteligencia que mensura
La duración de todo a su talento.

Flor la vimos primero hermosa y pura,
Luego materia acerba y desabrida,
Y perfecta después, dulce y madura;

He, even he, can scarcely buy the ways
Of sin; but virtue is more cheaply won,
She, by herself alone, courts everyone.

Alas for him, but poor is he that seeks
For gold and silver over sea and land,
In every clime, and travels far and wide!

Enough for me a corner by my hearth,
A book, a friend and a brief time for sleep
Quite undisturbed by creditors and sorrows.

And this is all that mother nature owes
To him who is a prudent, simple man,
With some plain dish of decent, homely food.

But not because I write you thus are you
To think that I achieve to such great virtue;
For Epictetus even this was hard.

Enough for the beginner to hate vice
And teach his soul to love humility;
For heaven will be more favorable then.

To scorn pleasure is not to be assumed
Of sound virtue, for even of himself
The vicious man knows it to be unprofitable.

But you cannot deny, there is no choice,
One must follow this path if he would reach
That lofty seat, the home of peace and rest.

The mind that measures time for everything,
With a supreme intelligence, does not
Mature the unripe fruit all in a moment.

We saw the flower first, so fair and pure,
Then the hard substance, bitter to the taste,
At last the perfect fruit, quite ripe and sweet.

Tal la humana prudencia es bien que mida
Y dispense y comparta las acciones
Que han de ser compañeras de la vida.

No quiera Dios que imite estos varones
Que moran nuestras plazas macilentos,
De la virtud infames histriones;

Esos inmundos trágicos, atentos
Al aplauso común, cuyas entrañas
Son infaustos y oscuros monumentos.

¡Cuán callada que pasa las montañas
El aura, respirando mansamente!
¡Qué gárrula y sonante por las cañas!

¡Qué muda la virtud por el prudente!
¡Qué redundante y llena de ruido
Por el vano, ambicioso y aparente!

Quiero imitar al pueblo en el vestido,
En las costumbres sólo a los mejores,
Sin presumir de roto y mal ceñido.

No resplandezca el oro y los colores
En nuestro traje, ni tampoco sea
Igual al de los dóricos cantores.

Una mediana vida yo posea,
Un estilo común y moderado,
Que no lo note nadie que lo vea.

En el plebeyo barro mal tostado
Hubo ya quien bebió tan ambicioso
Como en el vaso Múrino preciado;

Y alguno tan ilustre y generoso
Que usó, como si fuera vil gaveta,
Del cristal transparente y luminoso.

It would be well that prudent men should so
Distribute, temper and divide the actions
That are to be companions on life's way.

May God forbid that I copy these pale,
Lean men that haunt our squares, infamous actors
That bring disgrace on the fair name of virtue;

Unclean tragedians seeking for applause
Of men, whose hearts accursèd are within,
Sad monuments of darkness and of gloom.

How silently the gentle breeze blows through
The mountains, breathing, oh so quietly!
But how it chatters when it sways the reeds!

How mute is virtue in the prudent soul,
But how superfluous and full of noise
It does show off in vain, ambitious one!

In dress would I copy the average man,
In manners imitate the best alone,
Not boasting in untidy gown and tatters.

Nor would I that our garb be richly decked
With glittering gold and hues of brilliant shade,
Nor yet as simple as the Doric singers.

A modest way of living do I choose,
A middle course that suits the moderate man,
That nobody that passes will remark.

For one who drinks from crude, plebeian cup
Of clay, may be as covetous and greedy
As were it precious goblet of the ancients.

Another one, illustrious and noble,
May use, as if it were a vile container,
A chalice of the most translucent crystal.

Sin la templanza ¿viste tú perfeta
Alguna cosa? ¡Oh muerte! ven callada,
Como sueles venir en la saeta,

No en la tonante máquina preñada
De fuego y de rumor; que no es mi puerta
De doblados metales fabricada.

Así, Fabio, me muestra descubierta
Su esencia la verdad, y mi albedrío
Con ella se compone y se concierta.

No te burles de ver cuánto confío,
Ni al arte de decir, vana y pomposa,
El ardor atribuyas de este brío.

¿Es por ventura menos poderosa
Que el vicio la virtud? ¿Es menos fuerte?
No la arguyas de flaca y temerosa.

La codicia en las manos de la suerte
Se arroja al mar, la ira a las espadas,
Y la ambición se ríe de la muerte.

Y ¿no serán siquiera tan osadas
Las opuestas acciones, si las miro
De más ilustres genios ayudadas?

Ya, dulce amigo, huyo y me retiro
De cuanto simple amé; rompí los lazos.
Ven y verás al alto fin que aspiro,
Antes que el tiempo muera en nuestros brazos.

Did ever anything attain perfection
Without temperance? Oh death, come silently!
As by the arrow you are wont to come,

Not in the thundering engine charged with fire
And fearful sound: because my gate is humble,
It is not made of heavy brass and iron.

Thus Fabio, does truth unveil to me
Its very essence, and my will agrees
With it and in accord with self grows calm.

Scoff not nor jeer to see how much I trust;
Nor to the vain and pompous art of rhetoric
Should you ascribe the fervor of this speech.

Has virtue, peradventure, less of force
Than vice? Is she indeed less full of power?
Do not imply that she is timid, frail.

Wrath throws itself against the enemy's sword,
Greed in the hands of destiny does brave
The deep, the while ambition laughs at death.

And the opposite actions helped by more
Illustrious spirits, if I look at them,
Will they not be at least as full of courage?

Now, my dear friend, I flee and I retire
From all I, artless, loved; I broke my ties.
Come, you shall see what is that noble end
Toward which I aim, ere time die in our arms.

                                        E. L. T.

The Baroque Period

Luis de Góngora

The Italianate type of poetry introduced at the beginning of the six-teenth century prevailed for many years and indeed was the only Spanish poetical school. The mystics, as well as the secular poets, were faithful, each in his own way, and in accordance with his subject-matter, to the poetic norms of the Renaissance. But early in the seventeenth century something happened which was equivalent to a new poetic revolution in Spanish literary history. The event was the publication of two poems by Luis de Góngora, *Las Soledades* and *Fábula de Polifemo y Galatea*. With these a new poetry, a new literary school was established, *cultismo* (cultivated obscurity of style).

The obscurity in Góngora is not of thought but of language. In *Las Soledades* narration is a pretext, he makes constant digressions. The poem is a series of immense parentheses. Like Velázquez, he is a painter of profound superficiality. The necessity for lyricism is ever present with him, it spreads over his poetry as the ivy over the oak, and in the end covers it almost completely.

1561–1627

Has the poetry of Góngora basic reality? It is undeniable that it unfolds one reality after another, it is not wielding concepts but realities. But for him reality is not enough, and as he cannot combine it with mystical ideas, he has to create another reality to destroy the first. He has great wealth of metaphor, he escapes from one allusion to another.

Every poet feels the need of presenting things in his own manner, and the manner of Góngora is the most extraordinary that there is, it is oriental. As in Arabic art it was prohibited to represent objects in nature, the Arabs created arabesques. So Góngora did not permit himself to speak of things by their names, but created images in arabesque forms.

All the poets of the Golden Age can be classified in one or other of these three currents: Neo-Platonism, as in Garcilaso and Herrera; Catholic Spiritualism pure or combined with Neo-Platonism as in the mystics; and Moral Philosophy, reflexions on the brevity of human life etc. But Góngora though a priest, belongs to none of these categories, his poetry is exceedingly pagan.

From notes

86   *LAS SOLEDADES*

Dedicatoria al duque de Bejar

Pasos de un peregrino son errante
cuantos me dictó versos dulce musa:
en soledad confusa
perdidos unos, otros inspirados.

¡Oh tú, que, de venablos impedido
—muros de abeto, almenas de diamante—,
bates los montes, que, de nieve armados,
gigantes de cristal los teme el cielo;
donde el cuerno, del eco repetido,
fieras te expone, que—al teñido suelo,
muertas, pidiendo términos disformes—
espumoso coral le dan al Tormes!:

arrima a un fresno el fresno—cuyo acero,
sangre sudando, en tiempo hará breve
purpurear la nieve—
y, en cuanto da el solícito montero
al duro robre, al pino levantado
—émulos vividores de las peñas—
las formidables señas
del oso que aun besaba, atravesado,
la asta de tu luciente jabalina,
—o lo sagrado supla de la encina
lo augusto del dosel; o de la fuente
la alta cenefa, lo majestuoso
del sitïal a tu deidad debido—,
¡oh Duque esclarecido!,
templa en sus ondas tu fatiga ardiente,
y, entregados tus miembros al reposo
sobre el de grama césped no desnudo,
déjate un rato hallar del pie acertado
que sus errantes pasos ha votado
a la real cadena de tu escudo.

THE SOLITUDES   86

Dedication to the Duke of Bejar

Dictated by the Muse, these verses know,
As many footsteps as the pilgrim made;
Though some in solitude confused have strayed
    Others inspired were born.

Oh, thou, whom hindering javelins surround
—Diamond battlements, of fir the walls—
Who beatest the high mountains (armed with snow
This crystal giant crew the heavens appals);
Where with repeated echo now the horn
Displays wild beasts, that, to the crimson ground,
Dead, for much greater boundaries appeal,
And foaming coral add to Tormes' flood:

Lean 'gainst an ash thy ashen spear—whose steel
In few short minutes will, by sweating blood,
    The snow with purple dye—
And, while the careful beater may apply
To the hard oak and elevated pine
(That living emulate the very stones)
    The formidable bones
Of bears transfixed before by thy proud shaft
(They even then would kiss the shining haft),
—Either the ilex with its shade divine
A new but regal canopy may bring,
Or let the lofty margin of the spring
Supply thy godhead with majestic throne—
    Oh most illustrious peer!
Burning fatigue shall soon sweet coolness find,
And to repose thy limbs delivered here
    Upon the turfy ground,
Let thyself by the wandering feet be found,
Sure paces offered unto thee alone
And to the royal chains upon thy shield.

Honre süave, generoso nudo
libertad, de fortuna perseguida:
que, a tu piedad Euterpe agradecida,
su canoro dará dulce instrumento,
cuando la Fama no su trompa al viento.

87   *DE LA SOLEDAD PRIMERA*

Era del año la estación florida
en que el mentido robador de Europa
—media luna las armas de su frente,
y el Sol todos los rayos de su pelo—,
         luciente honor del cielo,
en campos de zafiro pace estrellas;
cuando el que ministrar podía la copa
a Júpiter mejor que el garzón de Ida,
—náufrago y desdeñado, sobre ausente—
lagrimosas de amor dulces querellas
         da al mar; que condolido,
         fué a las ondas, fué al viento
         el mísero gemido,
segundo de Arión dulce instrumento.

Del siempre en la montaña opuesto pino
         al enemigo Noto,
         piadoso miembro roto
—breve tabla—delfín no fué pequeño
al inconsiderado peregrino
que a una Libia de ondas su camino
         fió, y su vida a un leño.

Del Océano pues antes sorbido,
         y luego vomitado
no lejos de un escollo coronado
de secos juncos, de calientes plumas,
         —alga todo y espumas—,
halló hospitalidad donde halló nido
         de Júpiter el ave.

And let their soft and generous bond embrace
Him, who when free was dogged by Fortune blind:
Euterpe, flattered by thy pitying grace,
Her sweet canorous instrument shall yield
If Fame deny her trumpet to the wind.

Edward Meryon Wilson

A SHIPWRECKED YOUTH REACHES LAND   87

It was the flowery season of the year
In which Europa's perjured robber strays
—Whose brow the arms of the half-moon adorn,
The sun the shining armour of his hide—
Through sapphire fields to feast on stellar corn,
When, fitter cupbearer than Ganymede
For Jupiter, the lovesick boy gave tears
(Absent, disdained and shipwrecked) to the tide
And winds, which moved by his complaining lays
As to a second Arion's harp gave heed.

A pitying limb from mountain pine, opposed,
The constant enemy to Notus' strife,
Became no puny dolphine on that day
To the unthinking traveller who reposed,
Trusting to miserable boards his life,
And to an Ocean's Lybia his way.

Close by a headland, crowned
With sheltering feathers and dry rushes, he,
Engulfed before, then spewed up by the sea,
(Covered with foam, with seaweed girded) found
        A hospitable rest,
Where built the bird of Jupiter his nest.

Besa la arena, y de la rota nave
aquella parte poca
que le expuso en la playa dió a la roca:
que aun se dejan las peñas
lisonjear de agradecidas señas.

88   *Ven, Himeneo, ven*

Ven, Himeneo, ven donde te espera
con ojos y sin alas un Cupido,
cuyo cabello intonso dulcemente
niega el vello que el vulto ha colorido:
el vello, flores de su primavera,
y rayos el cabello de su frente.
Niño amó la que adora adolescente,
villana Psiques, ninfa labradora
de la tostada Ceres. Esta, ahora,
en los inciertos de su edad segunda
crepúsculos, vincule tu coyunda
a su ardiente deseo.
Ven, Himeneo, ven; ven, Himeneo.

Ven, Himeneo, donde, entre arreboles
de honesto rosicler, previene el día
—aurora de sus ojos soberanos—
virgen tan bella, que hacer podría
tórrida la Noruega con dos soles,
y blanca la Etiopia con dos manos.
Claveles del abril, rubíes tempranos,
cuantos engasta el oro del cabello,
cuantas—del uno ya y del otro cuello
cadenas—la concordia engarza rosas,
de sus mejillas, siempre vergonzosas,
purpúreo son trofeo.
Ven, Himeneo, ven; ven, Himeneo.

274

And, having kissed the sand,
The fragment from the shivered hull he gave
As offering to the rocks, now from the wave
    Safe, and restored to land;
    For even boulders rude
Are flattered by marks of gratitude.

Edward Meryon Wilson

A WEDDING HYMN   88

Come Hymen come, for here to thee we bring
With eyes but without wings a god of love,
Whose unshorn locks that sweetly hang above
Conceal the down upon his visage fair;
His down the flowers of a youthful spring,
And sunbeams from his forehead are his hair.
A boy he loved her, but adores today
This Psyche of the village, nymph to wage
For parchèd Ceres. Join her now, we pray,
Who in the twilight of her second age
Uncertain is, join in thy yoke to stay
    At his desire sincere,
    Come Hymen, Hymen here.

Come Hymen come, where in the morning skies
Of candid roses, day is now foretold
By such a beautiful young virgin, she
—Herself the Aurora of her sovereign eyes—
Could warm with her two suns Norwegian lands,
And whiten Ethiopia with two hands.
April carnations, early rubies, see
As many as are set in hair of gold,
With flowers that chain the lovers' necks—behold
The links of concord in the chain of rose—
These to her cheeks, that modesty disclose,
    The purple spoil appear,
    Come Hymen, Hymen here.

Ven, Himeneo, y plumas no vulgares
al aire los hijuelos den alados
de las que el bosque bellas ninfas cela;
de sus carcajes, éstos, argentados,
flechen mosquetas, nieven azahares;
vigilantes aquéllos, la aldehuela
rediman del que más o tardo vuela,
o infausto gime pájaro nocturno;
mudos coronen otros por su turno
el dulce lecho conyugal, en cuanto
lasciva abeja al virginal acanto
       néctar le chupa hibleo.
Ven, Himeneo, ven; ven, Himeneo.

. . . . .

89   *DE LA SOLEDAD SEGUNDA*

Éntrase el mar por un arroyo breve
que a recibillo con sediento paso
de su roca natal se precipita,
y mucha sal no sólo en poco vaso,
       mas su rüina bebe,
y su fin, cristalina mariposa
       —no alada, sino undosa—,
en el farol de Tetis solicita.

Muros desmantelando, pues, de arena,
centauro ya espumoso el Ocëano
       —medio mar, medio ría—
dos veces huella la campaña al día,
escalar pretendiendo el monte en vano,
       de quien es dulce vena
       el tarde ya torrente
arrepentido, y aun retrocedente.

Come Hymen come, and may each wingèd son
Of every lovely nymph the woods can show
Render no common feathers to the air;
Some, from the silvered quivers that they bear,
Shoot musket roses, orange blossom snow;
Let others keep the hamlet safe from one,
The most unlucky of nocturnal fowls,
That flies too slowly and ill-boding howls;
And in their flight let some crown silently
The marriage-bed, while the lascivious bee
From virginal acanthus sips the rare
      Hyblaean nectar there,
     Come Hymen, Hymen here.

. . . . .

Edward Meryon Wilson

A STREAMLET FLOWS INTO THE SEA   89

The sea through a brief streamlet seeks to pass,
Which with a thirsty pace to meet it flows
As from the natal rock itself it throws;
Much salt not only in a little glass
      It drinks, but ruin too,
      A crystal butterfly
     —Not winged, but wavy—who
Begs that it may in Tethys' lantern die.

     Dismantling sandy walls,
The Ocean now a spumy centaur, see,
     —Half sea, half estuary—
Twice in a day tread underfoot the plain,
Pretending too to scale the mount, in vain,
Whose gentle vein the tardy torrent falls,
Repentant, even drawing back again.

Eral lozano así novillo tierno,
de bien nacido cuerno
mal lunada la frente,
retrógrado cedió en desigual lucha
a duro toro, aun contra el viento armado:
no pues de otra manera
a la violencia mucha
del padre de las aguas, coronado
de blancas ovas y de espuma verde,
resiste obedeciendo, y tierra pierde.

90   *LETRILLA*

La más bella niña
de nuestro lugar,
hoy viuda y sola
y ayer por casar,
viendo que sus ojos
a la guerra van,
a su madre dice
que escucha su mal.
Dejadme llorar
orillas del mar.

Pues me distes, madre,
en tan tierna edad,
tan corto el placer,
tan largo el pesar,
y me cautivastes
de quien hoy se va
y lleva las llaves
de mi libertad,
dejadme llorar
orillas del mar.

And thus might we a lusty bullock find,
Young two-year old—whose noble horns have now
Hardly their crescent set upon his brow—
Receding in an unequal fight, give way
To a fierce bull, armed ev'n against the wind:
      The stream, no other way,
Resists obeying, as it loses ground
The violence of the watery father, crowned
With foam and weeds, in green and white display.

               Edward Meryon Wilson

LET ME WALK ALONE WHERE BREAKS THE SEA   90

The loveliest girl in all the country-side,
To-day forsaken, yesterday a bride,
Seeing her love ride forth to join the wars,
With breaking heart and trembling lips implores:
" My hope is dead, my tears
      are blinding me,
Oh let me walk alone
      where breaks the sea!

" You told me, Mother, what too well I know,
How grief is long, and joy is quick to go,
But you have given him my heart that he
Might hold it captive with love's bitter key,—
My hope is dead, my tears
      are blinding me,
Oh let me walk alone
      where breaks the sea!

En llorar conviertan
mis ojos de hoy más
el sabroso oficio
del dulce mirar,
    pues que no se pueden
mejor ocupar,
yéndose a la guerra
quien era mi paz:
dejadme llorar
orillas del mar.

No me pongáis freno
ni queráis culpar,
que lo uno es justo,
lo otro por demás;
    si me queréis bien
no me hagáis mal,
harto peor fuera
morir y callar,
dejadme llorar
orillas del mar.

Dulce madre mía,
¿quién no llorará,
aunque tenga el pecho
como un pedernal,
    y no dará voces
viendo marchitar,
los más verdes años
de mi mocedad?
Dejadme llorar
orillas del mar.

Váyanse las noches,
pues ido se han
los ojos que hacían
los míos velar.
    Váyanse, y no vean
tanta soledad,
despues que en mi lecho
sobra la mitad:
dejadme llorar
orillas del mar.

"My eyes are dim, that once were full of grace,
And ever bright with gazing on his face,
But now the tears come hot and never cease,
Since he is gone in whom my heart found peace,
My hope is dead, my tears
        are blinding me,
Oh let me walk alone
        where breaks the sea!

"Then do not seek to stay my grief, nor yet
To blame a sin my heart must needs forget;
For though the blame were spoken in good part,
Yet speak it not, lest you should break my heart.
My hope is dead, my tears
        are blinding me,
Oh let me walk alone
        where breaks the sea!

"Sweet mother mine, who would not weep to see
The glad years of my youth so quickly flee,
Although his heart were flint, his breast a stone?
Yet here I stand, forsaken and alone.
My hope is dead, my tears
        are blinding me,
Oh let me walk alone
        where breaks the sea!

"And still may night avoid my lonely bed,
Now that my eyes are dull, my soul is dead.
Since he is gone for whom they vigil keep,
Too long is night, I have no heart for sleep,
My hope is dead, my tears
        are blinding me,
Oh let me walk alone
        where breaks the sea!"

John Pierrepont Rice

LETRILLA

No son todos ruiseñores
los que cantan entre las flores,
sino campanitas de plata,
que tocan a la Alba;
sino trompeticas de oro,
que hacen la salva
a los Soles que adoro.

No todas las voces ledas
son de Sirenas con plumas,
cuyas húmidas espumas
son las verdes alamedas.
Si suspendido te quedas
a los süaves clamores,
 no son todos ruiseñores
 los que cantan entre las flores,
 sino campanitas de plata,
 que tocan a la Alba,
 sino trompeticas de oro,
 que hacen la salva
 a los Soles que adoro.

Lo artificioso que admira,
y lo dulce que consuela,
no es de aquel violín que vuela
ni de esotra inquieta lira;
otro instrumento es quien tira
de los sentidos mejores:
 No son todos ruiseñores
 los que cantan entre las flores,
 sino campanitas de plata,
 que tocan a la Alba,
 sino trompeticas de oro,
 que hacen la salva
 a los Soles que adoro.

ROUNDELAY   91

They are not only nightingales,
They who sing in flowery dales,
But little silver bells that play
    To welcome day,
And little golden horns that blow
    A greeting gay
    To eyes aglow.

Not every song upon the breeze
Comes from feathered songster's throat,
Sung by siren birds who float
Atop the spray of crested seas,
Green foliage of poplar trees,
Should you hearken to their tales.
  They are not only nightingales,
  They who sing in flowery dales,
  But little silver bells that play
      To welcome day,
  And little golden horns that blow
      A greeting gay
      To eyes aglow.

This artful charm, this dulcet choir
Of soft melodious decrial
Against despair; no winged viol
Plays this, nor any restless lyre.
But other melodies inspire
And stir one's heart, so good prevails.
  They are not only nightingales,
  They who sing in flowery dales,
  But little silver bells that play
      To welcome day,
  And little golden horns that blow
      A greeting gay
      To eyes aglow.

Alice Jane McVan

92   *VANA ROSA*

Ayer naciste, y morirás mañana.
¿Para tan breve ser, quién te dió vida?
¿Para vivir tan poco estás lucida,
y para no ser nada estás lozana?
Si te engañó tu hermosura vana,
bien presto la verás desvanecida
porque en tu hermosura está escondida
la ocasión de morir muerte temprana.
Cuando te corte la robusta mano,
ley de la agricultura permitida,
grosero aliento acabará tu suerte.
No salgas, que te aguarda algún tirano;
dilata tu nacer para tu vida,
que anticipas tu ser para tu muerte.

93   *LETRILLA*

Oveja perdida, ven
sobre mis hombros, que hoy
no sólo tu pastor soy,
sino tu pasto también.

Por descubrirte mejor,
cuando balabas perdida,
dejé en un árbol la vida,
donde me subió el amor,
si prenda quieres mayor,
mis obras hoy te la den.
Oveja perdida, ven
sobre mis hombros, que hoy
no sólo tu pastor soy,
sino tu pasto también.

A ROSE   92

Blown in the morning, thou shalt fade ere noon.
What boots a life which in such haste forsakes thee?
Thou'rt wondrous frolic, being to die so soon,
And passing proud a little colour makes thee.
If thee thy brittle beauty so deceives,
Know then the thing that swells thee is thy bane;
For the same beauty doth, in bloody leaves,
The sentence of thy early death contain.
Some clown's coarse lungs will poison thy sweet flower,
If by the careless plough thou shalt be torn;
And many Herods lie in wait each hour
To murder thee as soon as thou art born—
　　Nay, force thy bud to blow—their tyrant breath
　　Anticipating life, to hasten death!

Sir Richard Fanshawe

[We include this well-known sonnet which has been attributed to Góngora, and its excellent translation by Sir Richard Fanshawe, in spite of the fact that the translator has misunderstood the meaning of the Spanish word *dilata*, which in this case means *delay* and not *dilate*, or *blow* as he has it.]

COME, WANDERING SHEEP   93

Come, wandering sheep! O, come!
　　I'll bind thee to my breast,
I'll bear thee to thy home
　　And lay thee down to rest.

I saw thee stray forlorn,
　　And heard thee faintly cry,
And on the tree of scorn,
　　For thee, I deigned to die:
　　What greater proof could I
Give, than to seek the tomb?
Come, wandering sheep! O, come!

Pasto, al fin, hoy tuyo hecho,
¿cuál dará mayor asombro,
o el traerte yo en el hombro,
o el traerme tú en el pecho?
Prendas son de amor estrecho,
que aun los más ciegos las ven.
　　Oveja perdida, ven
　　sobre mis hombros, que hoy
　　no sólo tu pastor soy,
　　sino tu pasto también.

94　　*AL NACIMIENTO DE CRISTO NUESTRO SEÑOR*

Caído se le ha un clavel
hoy a la Aurora del seno:
¡qué glorioso que está el heno,
porque ha caído sobre él!

Cuando el silencio tenía
todas las cosas del suelo,
y coronada del yelo
reinaba la noche fría
en medio la monarquía
de tiniebla tan cruel,
　　caído se le ha un clavel
　　hoy a la Aurora del seno:
　　¡qué glorioso que está el heno,
　　porque ha caído sobre él!

De un solo clavel ceñida
la Virgen, aurora bella,
al mundo se le dió, y ella
quedó cual antes florida;
a la púrpura caída
solo fué el heno fiel.
　　Caído se le ha un clavel
　　hoy a la Aurora del seno:
　　¡qué glorioso que está el heno,
　　porque ha caído sobre él!

.　.　.　.　.　.　.

I shield thee from alarms,
   And wilt thou not be blest?
I bear thee in my arms,—
   Thou bear me in thy breast!
   O, this is love!—Come rest!
This is a blissful doom.
Come, wandering sheep! O, come!

John Bowring

THE NATIVITY OF CHRIST   94

Today from the Aurora's bosom
A pink has fallen—a crimson blossom;
And oh, how glorious rests the hay
On which the fallen blossom lay!

When silence gently had unfurled
Her mantle over all below,
And crowned with winter's frost and snow,
Night swayed the sceptre of the world,
Amid the gloom descending slow
   Upon the monarch's frozen bosom
   A pink has fallen,—a crimson blossom.

The only flower the Virgin bore
(Aurora fair) within her breast,
She gave to earth, yet still possessed
Her virgin blossom as before;
That hay that colored drop caressed,—
   Received upon its faithful bosom
   That single flower,—a crimson blossom.

. . . .

El heno, pues, que fué dino,
a pesar de tantas nieves,
de ver en sus brazos leves
este rosicler divino,
para su lecho fué lino,
oro para su dosel.
    Caído se le ha un clavel
    hoy a la Aurora del seno:
    ¡qué glorioso que está el heno,
    porque ha caído sobre él!

The manger, unto which 'twas given,
Even amid wintry snows and cold,
Within its fostering arms to fold
The blushing flower that fell from heaven,
Was as a canopy of gold.—
    A downy couch,—where on its bosom
    That flower had fallen,—that crimson blossom.

Henry W. Longfellow

Lope de Vega

Because of his moral, sentimental and esthetic instability, Lope de Vega is the precursor of modernism, a man in constant struggle with himself. There is a great deal of the romantic in him. The romantic, for his direct awareness, converts his own vital experience into poetry; the classic poet has a feeling of shyness or modesty in presenting himself as a literary theme and therefore lacks this immediacy. For the classic poet, the poem is like the flower of an organism from which nothing is known of the tree or its roots. In his poems there is very little that tells of his life history. Lope is quite the contrary, he affirms the spontaneous reaction before the idealized or the esthetic of the artist. He was extremely natural, but he

1562–1635

was also a man of culture who aspired to express in a certain ordered way that natural element converted into poetry. Hence the resemblance between the man and the poet, and also the variety and contradiction of his work. If in the man good and evil struggled, in the poet the classic and romantic were at strife.

His great theme is love, the capacity for loving. Hence his is a lyric of love, or of loves that move in all directions. But his poetry is not mystical; it expresses the reverse of amorous poetry; it is the poetry of the sinner and as in Spain, sin is the foundation stone of the whole conception of man, therefore Lope, the sinner, is such a real Spanish poet.

From notes

95   *TRÉBOLE*

Trébole, ¡ay Jesús, cómo huele!
Trébole, ¡ay Jesús, qué olor!
Trébole de la casada
que a su esposo quiere bien;
de la doncella también
entre paredes guardada,
que fácilmente engañada
sigue su primer amor.
  Trébole, ¡ay Jesús, cómo huele!
  Trébole, ¡ay Jesús, qué olor!

Trébole de la soltera
que tantos amores muda;
trébole de la viuda
que otra vez casarse espera,
tocas blancas por defuera
y faldellín de color.
  Trébole, ¡ay Jesús, cómo huele!
  Trébole, ¡ay Jesús, qué olor!

96   *SONETO*

Pastor que con tus silbos amorosos
me despertaste del profundo sueño:
tú, que hiciste cayado de ese leño
en que tiendes los brazos poderosos,
  vuelve los ojos a mi fe piadosos,
pues te confieso por mi amor y dueño
y la palabra de seguirte empeño
tus dulces silbos y tus pies hermosos.
  Oye, pastor, pues por amores mueres,
no te espante el rigor de mis pecados
pues tan amigo de rendidos eres.
  Espera, pues, y escucha mis cuidados . . .
Pero ¿cómo te digo que me esperes
si estás para esperar los pies clavados?

CLOVER   95

Clover, dear Christ, what fragrance!
Clover, dear Christ, how sweet!

Clover for you who are wed
And love your husband well;
And for the damoiselle
In the cloistered garden bred,
Who is easily misled
By the first love she may meet.
   Clover, dear Christ, what fragrance!
   Clover, dear Christ, how sweet!

Clover for you who are wooed
By many but marry none;
And for the widowed one
Who would marry if she could,
With the little white peaked hood
And the petticoat's red pleat.
   Clover, dear Christ, what fragrance!
   Clover, dear Christ, how sweet!

Jessie Read Wendell

THE GOOD SHEPHERD   96

Shepherd! who with thine amorous, sylvan song
Hast broken the slumber that encompassed me,
Who mad'st Thy crook from the accursèd tree
On which Thy powerful arms were stretched so long!
  Lead me to mercy's ever-flowing fountains;
For Thou my shepherd, guard, and guide shalt be;
I will obey Thy voice, and wait to see
Thy feet all beautiful upon the mountains.
  Hear, Shepherd, Thou who for Thy flock art dying,
Oh, wash away these scarlet sins, for Thou
Rejoicest at the contrite sinner's vow!
  Oh, wait! to Thee my weary soul is crying,
Wait for me: Yet why ask it, when I see,
With feet nailed to the cross, Thou'rt waiting still for me!

Henry W. Longfellow

97   *SONETO*

¿Qué tengo yo que mi amistad procuras?
¿Qué interés se te sigue, Jesús mío,
que a mi puerta, cubierto de rocío
pasas las noches del invierno escuras?

¡Oh, cuanto fueron mis entrañas duras
pues no te abrí! ¡Qué extraño desvarío
si de mi ingratitud el yelo frío
secó las llagas de tus plantas puras!

¡Cuántas veces el ángel me decía:
Alma, asómate agora a la ventana,
verás con cuanto amor llamar porfía!

¡Y cuántas, hermosura soberana,
"Mañana le abriremos" respondía,
para lo mismo responder mañana!

98   *SONETO*

Un soneto me manda hacer Violante,
que en mi vida me he visto en tanto aprieto;
catorce versos dicen, que es soneto;
burla burlando van los tres delante.

Yo pensé que no hallara consonante,
y estoy a la mitad de otro cuarteto,
mas si me veo en el primer terceto,
no hay cosa en los cuartetos que me espante.

Por el primer terceto voy entrando,
y parece que entré con pie derecho,
pues fin con este verso le voy dando.

Ya estoy en el segundo, y aun sospecho
que voy los trece versos acabando;
contad si son catorce, y está hecho.

Come, Wandering Sheep — Luis de Góngora

The nativity of Christ — Luis de Góngora

TOMORROW   97

Lord, what am I, that with unceasing care
Thou did'st seek after me, that Thou did'st wait
Wet with unhealthy dews before my gate,
And pass the gloomy nights of winter there?
    Oh, strange delusion, that I did not greet
Thy blest approach, and oh, to heaven how lost
If my ingratitude's unkindly frost
Has chilled the bleeding wounds upon Thy feet.
    How oft my guardian angel gently cried,
" Soul from thy casement look, and thou shalt see
How He persists to knock and wait for thee! "
    And oh, how often to that Voice of sorrow,
" Tomorrow we will open," I replied,
And when the morrow came I answered still " Tomorrow."

Henry W. Longfellow

SONNET ON A SONNET   98

To write a sonnet doth Juana press me,
I've never found me in such stress and pain;
A sonnet numbers fourteen lines 'tis plain,
And three are gone ere I can say, God bless me!
    I thought that spinning rhymes might sore oppress me,
Yet here I'm midway in the last quatrain;
And if the foremost tercet I can gain,
The quatrains need not any more distress me.
    To the first tercet I have got at last,
And travel through it with such right good-will,
That with this line I've finished it, I ween.
    I'm in the second now, and see how fast
The thirteenth line comes tripping from my quill—
Hurrah, 'tis done! Count if there be fourteen.

James Young Gibson

99

CANTARCILLO DE LA VIRGEN

Pues andáis en las palmas,
ángeles santos,
que se duerme mi niño,
tened los ramos.

Palmas de Belén
que mueven airados
los furiosos vientos
que suenan tanto:
no le hagáis ruido,
corred más paso,
que se duerme mi niño,
tened los ramos.

El niño divino,
que está cansado
de llorar en la tierra
por su descanso,
sosegar quiere un poco
del tierno llanto.
Que se duerme mi niño,
tened los ramos.

Rigurosos yelos
le están cercando;
ya veis que no tengo
con qué guardarlo.
Ángeles divinos
que váis volando,
que se duerme mi niño,
tened los ramos.

A CHRISTMAS CRADLESONG   99

Holy angels and blest,
  Through the palms as ye sweep
Hold their branches at rest
  For my babe is asleep.

And ye Bethlehem palm-trees,
  As stormy winds rush
In tempest and fury
  Your angry noise hush;—
Move gently, move gently,
  Restrain your wild sweep;
Hold your branches at rest
  My babe is asleep.

My babe all divine,
  With earth's sorrows oppressed,
Seeks in slumber an instant
  His grievings to rest;
He slumbers,— he slumbers,—
  O, hush then and keep
Your branches all still,—
  My babe is asleep.

Cold blasts wheel about him,—
  A rigorous storm,—
And ye see how, in vain,
  I would shelter his form;—
Holy angels and blest
  As above me ye sweep,
Hold these branches at rest,—
  My babe is asleep.

George Ticknor

100

Hoy la Nave del deleite

Hoy la Nave del deleite
se quiere hacer a la mar;—
¿hay quién se quiere embarcar?
Hoy la Nave del contento
con viento en popa de gusto,
donde jamás hay disgusto,
penitencia, ni tormento,
viendo que hay próspero viento,
se quiere hacer a la mar.
¿Hay quién se quiere embarcar?

Holloa! the good Ship of Delight   100

 Holloa! the good ship of Delight
Spreads her sails for the sea today;
Who embarks? who embarks, I say?
 Today the good ship of Content,
With a wind at her choice for her course,
To a land where no troubles are sent,
Where none knows the stings of remorse,
With a wind fair and free takes her flight;—
Who embarks? who embarks, I say?

George Ticknor

Francisco de Quevedo

Francisco de Quevedo lived at one of the most critical moments of Spain's history. He is a symbol of a tormented conscience in a world that was crumbling. His work was born of a state of sensitivity very living and human. All within him obeyed the strong wind of the Baroque—life in movement, full of contrast, dynamic. He knew all the changes of fortune; he was a clever courtier and diplomatist, but later a persecuted man, exiled from the court. He was moreover a great moralist who learned to live by the stoic philosophy, a great satirist, a soul of much nobility, with the fluctuations and contrasts typical of a man of the baroque period.

1580–1645

Quevedo was a great poet of death and of the passage of time, one tormented, who in spite of his fear of death, had a very real faith in salvation. He was a man with a pessimistic concept of life, in which he saw only confusion, "a poor and turbid river that the black sea swallows with engulfing waves." Towards that black sea of death he saw all things rushing. Nevertheless, in this horror at the thought of death, Quevedo struck a Christian note of conformity that accepted it as the inescapable law for all.

From notes

101   *MADRIGAL*

                    Amante sin reposo

Está la ave en el aire con sosiego,
en la agua el pez, la salamandra en fuego,
y el hombre, en cuyo ser todo se encierra,
está en sola la tierra.
Yo sólo, que nací para tormentos,
estoy en todos estos elementos:
la boca tengo en aire suspirando,
el cuerpo en tierra está peregrinando,
los ojos tengo en agua noche y día,
y en fuego el corazón y la alma mía.

102   *SONETO*

En crespa tempestad del oro undoso
nada golfos de luz ardiente y pura
mi corazón, sediento de hermosura,
si el cabello deslazas generoso.

Leandro en mar de fuego proceloso
su amor ostenta, su vivir apura;
Ícaro en senda de oro mal segura
arde sus alas por morir glorioso.

Con pretensión de fénix, encendidas
sus esperanzas, que difuntas lloro,
intenta que su muerte engendre vidas.

Avaro y rico, y pobre en el tesoro,
el castigo y la hambre imita a Midas,
Tántalo en fugitiva fuente de oro.

MADRIGAL

101

The Restless Lover

The birds to wanton in the air desire;
The salamander sports himself in fire;
The fish in water plays; and of the earth,
Man ever takes possession at his birth:
Only unhappy I, who born to grieve,
In all these elements at once do live:
Grief does with air of sighs my mouth supply,
My wretched body on cold earth does lie,
The streams which from mine eyes flow night and day
Cannot the fire which burns my heart allay.

Philip Ayres

LISA'S GOLDEN HAIR

102

When you shake free your hair from all controlling
Such thirst of beauty quickens my desire
That on its surge in red tornadoes rolling
My heart goes surfing over waves of fire.
    Leander, who for love the tempest dares,
It lets a sea of flames its life consume;
Icarus, at a sun whose rays are hairs,
Ignites its wings and glories in its doom.
    Firing its hopes (whose death I mourn) it strives
To fan their ash into fresh phoenix-lives
That, dying of delight, new hopes embolden.
    A miser rich, the crime and fate it measures
Of Midas, starved and mocked with stacks of treasures,
Or Tantalus—with streams that shone as golden.

Roy Campbell

103   *LETRILLA*

Poderoso caballero
es don Dinero.

Madre, yo al oro me humillo;
él es mi amante y mi amado,
pues de puro enamorado,
de contino anda amarillo;
que pues, doblón o sencillo,
hace todo cuanto quiero,
poderoso caballero
es don Dinero.

Nace en las Indias honrado,
donde el mundo lo acompaña;
viene a morir en España,
y es en Génova enterrado.
Y pues quien le trae al lado
es hermoso, aunque sea fiero,
poderoso caballero
es don Dinero.

Es galán y es como un oro,
tiene quebrado el color,
persona de gran valor,
tan cristiano como moro.
Pues que da quita el decoro
y quebranta cualquier fuero,
poderoso caballero
es don Dinero.

Son sus padres principales,
y es de nobles descendiente,
porque en las venas de Oriente
todas las sangres son reales;
y pues es quien hace iguales
al rico y al pordiosero,
poderoso caballero
es don Dinero.

THE LORD OF DOLLARS   103

Over kings and priests and scholars
Rules the mighty Lord of Dollars.

Mother, unto gold I yield me,
He and I are ardent lovers;
Pure affection now discovers
How his sunny rays shall shield me!
For a trifle more or less
All his power will confess,—
Over kings and priests and scholars
Rules the mighty Lord of Dollars.

In the Indies did they nurse him,
While the world stood round admiring;
And in Spain was his expiring;
And in Genoa did they hearse him;
And the ugliest at his side
Shines with all of beauty's pride;
Over kings and priests and scholars
Rules the mighty Lord of Dollars.

He's a gallant, he's a winner,
Black or white be his complexion;
He is brave without correction
As a Moor or Christian sinner.
He makes cross and medal bright,
And he smashes laws of right,—
Over kings and priests and scholars
Rules the mighty Lord of Dollars.

Noble are his proud ancestors
For his blood-veins are patrician;
Royalties make the position
Of his Orient investors;
So they find themselves preferred
To the duke or country herd,—
Over kings and priests and scholars
Rules the mighty Lord of Dollars.

¿A quién no le maravilla
ver en su gloria sin tasa
que es lo más ruin de su casa
doña Blanca de Castilla?
Mas pues que su fuerza humilla
al cobarde y al guerrero,
poderoso caballero
es don Dinero.

Sus escudos de armas nobles
son siempre tan principales,
que sin sus escudos reales
no hay escudos de armas dobles;
y pues a los mismos nobles
da codicia su minero,
poderoso caballero
es don Dinero.

Por importar en los tratos
y dar tan buenos consejos,
en las casas de los viejos
gatos le guardan de gatos.
Y pues él rompe recatos
y ablanda al juez más severo,
poderoso caballero
es don Dinero.

Es tanta su majestad
(aunque son sus duelos hartos),
que aun con estar hecho cuartos,
no pierde su calidad;
pero pues da autoridad
al gañán y al jornalero,
poderoso caballero
es don Dinero.

Nunca vi damas ingratas
a su gusto y afición;
que a las caras de un doblón
hacen sus caras baratas;

Of his standing who can question
When there yields unto his rank, a
Hight-Castillian Doña Blanca,
If you follow the suggestion?—
He that crowns the lowest stool,
And to hero turns the fool,—
Over kings and priests and scholars
Rules the mighty Lord of Dollars.

On his shields are noble bearings;
His emblazonments unfurling
Show his arms of royal sterling
All his high pretensions airing;
And the credit of his miner
Stands behind the proud refiner,—
Over kings and priests and scholars
Rules the mighty Lord of Dollars.

Contracts, bonds, and bills to render,
Like his counsels most excelling,
Are esteemed within the dwelling
Of the banker and the lender.
So is prudence overthrown,
And the judge complaisant grown,—
Over kings and priests and scholars
Rules the mighty Lord of Dollars.

Such indeed his sovereign standing
(With some discount in the order),
Spite the tax, the cash-recorder
Still his value fixed is branding.
He keeps rank significant
To the prince or man in want,—
Over kings and priests and scholars
Rules the mighty Lord of Dollars.

Never meets he dames ungracious
To his smiles or his attention,
How they glow but at the mention
Of his promises capacious!

y pues las hace bravatas
desde una bolsa de cuero,
poderoso caballero
es don Dinero.

Más valen en cualquier tierra
(¡mirad si es harto sagaz!)
sus escudos en la paz
que rodelas en la guerra.
Pues al natural destierra
y hace propio al forastero,
poderoso caballero
es don Dinero.

104   *SONETO*

¡Ah de la vida! ¿Nadie me responde?
Aquí de los antaños que he vivido;
la Fortuna mis tiempos ha mordido,
las Horas mi locura las esconde.
¡Que, sin poder saber cómo ni adónde,
la salud y la edad se hayan huído!
Falta la vida, asiste lo vivido,
y no hay calamidad que no me ronde.
Ayer se fué; Mañana no ha llegado;
Hoy se está yendo sin parar un punto:
soy un Fué y un Será y un Es cansado.
En el hoy y mañana y ayer, junto
pañales y mortaja, y he quedado
presentes sucesiones de difunto.

And how bare-faced they become
To the coin beneath his thumb!—
Over kings and priests and scholars
Rules the mighty Lord of Dollars.

   Mightier in peaceful season
(And in this his wisdom showeth)
Are his standards, than when bloweth
War his haughty blasts and breeze on;
In all foreign lands at home,
Equal e'en in pauper's loam,—
Over kings and priests and scholars
Rules the mighty Lord of Dollars.

Thomas Walsh

LIFE'S BREVITY   104

   Ah, what of life! Does no one answer me?
Ye days of yore, that I have lived, draw near;
My times has Fortune swallowed, the severe,
The hours, my madness hides, my lunacy.
   I know that health and years from me did flee,
But how and where they fled does not appear.
Life fails me, the already lived is here,
And I am haunted by calamity.
   Yesterday's gone, Tomorrow does delay,
Today is going, in a breath does pass,
I am a Was, Shall be, Is, sore bestead.
   In Tomorrow, Today and Yesterday
Joined, swaddling clothes and shroud, I am, alas,
Now naught but a succession of the dead.

E. L. T.

105   *SONETO*

Miré los muros de la patria mía,
si un tiempo fuertes, ya desmoronados,
de la carrera de la edad cansados,
por quien caduca ya su valentía.

Salíme al campo, vi que el Sol bebía
los arroyos del yelo desatados,
y del monte quejosos los ganados,
que con sombras hurtó su luz al día.

Entré en mi casa; vi que, amancillada,
de anciana habitación era despojos;
mi báculo, más corvo y menos fuerte.

Vencida de la edad sentí mi espada,
y no hallé cosa en que poner los ojos
que no fuese recuerdo de la muerte.

106   *A ROMA SEPULTADA EN SUS RUINAS*

Buscas en Roma a Roma, ¡oh peregrino!,
y en Roma misma a Roma no la hallas:
cadáver son las que ostentó murallas,
y tumba de sí propio el Aventino.

Yace donde reinaba el Palatino;
y, limadas del tiempo las medallas,
más se muestran destrozo a las batallas
de las edades que blasón latino.

Sólo el Tibre quedó, cuya corriente,
si ciudad la regó, ya sepoltura
la llora con funesto son doliente.

¡Oh Roma! En tu grandeza, en tu hermosura,
huyó lo que era firme, y solamente
lo fugitivo permanece y dura.

SONNET: DEATH-WARNINGS   105

I saw the ramparts of my native land
One time so strong, now dropping in decay,
Their strength destroyed by this new age's way
That has worn out and rotted what was grand.
  I went into the fields; there I could see
The sun drink up the waters newly thawed;
And on the hills the moaning cattle pawed,
Their miseries robbed the day of light for me.
  I went into my house; I saw how spotted,
Decaying things made that old home their prize;
My withered walking-staff had come to bend.
  I felt the age had won; my sword was rotted;
And there was nothing on which I set my eyes
That was not a reminder of the end.

John Masefield

ROME IN HER RUINS   106

  Amidst these scenes, O Pilgrim, seek'st thou Rome?
Vain is thy search—the pomp of Rome is fled;
Her silent Aventine is glory's tomb;
Her walls, her shrines, but relics of the dead.
  That hill, where Cæsars dwelt in other days,
Forsaken mourns where once it towered sublime;
Each mouldering medal now far less displays
The triumphs won by Latium, than by Time.
  Tiber alone survives;—the passing wave
That bathed her towers now murmurs by her grave,
Wailing with plaintive sound her fallen fanes.
  Rome! of thine ancient grandeur all is past
That seemed for years eternal framed to last;—
Nought but the wave, a fugitive, remains.

Felicia D. Hemans

Calderón de la Barca

What is to be found in utter completeness in the *Ode on the Death of his Father* (see page 49) by Jorge Manrique, we shall not find expressed in Spanish literature again with the same simplicity and austerity. But in the xviiith century a work, whose conception is of insuperable grandeur, treats the same theme in dramatic form. It is *La Vida es sueño* by Calderón de la Barca. Two centuries had passed since Manrique. The Renaissance had passed over human consciousness discovering continents, altering beliefs, widening horizons. Man feels better, knows more, expresses with greater exactness and beauty his inner life. But he pays for his growing spiritual contrasts with an ever greater complexity of mind, a more dramatic sense of conflict between world and man. The conflict is the same, but what the poet saw purely and directly, the dramatist sees across a whole new scaffolding of intricate concepts.

Is life a dream, a deceptive appearance, nothing more? Can man have any certainty that he lives? No, perhaps not. But nevertheless, just in case life should be real, we should live it honorably. If life is a dream,

1600–1681

let us dream without ceasing to remember that some day we are to awaken. Let us remember that all our power is lent and must be returned to the Giver one day. After the symbol of the dream we have the Christian position: living or dreaming is an earthly existence; awakening is death, the passage to another life. Man contemplates life within him, perceives its transitory, fleeting character, is not even sure it is anything more than a dream. But that will not stop him. One must boldly dare all. One must live in good acts. For the only thing that man can be sure of is his capacity to act well, his power over his own acts.

Those who demand stability, permanence, eternity are all wrong. So also those who exert their efforts in the attainment of triumphs of this world. But those are in error too who renounce life, who withdraw from the vital duty, for fear that it may pass or that it may be a dream. This poetic attitude seems to end with the following lesson: accept reality with all its risk of being transitory and unreal, with all its dream-like adventure. Only he who accepts death and dreams accepts life.

P. S.

107   *LA VIDA ES SUEÑO*

Segismundo   Es verdad; pues reprimamos
esta fiera condición,
esta furia, esta ambición,
por si alguna vez soñamos;
y sí haremos, pues estamos
en mundo tan singular,
que el vivir sólo es soñar;
y la experiencia me enseña
que el hombre que vive, sueña
lo que es, hasta despertar.
Sueña el rey que es rey, y vive
con este engaño mandando,
disponiendo y gobernando;
y este aplauso, que recibe
prestado, en el viento escribe;
y en cenizas le convierte
la muerte (¡desdicha fuerte!):
¿que hay quien intente reinar,
viendo que ha de despertar
en el sueño de la muerte?
Sueña el rico en su riqueza,
que más cuidados le ofrece;
sueña el pobre que padece
su miseria y su pobreza;
sueña el que a medrar empieza,
sueña el que afana y pretende,
sueña el que agravia y ofende,
y en el mundo, en conclusión,
todos sueñan lo que son,
aunque ninguno lo entiende.
Yo sueño que estoy aquí
de estas prisiones cargado,
y soñé que en otro estado
más lisonjero me vi.
¿Qué es la vida? Un frenesí.
¿Qué es la vida? Una ilusión,
una sombra, una ficción,
y el mayor bien es pequeño;
que toda la vida es sueño,
y los sueños, sueño son.

LIFE'S A DREAM   107

Segismundo   Truth—and let us then restrain
This the fierceness of our pride,
Lay this wilfulness aside,
Lest perchance we dream again:
And we shall so, who remain
In a world of wonder thrown,
Where to live and dream are one.
For experience tells me this,
Each is dreaming what he is,
Till the time his dream is done.
The king dreams himself a king,
And in this conceit he lives,
Lords it, high commandment gives,
Till his lent applause takes wing,
Death on light winds scattering,
Or converting (oh, sad fate!)
Into ashes all his state:
How can men so lust to reign,
When to waken them again
From their false dream Death doth wait?
And the rich man dreams no less
'Mid his wealth which brings more cares;
And the poor man dreams he bears
All his want and wretchedness;
Dreams, whom anxious thoughts oppress,
Dreams, who for high place contends,
Dreams, who injures and offends;
And though none are rightly ware,
All are dreaming that they are
In this life, until death ends.
I am dreaming I lie here,
Laden with this fetter's weight,
And I dreamed that I of late
Did in fairer sort appear.
What is life? a frenzy mere;
What is life? e'en that we deem;
A conceit, a shadow all,
And the greatest good is small:
Nothing is, but all doth seem—
Dreams within dreams, still we dream!

Richard C. Trench

Danïel. ¿Quién eres?
Muerte. Yo, divino profeta Danïel
De todo lo nacido soy el fin;
Del pecado y de la envidia hijo cruel,
Abortado por áspid de un jardín.
La puerta para el mundo me dió Abel,
Mas quien me abrió la puerta fué Caín,
Donde mi horror introducido ya,
Ministro es de las iras de Jehová.

Del pecado y la envidia, pues, nací,
Porque dos furias en mi pecho estén:
Por la envidia caduca muerte di
A cuantos de la vida la luz ven;
Por el pecado muerte eterna fuí
Del alma, pues que muere ella también;
Si de la vida es muerte el espirar,
La muerte así del alma es el pecar.

Si *Juicio,* pues, *de Dios,* tu nombre fué,
Y del juicio de Dios rayo fatal
Soy yo, que a mi furor postrar se ve
Vegetable, sensible y racional,
¿Por qué te asombras tú de mí? ¿Por qué
La porción se estremece en ti mortal?
Cóbrate, pues, y hagamos hoy los dos,
De Dios tú el juicio, y yo el poder de Dios.

Aunque no es mucho que te asombres, no,
Aun cuando fueras Dios, de verme a mí;
Pues cuando El de la flor de Jericó
Clavel naciera en campos de alhelí,
Al mismo Dios le estremeciera yo
La parte humana, y al rendirse a mí
Turbaran las estrellas su arrebol,
Su faz la luna y su semblante el sol.

DEATH SPEAKS   108

Daniel. Who are you?
Death. O holy and prophetic Daniel,
Of all things that are born I am the end,
The son of sin and of envy cruel,
Aborted by a serpent in a garden.
The door into the world gave me Abél
But he who opened it for me was Cain,
By which my horror having entered once
Became the instrument of Jahweh's wrath.

Of envy was I born then and of sin,
And so there are two furies in my breast.
Because of envy I gave wretched death
To all who saw the light: because of sin
I am the death eternal of the soul,
Since you must know that that may die as well.
For if of life death is the parting breath,
Sin to the soul is therefore death itself.

If *Judgement of God* is then your name
And of God's Judgement the fatal ray
Am I, at whose furie you see laid low
Things vegetable, sensible and rational,
Why do you stand amazéd thus, and why
Does your O mortal part tremble at me?
Collect yourself and let us act the two,
I the power of God, his judgement you.

Yet it would not be strange that you should fear,
Even though you were God, to look on me;
Since when He, from the flower of Jericho,
Carnation is born in fields of *alhelí*,
I shall make tremble even of God himself
The human part, and when He yields to me,
The stars will falter and their color change,
Its face the moon and the sun its semblance.

Titubeara esa fábrica infeliz,
Y temblara esa forma inferïor;
La tierra desmayara su cerviz,
Luchando piedra a piedra y flor a flor;
A media tarde, joven e infeliz
Espirara del día el resplandor.
Y la noche su lóbrego capuz
Vistiera por la muerte de la luz. . . .

  .   .   .   .

Yo abrasaré los campos de Nembrot,
Yo alteraré las gentes de Babel,
Yo infundiré los sueños de Behemot,
Yo verteré las plagas de Israel,
Yo teñiré la viña de Nabot,
Y humillaré la frente a Jezabel,
Yo mancharé las mesas de Absalón
Con la caliente púrpura de Amón.

Yo postraré la majestad de Acab,
Arrastrado en su carro de rubí;
Yo con las torpes hijas de Moab
Profanaré las tiendas de Zambrí;
Yo tiraré los chozos de Joab;
Y si mayor aplauso fías de mí
Yo inundaré los campos de Senar
Con la sangre infeliz de Baltasar.

Then that unhappy fabric will be rocked,
And shaken too that form inferior;
The fainting earth will low bow down its neck,
Contesting stone by stone and flower by flower.
In the mid afternoon, unhappy and brief,
The splendour of the daytime will expire,
And its lugubrious hooded cloak the night
Put on in mourning for the death of light. . . .

     .   .   .   .   .

I shall dry up the pastures of Nembroth,
I shall confound the people of Babél,
I shall unloose the dreams of Behemoth,
I shall pour out the plagues of Israel,
I shall infect the vineyards of Naboth,
I shall bring low the forehead of Jezebel,
I shall defile the tables of Absalóm
With the incestuous purple of Amnon.

I shall bring low the majesty of Ahab,
Hurling him from his chariot of ruby;
And with the shameless daughters of Moab
I shall profane and soil the tents of Zimri;
I shall thrust home the javelins of Joab,
And, if a greater fame you demand of me,
I shall bedrench the lowlands of Shinar
With the unhappy blood of Belshazzar.

Gerald Brenan

109

LA CRUZ

    Árbol donde el cielo quiso
dar el fruto verdadero
contra el bocado primero,
flor del nuevo paraíso,
arco de luz, cuyo aviso
en piélago más profundo
la paz publicó del mundo,
planta hermosa, fértil vid,
arpa del nuevo David,
tabla del Moisés segundo:
pecador soy, tus favores
pido por justicia yo;
pues Dios en ti padeció
sólo por los pecadores.

SONETO

    Éstas, que fueron pompa y alegría,
despertando al albor de la mañana,
a la tarde serán lástima vana,
durmiendo en brazos de la noche fría.
    Este matiz, que al cielo desafía,
iris listado de oro, nieve y grana,
será escarmiento de la vida humana:
¡tanto se emprende en término de un día!
    A florecer las rosas madrugaron,
y para envejecerse florecieron:
cuna y sepulcro en un botón hallaron.
    Tales los hombres sus fortunas vieron:
en un día nacieron y expiraron;
que pasados los siglos, horas fueron.

THE CROSS   109

Tree which heaven has willed to dower
With that true fruit whence we live,
As that other death did give;
Of new Eden loveliest flower;
Bow of light, that in worst hour
Of the worst flood signal true
O'er the world, of mercy threw;
Fair plant, yielding sweetest wine;
Of our David harp divine;
Of our Moses tables new;
Sinner am I, therefore I
Claim upon thy mercies make;
Since alone for sinners' sake
God on thee endured to die.

Richard C. Trench

SONNET   110

These flowers that were resplendent, a delight
Awaking at the dawning of the day,
Will be at evening but a sad display
Of blooms asleep in the cold arms of night.
These tints that rival heaven's rainbow bright,
This iris, gold, snow-white and rose, convey
A lesson to our human life today:
So much that passes in a short day's flight!
At early dawn the rose began to bloom,
It was but to grow old, that blossoming,
For in the bud were found cradle and tomb.
And thus man saw his birth foreshadowing
His death, and this to be his cruel doom:
Long ages passed like hours perishing.

E. L. T.

SONETO

Esos rasgos de luz, esas centellas,
que cobran con amagos superiores,
alimentos del sol en resplandores,
aquello viven, que se duele de ellas.

Flores nocturnas son; aunque tan bellas,
efímeras padecen sus ardores;
pues si un día es el siglo de las flores,
una noche es la edad de las estrellas.

De esa, pues, primavera fugitiva
ya nuestro mal, ya nuestro bien se infiere:
registro es nuestro, o muera el sol o viva.

¿Qué duración habrá que el hombre espere,
o qué mudanza habrá que no reciba
de astro, que cada noche nace y muere?

SONNET   III

Those flakes of fire, brilliant sparks of light,
Receive their shining radiance from the sun
With hints of more; and thus, their life begun,
Lasts but as he shows pity with his might.
    And so, though beautiful those blooms of night,
Their lustrous gleam is but a passing one;
For stars a life-time in one night is run,
As flowers live an age in one day's flight.
    That fleeting spring is image of our life,
From it our ill, our good do we perceive,
By when the sun goes down or it doth rise.
    How long may man expect to live in strife,
What change is there that he may not receive
From star that night by night is born and dies?

E. L. T.

Neo-Classicism

Juan Meléndez Valdés

Juan Meléndez Valdés was born in Ribera del Fresno, Province of Badajoz, in 1754. As a young man he studied law at the University of Salamanca, where he later became a professor of the Humanities. While still a student, his poetic gift won him the friendship of Cadalso and Jovellanos, two of the most outstanding and talented writers of Spain at the time. Under their guidance and encouragement Meléndez devoted himself to his poetry and soon came to enjoy national renown.

In 1789 he left Salamanca to become a judge; from then on he was subjected to the political uncertainties of the turbulent times in which he lived. During the Napoleonic invasion he, like many other sincere but misguided Spaniards, supported the French, and when Spain re-

1754-1817

gained her independence he had to go into exile in France, where he died in 1817.

At a moment in which Spanish poetry had become merely a mechanical imitation of the style of Góngora and the satirical verse of Quevedo, Meléndez appeared with an ideal of poetic grace and simplicity. His themes reflected the mood of the era: erotic poems in the playful manner of Anacreon, philosophical odes, elegies and Night poems reminiscent of Gray and Young. His charm and his defects are also those of his time: elegance, superficiality, delicate voluptuousness and sentimentalism. Juan Meléndez Valdés is at once the best and the most representative Spanish poet of his century.

From notes

DE MIS NIÑECES

Siendo yo niño tierno,
Con la niña Dorila
Me andaba por la selva
Cogiendo florecillas.

De que alegres guirnaldas
Con gracia peregrina,
Para ambos coronarnos
su mano disponía.

Así en niñeces tales
De juegos y delicias
Pasábamos felices
Las horas y los días.

Con ellos poco a poco
La edad corrió de prisa;
Y fué de la inocencia
Saltando la malicia.

Yo no sé; mas al verme
Dorila se reía;
Y a mí de sólo hablarla
También me daba risa.

Luego al darle las flores
El pecho me latía;
Y al ella coronarme
Quedábase embebida.

Una tarde tras esto
Vimos dos tortolitas,
Que con trémulos picos
Se halagaban amigas.

Y de gozo y deleite,
Cola y alas caídas,
Centellantes sus ojos,
Desmayadas gemían.

OF LOVE'S AWAKENING 112

When I was yet a child,
　A child Dorila too,
To gather there the flowerets wild,
　We roved the forest through.

And gaily garlands then,
　With passing skill displayed,
To crown us both, in childish vein,
　Her little fingers made.

And thus our joys to share,
　In such our thoughts and play,
We passed along, a happy pair,
　The hours and days away.

But e'en in sports like these,
　Soon age came hurrying by!
And of our innocence the ease
　Malicious seemed to fly.

I knew not how it was,
　To see me she would smile;
And but to speak to her would cause
　Me pleasure strange the while.

Then beat my heart the more,
　When flowers to her I brought;
And she, to wreathe them as before,
　Seemed silent, lost in thought.

One evening after this
　We saw two turtle-doves,
With trembling throat, who, wrapt in bliss,
　Were wooing in their loves.

In manifest delight,
　With wings and feathers bowed,
Their eyes fixed on each other bright,
　They languished, moaning loud.

Alentónos su ejemplo;
Y entre honestas caricias
Nos contamos turbados
Nuestras dulces fatigas;

Y en un punto cual sombra
Voló de nuestra vista
La niñez; mas en torno
Nos dió el Amor sus dichas.

EL DESPECHO

Los ojos tristes, de llorar cansados,
Alzando al cielo, su clemencia imploro;
Mas vuelven luego al encendido lloro,
Que el grave peso no les sufre alzados;
   Mil dolorosos ayes desdeñados
Son ¡ay! trasunto de la luz que adoro;
Y ni me alivia el día ni mejoro
Con la callada noche mis cuidados.
   Huyo a la soledad y va conmigo
Oculto el mal, y nada me recrea;
En la ciudad en lágrimas me anego;
Aborrezco mi ser; y aunque maldigo
La vida, temo que la muerte aun sea
Remedio débil para tanto fuego.

The example made us bold,
    And with a pure caress,
The troubles we had felt we told,
    Our pains and happiness.

And at once from our view
    Then, like a shadow, fled
Our childhood and its joys, but new,
    Love gave us his instead.

James Kennedy

DESPAIR   113

   Worn out with weeping my sad eyes I raise
To heaven, its compassion I implore;
But then those eyes are bathed in tears once more,
Weighted with woe they cannot upward gaze;
   My sorrowful sighing disdained betrays
Reflection of the light that I adore;
And neither does the day relieve me nor
Is silent night less tearful than my days;
   Nought gives me joy; in crowds are tears and strife
And hidden sorrow ever goes with me
When grieving I to solitude retire;
   I hate my being; and although my life
I curse, I fear that even death may be
But a weak remedy for so much fire.

                                             E. L. T.

114   EL PENSAMIENTO

Cual suele abeja inquieta, revolando
Por florido pensil entre mil rosas,
Hasta venir a hallar las más hermosas,
Andar con dulce trompa susurrando;
    Mas luego que las ve, con vuelo blando
Baja y bate las alas vagorosas,
Y en medio de sus hojas olorosas
El delicado aroma está gozando;
    Así, mi bien, el pensamiento mío
Con dichosa zozobra, por hallarte,
Vagaba, de amor libre, por el suelo;
    Pero te vi, rendíme, y mi albedrío,
Abrasado en tu luz goza al mirarte
Gracias que envidia de tu rostro el cielo.

115   LA FUGA INÚTIL

Tímido corzo, de crüel acero
El regalado pecho traspasado,
Ya el seno de la hierba emponzoñado,
Por demás huye del veloz montero.
    En vano busca el agua y el ligero
Cuerpo revuelve hacia el doliente lado
Cayó y se agita y lanza acongojado
La vida en un bramido lastimero.
    Así la flecha al corazón clavada,
Huyo en vano la muerte, revolviendo
El ánima a mil partes dolorida;
    Crece el veneno, y de la sangre helada
Se va el herido corazón cubriendo,
Y el fin se llega de mi triste vida.

A THOUGHT   114

As flits the restless bee around the fair,
Blossoming garden midst a thousand roses,
Humming from flower to flower till he with honied
Proboscis finds of all the most desired;
   But when he sees it, with rapturous flight
Swoops down and beats his swift quivering wings
In a profusion of sweet-scented petals
Rejoicing in their exquisite perfume;
   E'en thus, dear one, my thought by love untroubled,
With happy, though anxious anticipation,
In search of you went roving through the earth;
   But I saw you, surrendered and my soul,
Glowing in your light when it has seen you
Enjoys the beauties of the face heaven envies.

E. L. T.

THE USELESS FLIGHT   115

The timid fallow deer, his tender breast
Pierced through by cruel steel, and the fair grass
Already poisoned by his blood, alas,
Does uselessly flee from the hunter's quest!
   In vain he seeks the water, sad, alone,
He turns his body towards his suffering side;
Now he has fallen, trembling, terrified
He yields his life with a despairing moan.
   Thus I, the arrow now piercing my heart
Do flee in vain from death, turning my grieving
Spirit towards many a sensitive spot;
   The poison grows, my flowing blood does start
To freeze in my wounded breast, I perceiving
Now that the end is near of my sad lot.

E. L. T.

Romanticism

José de Espronceda

The poet who best represents romanticism in Spain is José de Espronceda. What is the world for this romantic? In the first place, a mystery whose key lies in the hands of a superior being, God, toward whom man turns in an attitude of questioning, of challenge. The conception of the world as mystery is one of the most profound impulses of the romantic soul. The key to this mystery is simply death. But death is final, the absolute end of life, and not a passage to a higher and eternal life. It is the death of the romantic in open revolt, in despair, the terrible death without future life.

Let us consider the *Canto a Teresa*, the elegy he wrote to the woman who was the great love of his life. It is a very important poem among Spanish lyrics, a kind of breviary for the romantic, a vivid document of the innermost soul. We find there almost all the great themes of romantic poetry, but naturally the theme of love stands out. That love is described in the beginning as illusion, delirium, infinite longing, flights of imagination that touch upon realities without ever pausing upon any. And that is because the romantic desires all, hence his tragedy.

1808–1842

According to the poet, love was born in paradise and was dragged thence, and seeks for fulfillment without its being possible, because it is not of this earth.

It is interesting the way in which that love moves around the woman. Because she appears mysterious, anti-sensual, a phantom, she is only an illusion and therefore unattainable. For the romantic there is no woman that fulfils his rapture and consequently his is a tragic love. In the *Canto* we see clearly the three stages of the feminine figure: first the illusory woman, then the real woman who approaches the possibility of realizing the illusion of love, and finally the sadly real woman. What does the poet find in that heaven into which he threw himself? Nothing but doubt, that celestial beauty has become an illusion of air. Reality can produce nothing of what the inner life has forged. His poetic world tried, touched the real world, and from this contact drew only hatred and malediction. There is no way out but death. This is the romantic attitude: despair, hatred, death while rebelling. Man has no choice but to die or to go on living externally.

From notes

EL SOL

Pára y óyeme ¡oh sol! yo te saludo
Y extático ante ti me atrevo a hablarte:
Ardiente como tú mi fantasía,
Arrebatada en ansia de admirarte
Intrépidas a ti sus alas guía.
¡Ojalá que mi acento poderoso,
Sublime resonando,
Del trueno pavoroso
La temerosa voz sobrepujando,
¡Oh sol! a ti llegara
Y en medio de tu curso te parara!

¡Ah! si la llama que mi mente alumbra
Diera también su ardor a mis sentidos;
Al rayo vencedor que los deslumbra,
Los anhelantes ojos alzaría,
Y en tu semblante fúlgido atrevidos,
Mirando sin cesar, los fijaría.
¡Cuánto siempre te amé, sol refulgente!
¡Con qué sencillo anhelo,
Siendo niño inocente,
Seguirte ansiaba en el tendido cielo,
Y extático te vía,
Y en contemplar tu luz me embebecía!

De los dorados límites de Oriente
Que ciñe el rico en perlas Oceano,
Al término sombroso de Occidente,
Las orlas de tu ardiente vestidura
Tiendes en pompa, augusto soberano,
Y el mundo bañas en tu lumbre pura,
Vívido lanzas de tu frente el día,
Y, alma y vida del mundo,
Tu disco en paz majestuoso envía
Plácido ardor fecundo,
Y te elevas triunfante,
Corona de los orbes centellante.

HYMN TO THE SUN   116

Hail to thee Sun! Oh, list and stay thy course!
To thee in ecstasy I make my prayer,
The while my soul, aglow with fire like thine,
Uplifts her wings and boldly cleaves the air,
To pay her tribute to thy power divine.
Oh, that this voice of mine in wondrous wise,
Rending the clouds asunder,
To thee, great Sun, might rise,
Drowning with words sublime the dreaded thunder,
And, in the heavens' blue vault,
Bidding thee in thy mighty journey halt!

Oh, that the inner flame which lights the mind
Would lend its virtue to my feeble sight,
So that no longer with thy beams made blind
Mine eager eyes I might undazzled raise,
And on thy radiant face, divinely bright,
Might even dare to rest my constant gaze!
How I have ever loved thee, glorious Sun!
A child, with wondering eyes,
My life but just begun,
How oft I longed to reach thee in the skies;
And on what rapture fed
As thy great chariot on its pathway sped!

From where the Orient rears his golden crest,
Whose borders Ocean girds with many a pearl,
E'en to the limits of the shadowy West
The dazzling hem of thy bright garment gleams,
And thou thy shining banner dost unfurl,
And bathest all the world in thy pure streams.
From thy broad brow the light of day thou sendest,
Great source of life the seat,
And of thy calm, majestic disk thou lendest
The fertilizing heat,
Amid the spheres on high
Rising triumphant in the azure sky.

Tranquilo subes del zenit dorado
Al regio trono en la mitad del cielo,
De vivas llamas y esplendor ornado,
Y reprimes tu vuelo:
Y desde allí tu fúlgida carrera
Rápido precipitas,
Y tu rica encendida cabellera
En el seno del mar trémula agitas
Y tu esplendor se oculta,
Y el ya pasado día
Con otros mil la eternidad sepulta.

¡Cuántos siglos sin fin, cuántos has visto
En su abismo insondable desplomarse!
¡Cuánta pompa, grandeza y poderío
De imperios populosos disiparse!
¿Qué fureon ante ti? Del bosque umbrío
Secas y levas hojas desprendidas,
Que en círculos se mecen
Y al furor de Aquilón desaparecen.

Libre tú de la cólera divina
Viste anegarse el universo entero,
Cuando las aguas por Jehová lanzadas,
Impelidas del brazo justiciero
Y a mares por los vientos despeñadas,
Bramó la tempestad: retumbó en torno
El ronco trueno y con temblor crujieron
Los ejes de diamante de la tierra:
Montes y campos fueron
Alborotado mar, tumba del hombre.
Se estremeció el profundo;
Y entonces tú, como señor del mundo,
Sobre la tempestad tu trono alzabas,
Vestido de tineblas,
Y tu faz engreías
Y a otros mundos en paz resplandecías.

Y otra vez nuevos siglos
Viste llegar, huir, desvanecerse
En remolino eterno, cual las olas

Calmly thou scal'st the Zenith's golden height,
In Heaven's high hall enthroned supreme thou reignest,
And there with living flames and splendour dight,
Thy fiery steeds thou reinest.
From thence full speedily thy way thou takest,
Till down the steep incline
Thy rich and trailing locks of gold thou shakest
On Ocean's heaving, tremulous floor of brine;
Then in deep, watery bowers
Thy glory dies away,
And one more day Eternity devours.

What ages, Sun, what ages hast thou seen,
Thus swallowed by the gulf no plummet measures,
What mighty nations, what imperial pride,
What pomp and splendour, and what heaped up treasures!
'Fore thee, what were they? Leaves blown far and wide
From the great forest—withered, light and sear,
Eddying, all tempest-tossed,
Till the blast drove them hence, and they were lost.

And thou, alone from wrath divine exempt,
Has seen submergèd all the sinful world,
When driving rains were by Jehovah poured
On man and beast; the pent up winds were hurled
O'er heaving seas, and loud the billows roared;
From rifted cloud the deafening thunder pealed
In dreadful menace; and in anguished throes
The Earth upon her diamond axle swayed;
O'er hill and plain uprose
The huge, tumultuous sea—a watery grave.
Trembled the mighty deep,
While thou, our lord, as one awake from sleep,
Above the stormy waste didst build thy throne,
Robed in funereal black,
With face that darkly gleams,
Till on new worlds thou sendest healing beams.

And wilt thou ever see
The ages rise and fall, and yield their place
In never-ending change like restless waves,

341

Llegan, se agolpan y huyen de Oceano,
Y tornan otra vez a sucederse;
Mientra inmutable tú, solo y radiante
¡Oh sol! siempre te elevas,
Y edades mil y mil huellas triunfante.

    ¿Y habrás de ser eterno, inextinguible,
Sin que nunca jamás tu inmensa hoguera
Pierda su resplandor, siempre incansable,
Audaz siguiendo tu inmortal carrera,
Hundirse las edades contemplando
Y solo, eterno, perenal, sublime,
Monarca poderoso, dominado?
No; que también la muerte,
Si de lejos te sigue,
No menos anhelante te persigue.
Quién sabe si tal vez pobre destello
Eres tú de otro sol que otro universo
Mayor que el nuestro un día
Con doble resplandor esclarecia!!!

    Goza tu juventud y tu hermosura,
¡Oh sol! que cuando el pavoroso día
Llegue que el orbe estalle y se desprenda
De la potente mano
Del Padre soberano,
Y allá a la eternidad también descienda,
Deshecho en mil pedazos, destrozado
Y en piélagos de fuego
Envuelto para siempre y sepultado;
De cien tormentas al horrible estruendo,
En tinieblas sin fin tu llama pura
Entonces morirá: noche sombría
Cubrirá eterna la celeste cumbre:
Ni aun quedará reliquia de tu lumbre!!!

That, hurrying o'er the Ocean, crowd and break,
Recede, then sweep along in their fierce chase?
Whilst thou, O Sun, triumphant and sublime,
In lonely splendour dwellst,
Eternal witness of the march of time.

And wilt thou unextinguished thus abide,
And will thy giant furnace burn for aye,
Its fierceness unconsumed? Wilt thou, O Sun,
Thus proudly through the heavens go thy way,
Watching the myriad ages wax and wane,
And be alone eternally unmoved,
Holding forever undisputed reign?
Not so—the Conqueror, Death,
Albeit in hour unknown,
Will overtake thee and claim thee for his own.
Perchance, who knows? Thou art but some poor spark
Of sun more vast, that on another world
Greater than ours, with light yet more divine,
And splendour unimagined once did shine!

Rejoice then, Sun, in this thy strength and youth,
For, when the dreaded day draws nigh at last,
The day when thou from thy great throne wilt fall
(Loosed from the mighty hands
Of Him that all commands,)
And in eternity shalt hide thy Ball,
In thousand fragments shattered, wrecked and torn
Immersed in seas of fire,
Thy course accomplished, and thy strength outworn,
Then thy pure flame in darkness, of a truth,
Will wholly cease, thy glory be o'erpast,
Shrouded for ever by the pall of night,
No vestige left of thy refulgent light.

Ida Farnell

343

CANCIÓN DEL PIRATA

Con diez cañones por banda,
Viento en popa a toda vela
No corta el mar, sino vuela
Un velero bergantín:
   Bajel pirata que llaman
Por su bravura el *Temido,*
En todo mar conocido
Del uno al otro confín.

   La luna en el mar rïela,
En la lona gime el viento,
Y alza en blanda movimiento
Olas de plata y azul;
   Y ve el capitán pirata,
Cantando alegre en la popa,
Asia a un lado, al otro Europa
Y allá a su frente Estambul.

"Navega, velero mío,
     Sin temor,
Que ni enemigo navío,
Ni tormenta, ni bonanza
Tu rumbo a torcer alcanza,
Ni a sujetar tu valor.

     "Veinte presas
     Hemos hecho
     A despecho
     Del inglés,
     Y han rendido
     Sus pendones
     Cien naciones
     A mis pies.

"Que es mi barco mi tesoro,
Que es mi Dios la libertad,
Mi ley la fuerza y el viento,
Mi única patria la mar.

PIRATE'S SONG

With cannon ten on port and starboard,
Wind just aft and strong,
Flying the sea, not plowing through,
A brigantine skims along,
     She is called the *Dreaded* by a host
And feared on every side,
From the eastern to the western coast,
Wherever she may ride.

     Across the sea the moonlight shines,
The wind goes wailing through,
Shrill in the canvas, ruffling waves
Of silver and of blue.
     There on the poop the captain sings
By whom the band is led,
With Asia left and Europe right
And Istambul ahead.

"Sail on, swift bark, at my command,
          So brave and bold,
No warship by your foemen manned,
Nor storm, nor calm, nor any force
Shall turn you from your chosen course
Nor daunt your hardy soul.

                    "A score of ships
                    We've seized aright
                    And this despite
                    The English fleet.
                    And I have forced
                    A hundred lords
                    To lay their swords
                    Beneath my feet.

"My only treasure a pirate ship,
My god but liberty,
My law, brute force and a hearty wind,
My land, the open sea.

"Allá muevan feroz guerra
         Ciegos reyes
Por un palmo más de tierra:
Que yo tengo aquí por mío
Cuanto abarca el mar bravío,
A quien nadie impuso leyes.

        "Y no hay playa,
        Sea cualquiera,
        Ni bandera
        De esplendor,
        Que no sienta
        Mi derecho
        Y dé pecho
        A mi valor.

"Que es mi barco mi tesoro. . . .

"A la voz de " ¡barco viene! "
         Es de ver
Como vira y se previene
A todo trapo a escapar:
Que yo soy el rey del mar,
Y mi furia es de temer.

        "En las presas
        Yo divido
        Lo cogido
        Por igual:
        Solo quiero
        Por riqueza
        La belleza
        Sin rival.

"Que es mi barco mi tesoro. . .

" ¡Sentenciado estoy a muerte!
         Yo me río:
No me abandone la suerte,
Y al mismo que me condena,
Colgaré de alguna entena,
Quizá en su propio navío.

"Kings are plunging into war,
            Unseeing fools,
To fight for land, for a trifle more,
While anything that sails the sea
Belongs by my own laws to me,
Unchecked by others' rules.

            "There nowhere lies
            A foreign land
            Or distant strand
            That does not feel,
            Whate'er its flag,
            My crushing might,
            Admit my right,
            And to me yield.

"My only treasure a pirate ship. . . .

"The cry, "A ship!" is a sudden threat.
            Watch them veer.
See how fast, full canvas set,
In desperate fright they try to flee:
I am king of all the sea,
My wrath inspires their fear.

            "The spoils of war
            That raids provide
            I then divide
            With justice fine,
            Unless I claim
            Some damsel rare,
            Surpassing fair,
            And make her mine.

"My only treasure a pirate ship. . . .

"And I have been condemned to die!
            I laugh at that.
Upon good fortune I rely,
And hope to hang him by the neck,
Perhaps from a yardarm on his deck,
Who sentenced me to die.

347

"Y si caigo,
¿Qué es la vida?
Por perdida
Ya la di,
Cuando el yugo
Del esclavo,
Como un bravo,
Sacudí.

"Que es mi barco mi tesoro. . .

"Son mi música mejor
    Aquilones;
El estrépito y temblor
De los cables sacudidos,
Del negro mar los bramidos
Y el rugir de mis cañones.

"Y del trueno
Al son violento,
Y del viento
Al rebramar,
Yo me duermo
Sosegado,
Arrullado
Por el mar.

"Que es mi barco mi tesoro,
Que es mi Dios la libertad,
Mi ley la fuerza y el viento,
Mi única patria la mar."

"If I should fall,
If life's the cost?
I'd count well lost
The life I gave.
I knew the risk
Yet with one stroke
Cast off the yoke
That held me slave.

"My only treasure a pirate ship. . . .

"Melodies in the wind abound:
        I love to hear
The cables' splashing, scraping sound,
The roar and bark of the loud Black Sea,
The crash of the cannon's battery,
Delightful to my ear.

"Rolls of thunder
Snap and growl
And seawinds howl
Across the deep.
I am calmed
As sounds grow dulled,
And by them lulled
I drift to sleep.

"My only treasure a pirate ship,
My god but liberty,
My law, brute force and a hearty wind,
My land, the open sea."

Alice Jane McVan

118 ROSAS Y ESPERANZAS

Fresca, lozana, pura y olorosa,
Gala y adorno del pensil florido,
Gallarda puesta sobre el ramo erguido,
Fragancia esparce la naciente rosa;
   Mas si el ardiente sol lumbre enojosa
Vibra del can en llamas encendido,
El dulce aroma y el color perdido,
Sus hojas lleva el aura presurosa.
   Así brilló un momento mi ventura
En alas del amor, y hermosa nube
Fingí tal vez de gloria y de alegría;
   Mas ¡ay! que el bien trocóse en amargura,
Y deshojada por los aires sube
La dulce flor de la esperanza mía.

119 A TERESA

   ¿Por qué volvéis a la memoria mía,
Tristes recuerdos del placer perdido,
A aumentar la ansiedad y la agonía
De este desierto corazón herido?
¡Ay! que de aquellas horas de alegría
Le quedó al corazón sólo un gemido,
¡Y el llanto que al dolor los ojos niegan,
Lágrimas son de hiel que el alma anegan!

   .   .   .

   Gorjeaban los dulces ruiseñores,
El sol iluminaba mi alegría,
El aura susurraba entre las flores,
El bosque mansamente respondía,
Las fuentes mumuraban sus amores . . .
¡Ilusiones que llora el alma mía!
¡Oh! ¡Cuán süave resonó en mi oído
El bullicio del mundo y su ruido!

SONNET   118

    Luxuriant, fragrant, fresh the new-blown rose,
The choicest blossom in the garden now,
Gracefully poised upon the upright bough,
Does scatter its sweet perfume as it grows;
    But should the sun annoying light impose,
Whose fire the kindled Dog-star doth endow,
Its fragrance lost and color, would allow
The gentle breeze its petals to dispose.
    Thus for one moment my good fortune shone
On wings of love, a beauteous cloud, maybe
Of glory and of joy conceived by me;
    Alas, my bliss was changed in bitter hour,
And stripped of petals, through the air upblown,
Is what was once my hope, that fragrant flower.

                                        E. L. T.

TO TERESA   119

Visions of days outworn, why do ye grow
    Thus ever more distinct round memory's page?
Would ye increase my heavy weight of woe,
    And 'gainst a broken heart new battle wage?
Alas! Of all the joy of long ago
    But groans remain, nor do dry eyes assuage
The ache of bitter grief; and tears repressed
Are tears of gall that flood the heavy breast.

                .   .   .

The nightingales sang loudly in those hours,
    The Sun shone brightly, and my full heart beat;
Gently the breezes whispered 'mid the flowers,
    The forests murmured low in answer sweet,
The fountains told of love in fragrant bowers.
    Illusions all it irks me to repeat!
Alas! How full of bright, entrancing joys
Appeared the world, its tumult and its noise.

Mi vida entonces, cual guerrera nave
Que el puerto deja por la vez primera
Y al soplo de los céfiros süave
Orgullosa desplega su bandera,
Y al mar dejando que a sus pies alabe
Su triunfo en roncos cantos, va velera,
Una ola tras otra bramadora
Hollando y dividiendo vencedora.

¡Ay! En el mar del mundo, en ansia ardiente
De amor volaba; el sol de la mañana
llevaba yo sobre mi tersa frente,
Y el alma pura de su dicha ufana:
Dentro de ella el amor cual rica fuente
Que entre frescura y arboledas mana,
Brotaba entonces abundante río
De ilusiones y dulce desvarío.

Yo amaba todo: un noble sentimiento
Exaltaba mi ánimo, y sentía
En mi pecho un secreto movimiento,
De grandes hechos generoso guía.
La libertad, con su inmortal aliento,
Santa diosa, mi espíritu encendía,
Contino imaginando en mi fe pura
Sueños de gloria al mundo y de ventura.

   .   .   .

Hay una voz secreta, un dulce canto,
Que el alma sólo recogida entiende,
Un sentimiento misterioso y santo
Que del barro al espíritu desprende:
Agreste, vago y solitario encanto
Que en inefable amor el alma enciende,
Volando tras la imagen peregrina
El corazón de su ilusión divina.

Yo, desterrado en extranjera playa,
Con los ojos extático seguía
La nave audaz que en argentada raya
Volaba al puerto de la patria mía:

This life of mine seemed in those happy days
   Like some tall vessel, that in all her pride
First leaves the port, and her gay flag displays,
   When, carried by the wind o'er waters wide;
The deep, hoarse voice of Ocean chants her praise,
   As she full merrily doth onward glide;
The surging billows leap around her bows,
While she triumphantly her pathway ploughs.

Ah me! O'er life's great sea I took my flight
   Aglow with love. On my smooth brow was seen
Youth's glorious sunshine; likewise shone the light
   Of early dawn within my soul, I ween;
And love abode there, like some fountain bright
   Amid the freshness of the woodland green;
And from that fountain came abundant streams
Of joyous aspirations and sweet dreams.

And love subdued me, filled me with desire
   Nobly to spend my days—A secret yearning
Grew ever stronger, mighty to inspire
   My inner self. My thoughts were ever turning
Toward all things great, and, with the holy fire
   That freedom's torch aye kindles, I was burning;
While, full of ardent faith, I sought to rise
To deeds of glory and of high emprise.

       .   .   .

There is a voice sweeter than tongue can tell,
   That speaks in hours of lonely reverie,
A pure and holy prompting, strong to quell
   All things of earth, and set the spirit free;
There is a potent and mysterious spell,
   That fires the mind with love and ecstasy,
And bids the palpitating heart to fly
After the wondrous vision pure and high.

Oft from an alien shore, I used to gaze
   On many a vessel riding o'er the foam,
That, seen afar in the Moon's silvery rays,
   Sailed for my native land, my well-beloved home;

353

Yo cuando en Occidente el sol desmaya,
Solo y perdido en la arboleda umbría,
Oír pensaba el armonioso acento
de una mujer, al suspirar del viento.

.   .   .

Mujer que amor en su ilusión figura,
Mujer que nada dice a los sentidos,
Ensueño de suavísima ternura,
Eco que regaló nuestros oídos:
De amor la llama generosa y pura,
Los goces dulces del placer cumplidos.
Que engalana la rica fantasía,
Goces que avaro el corazón ansía.

.   .   .

¡Oh Teresa! ¡Oh dolor! Lágrimas mías,
¡Ah! ¿dónde estáis que no corréis a mares?
¿Por qué, por qué como en mejores días
No consoláis vosotras mis pesares?
¡Oh! los que no sabéis las agonías
De un corazón que penas a millares
¡Ay! desgarraron, y que ya no llora,
Piedad tened de mi tormento ahora!

.   .   .

¿Quién pensara jamás, Teresa mía,
Que fuera eterno manantial de llanto
Tanto inocente amor, tanta alegría,
Tantas delicias y delirio tanto?
¿Quién pensara jamás llegase un día
En que perdido el celestial encanto,
Y caída la venda de los ojos,
Cuanto diera placer causara enojos?

Aun parece, Teresa, que te veo
Aérea como dorada mariposa,
En sueño delicioso del deseo,
Sobre tallo gentil temprana rosa,
Del amor venturoso devaneo,
Angélica, purísima y dichosa,
Y oigo tu voz dulcísima, y respiro
Tu aliento perfumado en tu suspiro.

354

Or, when the western sky was all ablaze,
  As the Sun sank, in solitude would roam
And roaming seemed to hear a woman's voice,
Whose gentle notes made my young heart rejoice.

              .   .   .

Woman, as love first sees in hours of sleep,
  A being to the soul alone appealing,
The echo of a tender whisper deep,
  Like strange, sweet music o'er the spirit stealing,
Woman, who bids love's ardent flame to leap,
  The joys that beckon from afar revealing,
Joys that the fancy decks in colours bright,
That fill the yearning heart with fond delight.

              .   .   .

Teresa! Fatal name! Alas my tears,
  Where are ye hidden, that ye do not flow?
Wherefore, oh, wherefore, as in other years
  Bring ye no comfort to my bitter woe?
O ye, who ne'er have felt the pain that sears
  And burns the tortured heart, who do not know
The anguish that in tears finds no relief,
Pity at least my torments and my grief!

              .   .   .

That to eternal pain, Teresa mine,
  Such bliss should change, what prophet had foretold,
Such innocent love, such gladness all divine,
  Such heavenly rapture and such dreams of gold?
Who might alas! forecast the day malign
  When, the spell broken, fate with fingers cold,
Should cause the bandage from our eyes to fall,
And turn our sometime mirth to bitter gall?

E'en now, Teresa, in thy loveliness,
  Like some fair butterfly with wings of flame
Thou hoverest before me, and I bless
  The beauty that my every sense o'ercame;
Thou art a dream no pen can e'er express.
  I see thee now, young rose, thou art the same;
Again I hear thy voice, I feel thee nigh
And breathe the perfumed sweetness of thy sigh.

Y aun miro aquellas ojos que robaron
A los cielos su azul, y las rosadas
Tintas sobre la nieve, que envidiaron
Las de mayo serenas alboradas;
Y aquellas horas dulces que pasaron
Tan breves ¡ay! como después lloradas,
Horas de confianza y de delicias,
De abandono, y de amor, y de caricias.

.   .   .

Y llegaron en fin . . . ¡Oh! ¿Quién, impío,
¡Ay! agostó la flor de tu pureza?
Tú fuiste un tiempo cristalino río,
Manantial de purísima limpieza;
Después torrente de color sombrío,
Rompiendo entre peñascos y maleza,
Y estanque, en fin, de aguas corrompidas,
Entre fétido fango detenidas.

¿Cómo caíste despeñado al suelo,
Astro de la mañana luminoso?
Ángel de luz ¿quién te arrojó del cielo
A este valle de lágrimas odioso?
Aun cercaba tu frente el blanco velo
Del serafín, y en ondas fulgoroso,
Rayos al mundo tu esplendor vertía
Y otro cielo el amor te prometía.

Mas, ¡ay!, que es la mujer ángel caído
O mujer nada más y lodo inmundo,
Hermoso ser para llorar nacido,
O vivir como autómata en el mundo:
Sí, que el demonio en el Edén perdido
Abrasara con fuego del profundo
La primera mujer, y ¡ay! aquel fuego,
La herencia ha sido de sus hijos luego.

Brota en el cielo del amor la fuente
Que a fecundar el universo mana,
Y en la tierra su límpida corriente
Sus márgenes con flores engalana;

Those lovely eyes, that stole from Heaven their blue,
  After long years I see before me still,
See too that colour, like the roseate hue
  Of snow new-fallen at Sunrise, that doth fill
With envy May's young morning, bathed in dew;
  And even now, alas! I feel the thrill
Of those brief hours of joy, unmixed with pain,
When early love held undivided reign.

Then came dark hours—What wretch without remorse
  Robbed thee of purity? Alas! Alas!
Of old thou wast of all things pure the source,
  A limpid rivulet, as clear as glass,
Later a torrent dark, with eddying course,
  Forcing its way 'mid crags and tangled grass,
And then a fetid pool of water slack
Losing itself in mire, corrupt and black.

Tell me, how camst thou on this earth to light,
  Cleaving the air, bright star of early morn?
Angel, who bade thee from the heavens take flight,
  And sojourn in this vale of tears forlorn?
Circling thy brow there floated dazzling white
  The seraph's veil, in heavenly mansion worn:
And bringing glory from the realms above
Another heaven didst thou find in love.

Ah me! A fallen angel, weak and frail
  Is woman, fashioned out of impure clay.
A beauteous being, born to weep and wail,
  Or soul-less in the world live out her day.
'Twas the first woman Satan did assail,
  When into Paradise he stole his way,
Within her kindling flame that many an age
Hath been of all her sons the heritage.

The fount of love in Heaven hath its start,
  And freely flows on earth, that all may drink;
And, as it flows, behold in every part
  Fair flowers of lively hue adorn its brink.

Mas, ¡ay!, huid: el corazón ardiente
Que el agua clara por beber se afana,
Lágrimas verterá de duelo eterno,
Que su raudal lo envenenó el infierno.

        .   .   .

Los años ¡ay! de la ilusión pasaron;
Las dulces esperanzas que trajeron,
Con sus blancos ensueños se llevaron,
Y el porvenir de oscuridad vistieron:
Las rosas del amor se marchitaron,
Las flores en abrojos convirtieron,
Y de afán tanto y tan soñada gloria,
Sólo quedó una tumba, una memoria.

        .   .   .

Y tú, feliz, que hallastes en la muerte
Sombra a que descansar en tu camino,
Cuando llegabas mísera a perderte
Y era llorar tu único destino;
Cuando en tu frente la implacable suerte
Grababa de los réprobos el sino . . .
¡Feliz! La muerte te arrancó del suelo,
Y otra vez ángel te volviste al cielo.

Roída de recuerdos de amargura,
Árido el corazón sin ilusiones,
La delicada flor de tu hermosura
Ajaron del dolor los aquilones:
Sola y envilecida, y sin ventura,
Tu corazón secaron las pasiones,
Tus hijos ¡ay! de ti se avergonzaran,
Y hasta el nombre de madre te negaran.

        .   .   .

¡Oh, cruel! ¡muy cruel! . . . ¡Ay!, yo, entretanto
Dentro del pecho mi dolor oculto,
Enjugo de mis párpados el llanto
Y doy al mundo el exigido culto:
Yo escondo con vergüenza mi quebranto,
Mi propia pena con mi risa insulto,
Y me divierto en arrancar del pecho
Mi mismo corazón pedazos hecho.

But oh, beware! for when the burning heart
  Would fain draw nigh, it needs must backward shrink;
The stream envenomed by the powers infernal
For them that taste thereof hath tears eternal.

                .   .   .

Alas! The years of dear illusion passed,
  And fond deceiving fancy vanishèd,
And all the hopes we cherished followed fast,
  While heavy loomed the coming years as lead.
It is but for a day love's roses last!
  The flowers turned into briars their leaves hung dead,
And of the glory that we thought to see
Alone remains a tomb, a memory!

                .   .   .

And thou art happy, that by death hast gained
  A place wherein to hide thee from the Sun,
When, fronted by despair, alone remained
  The bitterness of tears, thou wretched one;
When by a hapless fate thou wast constrained
  To bear the brand of shame, then, all undone,
Thou wast by death borne far away from strife,
To find beyond the grave a second life.

By memory pursued, by storm-winds tossed,
  In torture worse than death thy days were spent,
Thy flower-like beauty dimmed, thy fragrance lost,
  Thy life a desert, wherein came and went
The blast of passion, where an early frost
  Chilled thy poor heart, and left it dried and rent,
Thy very sons forsook thee for another,
Denying thee the sacred name of mother.

                .   .   .

Oh cruel, too cruel! Alas!—And I the while
  Mine anguish deep within my bosom hide;
Checking my tears, I force my lips to smile,
  And from the world no longer turn aside;
Concealing black despair, by many a wile,
  The rending pains with laughter I deride,
Divert myself with tearing shred by shred
The heart that lies within me cold and dead.

Gocemos sí; la cristalina esfera
Gira bañada en luz: ¡bella es la vida!
¿Quién a parar alcanza la carrera
Del mundo hermoso que al placer convida?
Brilla radiante el sol, la primavera
Los campos pinta en la estación florida:
Truéquese en risa mi dolor profundo . . .
Que haya un cadáver más, ¡qué importa al mundo!

Be glad while yet ye may! The crystal sphere
  Revolves in golden light, and life is fair,
Whoever yet could stay in her career
  The Earth, that bids rejoice? See, in mid air
The radiant sunbeams dance! See, year by year
  The fields and forests their Spring vesture wear!
Let then deep-seated sorrow change to mirth;
Who recks of one more corpse laid low in earth?

Ida Farnell

Gustavo Adolfo Bécquer

Bécquer is a late Romantic who, in an atmosphere dominated by anti-romantic models, was preserved like a strange, rare flower. He alone was great enough to express all the greatness of Romanticism. He reminds one of a palm tree of the tropics with a slender trunk, that because of its flexibility resists the hurricane and rises again as graceful as ever.

Bécquer is a great poet, perhaps the greatest of the xixth century. He is great because he is absolutely possessed by poetry. His poems, very short, are true distillations, essence of psychic and sentimental experiences that leave as residue in small space, a great power of emotion.

The work of Bécquer gives the impression of being unstudied, very simple and easy of attainment. But Bécquer is a cultivated, not spontaneous, but sensitive poet. He represents a selective and reactionary position in romanticism. His is a purified romanticism, free of pomp and show. He aspires to create pure poetry that makes its own forms, that is not prolonged by tedious commentaries, but concentrates on substance, that more than alluring the reader, fills him with noble thoughts.

1836–1870

Bécquer lived in a realistic outer world, but made his escape into a world of dreams. He is one of the greatest of love poets. He died at the age of thirty-four practically unknown, having published no books. His *Rimas* appeared in periodicals and only after his death were collected by his friends and published in book form. They are his only poems, though his *Leyendas* are poetry in prose form. It was his theory that poetry should be brief and without adornment; like an electric spark it should strike the senses and flee. With one idea an infinity of ideas is awakened. He is the poet whose "white hand" has touched the strings of his harp awaking ideas and sentiments that will never die.

His best known and most beautiful poem, "Volverán las oscuras golondrinas" (The swallows will return), is optimistic in tone. The poet has faith in his own love, it is this that saves him; life is not absolute disillusion; its outward aspects fly away, but love like his cannot change. The poem is in the form of a symmetric ballad. The future and the past alternate, and the future will never be as the past.

From notes

RIMAS

120   II

    Saeta que voladora
Cruza, arrojada al azar,
Y que no se sabe dónde
Temblando se clavará;

    Hoja que del árbol seca
Arrebata el vendaval,
Y que no hay quien diga el surco
Donde al polvo volverá;

    Gigante ola que el viento
Riza y empuja en el mar,
Y rueda y pasa y se ignora
Qué playa buscando va;

    Luz que en cercos temblorosos
Brilla, próxima a expirar,
Y que no se sabe de ellos
Cuál el última será;

    Eso soy yo, que al acaso
Cruzo el mundo, sin pensar
De dónde vengo, ni adónde
Mis pasos me llevarán.

121   VII

    Del salón en el ángulo oscuro,
De su dueña tal vez olvidada,
Silenciosa y cubierta de polvo
      Veíase el arpa.

    ¡Cuánta nota dormía en sus cuerdas,
Como el pájaro duerme en las ramas,
Esperando la mano de nieve
      Que sabe arrancarlas!

RHYMES

II

120

An aimless darting arrow
Through the distance flying,
Never knowing where
Its target may be lying;

A vagrant autumn leaf
By sea winds whirled around,
No one knowing where
It will fall upon the ground;

A towering ocean wave
Tossed in the storm's vast roar,
Swirling, passing, unaware
What beach it searches for;

A light that flickers, shines,
Wavers, all but dark,
Nor knows which trembling gleam
May be its final spark;

All of this am I;
I go my way unheeding,
Never knowing where
My footsteps may be leading.

Alice Jane McVan

VII

121

In a dark corner of the room the harp
Was seen, perchance there by its owner thrust
Away and forgotten beneath a thick
Covering of dust.

How many notes were slumbering in its strings,
Silent as some bird on the bough asleep,
Waiting until its owner's snow-white hand
The chords should sweep!

¡Ay! —pensé—, ¡cuántas veces el genio
Así duerme en el fondo del alma,
Y una voz como Lázaro, espera
Que diga: "¡Levántate y anda!"

122

IX

Besa el aura que gime blandamente
Las leves ondas que jugando riza;
El sol besa a la nube en Occidente
Y de púrpura y oro la matiza;
La llama en derredor del tronco ardiente
Por besar a otra llama se desliza,
Y hasta el sauce, inclinándose a su peso,
Al río que le besa, vuelve un beso.

123

X

Los invisibles átomos del aire
En derredor palpitan y se inflaman;
El cielo se deshace en rayos de oro;
La tierra se estremece alborozada;
Oigo flotando en olas de armonía
Rumor de besos y batir de alas;
Mis párpados se cierran . . . ¿Qué sucede?
—¡Es el amor que pasa!

124

XI

—Yo soy ardiente, yo soy morena,
Yo soy el símbolo de la pasión;
De ansia de goces mi alma está llena.
¿A mí me buscas?—No es a ti; no.

Alas, I thought, how often in the depths
Of his own soul there sleeps a genius' worth
Waiting, like Lazarus, to hear a voice
    Saying "come forth!"

E. L. T.

IX

122

The gentle breeze with a whispered cry
Kisses the water it ripples in fun;
The radiant clouds in the western sky
Are purple and gold from the kiss of the sun;
A flame slips round a tree trunk nigh
To kiss with ardour another one;
And the willow, trailing low its leaves,
Returns to the river the kiss it receives.

Alice Jane McVan

X

123

The quivering, unseen atoms of air
Are aglow with warmth, and all the sky
Dissolves in molten rays of gold.
Laughter shakes the earth; the sigh
Of kisses and wings comes floating down
On waves of harmony from on high.
My eyes are closed . . . What can it be?
    Love is passing by!

Alice Jane McVan

XI

124

"I am a passion; I am a flame;
I am a symbol of loves that go,
I am that desire which transcends shame—
Is it I you seek?" "Not you: no!"

—Mi frente es pálida; mis trenzas de oro;
Puedo brindarte dichas sin fin;
Yo de ternura guardo un tesoro.
¿A mí me llamas?—No; no es a ti.

—Yo soy un sueño, un imposible,
Vano fantasma de niebla y luz;
Soy incorpórea, soy intangible;
No puedo amarte.—¡Oh, ven; ven tú!

125   **XXI**

—¿Qué es poesía?—dices mientras clavas
  En mi pupila tu pupila azul;—
¿Qué es poesía? ¿Y tú me lo preguntas?
  Poesía . . . eres tú.

126   **LII**

Olas gigantes que os rompéis bramando
En las playas desiertas y remotas,
Envuelto entre las sábanas de espuma,
      ¡Llevadme con vosotros!

Ráfagas de huracán, que arrebatáis
Del alto bosque las marchitas hojas,
Arrastrado en el ciego torbellino,
      ¡Llevadme con vosotros!

Nubes de tempestad, que rompe el rayo
Y en fuego encienden las sangrientas orlas,
Arrebatado entre la niebla oscura,
      ¡Llevadme con vosotros!

Llevadme, por piedad, adonde el vértigo
Con la razón me arranque la memoria . . .
¡Por piedad! . . . ¡Tengo miedo de quedarme
      Con mi dolor a solas!

"My brow is pale, my hair is gold;
I can make your dreams come true.
Treasures of tenderness I hold—
Is it I you call?" "No: not you!"

"I am a mystery; I am a dream;
A fleeting phantom of light and gloom;
A mist; a shadow; not what I seem,—
I cannot love you!" "Oh, come, come!"

Muna Lee

XXI   125

What is poetry? you say,
Holding my eyes with yours of blue,
What is poetry? . . . You ask that?
      Poetry . . . It is you!

Ina D. Singleton

LII   126

Great waves, crashing on desert shores,
Wrapped in white sheets of foam,
Roaring afar to unseen lands,
      Carry me where you roam!

Hurricane blasts, that snatch the leaves
Whether they will or no,
Dragging them off with rope of wind,
      Carry me where you go!

Clouds that rend night with lightning's sword,
Vanish in mist from view,
Binding the ragged wounds with fire,
      Carry me off with you!

Take me and hide me, Waves, Wind and Clouds,
From merciless memory,
Take, in pity! . . . I fear to stay
      Alone with misery!

Ina D. Singleton

        LIII

Volverán las oscuras golondrinas
En tu balcón sus nidos a colgar,
Y otra vez con el ala a sus cristales
     Jugando llamarán;

Pero aquellas que el vuelo refrenaban
Tu hermosura y mi dicha al contemplar,
Aquellas que aprendieron nuestros nombres,
     Ésas . . . ¡no volverán!

Volverán las tupidas madreselvas
De tu jardín las tapias a escalar,
Y otra vez a la tarde, aún más hermosas,
     Sus flores se abrirán;

Pero aquellas, cuajadas de rocío,
Cuyas gotas mirábamos temblar
Y caer, como lágrimas del día . . .
     Ésas . . . ¡no volverán!

Volverán del amor en tus oídos
Las palabras ardientes a sonar;
Tu corazón de su profundo sueño
     Tal vez despertará;

Pero mudo y absorto y de rodillas,
Come se adora a Dios ante su altar,
Como yo te he querido . . . desengáñate,
     ¡Así no te querrán!

The dusky swallows will hang their nests
In your balcony once again,
And with their wings they will lightly tap,
As they flit past your window-pane;
But those who paused in their eager flight
And lingered our names to learn,
That viewed your beauty and my delight. . . .
Ah! these will not return!

Dense honeysuckle will scale the walls
Of your garden, and there once more
Will show its blossoms when evening comes,
Even lovlier than before;
But those dew-laden, whose drops we watched
Now tremble and fall, alack!
That we saw fall like the tears of day. . . .
Ah! these will not come back!

The burning, passionate words of love
Once again in your ears will sound;
And then your heart will perhaps awake,
Will be roused from its sleep profound;
But as one kneels at His altar, mute,
Adoring, with head bent low,
As I have loved you. . . . be undeceived,
Ah! they'll not love you so!

Mrs. W. S. Hendrix

Generation of 1898

Miguel de Unamuno

A monumental figure, Miguel de Unamuno lived in the kingdom of eternity. Few names in Spanish literature have attracted such international attention. Born in Bilbao in the Basque country of northern Spain, he studied philosophy and letters in Madrid, and was called to the chair of Greek language and literature in the University of Salamanca.

His life was an unceasing spiritual struggle which over a period of forty years was apparent in his diaries, articles, etc., for he was a prolific writer in all the literary genres: dramas, essays, novels and poetry. His most important and best known writings are prose, but he was also a poet, the most personal, most profound and greatest poet of the spiritual life of his time. His struggle was always for eternal life. "Sobrevivir" is the idea of his work and life. He wanted to live on in his poems, he gave them life, but they in turn would give him life. For him "poetry is a form of thinking in mystery, of sculpturing mist."

In *Castilla* (see page 376) Unamuno establishes a relation between the landscape and man. The mission of the poem, always the mission of Unamuno, is the spiritual mission to lift man up above the earth, where he lives, to heaven, the mystical.

For many years Unamuno was the heart of the life and thought of Salamanca. In the poem *Salamanca* (see page 376) he describes the university of which he was rector—"Tall grove of towers . . . great forest of stone that drew out the history from the deep recesses of mother

1864--1936

earth." Salamanca with its plateresque façades, grace of cloisters and patios, and its literary memories, is a luminous evocation of the ancient life of Spain.

Hermosura (see page 384) is another poem of Salamanca. The poet's soul has need of rest; his tormented spirit comes in contact with serenity, a vision of beauty, "blessed beauty, answer to the riddle."

En Gredos (see page 398) is related to the ideas of the generation of 1898, concern for the fate of Spain—renunciation of its history and a vision of life through its spiritual values.

Unamuno's finest poem, *El Cristo de Velázquez* (see page 394) is a series of eighty-eight lyrical meditations on the dying Christ. His inspiration for this poem was a painting by Velázquez that represents Christ on the cross in agony, but suffused with calm. It is interesting to know that Unamuno always carried a crucifix given him by his sister, a nun. The poem associates the agonizing Christ with all men. The comments upon his body show Him to be a "Man of flesh and bone." This is the greatest religious poem of Spain since the xviᵗʰ century. It contains the whole of Unamuno's thought—the implacable fighter struggling with his doubts, it is a war for peace —

> "only in fighting for heaven, Christ, shall
> we mortals be able to live in peace."

From notes

128

CASTILLA

Tú me levantas, tierra de Castilla,
en la rugosa palma de tu mano,
al cielo que te enciende y te refresca,
al cielo, tu amo.

Tierra nervuda, enjuta, despejada,
madre de corazones y de brazos,
toma el presente en ti viejos colores
del noble antaño.

Con la pradera cóncava del cielo
lindan en torno tus desnudos campos,
tiene en ti cuna el sol y en ti sepulcro
y en ti santuario.

Es todo cima tu extensión redonda
y en ti me siento al cielo levantado,
aire de cumbre es el que se respira
aquí, en tus páramos.

¡Ara gigante, tierra castellana,
a ese tu aire soltaré mis cantos,
si te son dignos bajarán al mundo
desde lo alto!

129

SALAMANCA

Alto soto de torres que al ponerse
tras las encinas que el celaje esmaltan
dora a los rayos de su lumbre el padre
Sol de Castilla;

bosque de piedras que arrancó la historia
a las entrañas de la tierra madre,
remanso de quietud, yo te bendigo,
¡mi Salamanca!

Miras a un lado, allende el Tormes lento,
de las encinas el follaje pardo
cual el follaje de tu piedra, inmoble,
denso y perenne.

CASTILE   128

Oh, land of Castile, you do raise me up
to the sky in the rough palm of your hand;
to the sky that burns and refreshes you,
   the sky, your master.

Parched land, sinewy land and land of clear
horizons, mother of hearts and of arms,
the present takes in you the ancient coloring
   of long past glories.

At their outer edges, your bare brown fields
touch heaven with its concave meadow of sky,
the burning sun has its cradle in you,
   its tomb, its sanctuary.

The rounded dome of your space is all summit,
in you I feel myself raised up to heaven,
I breathe here on your desolate waste lands
   air from high mountains.

You are a vast altar, land of Castile,
into your air I shall set free my songs,
if worthy of you to the world they'll come
   down from the uplands.
        E. L. T.

SALAMANCA   129

Tall grove of towers that as he goes down
back of the trees that embellish the cloudscape
the father Sun of Castile doth touch with
   his golden rays;

 great forest of stone that drew out the history
from the deep recesses of mother earth,
backwater of quietude, I bless thee,
   my Salamanca!

On one side, beyond the slow river Tormes,
thou dost see the dark foliage of the trees,
which like the foliage of thy stone is motionless,
   dense and perennial.

Y de otro lado, por la calva Armuña,
ondea el trigo, cual tu piedra, de oro,
y entre los surcos al morir la tarde
      duerme el sosiego.

Duerme el sosiego, la esperanza duerme,
de otras cosechas y otras dulces tardes,
las horas al correr sobre la tierra
      dejan su rastro.

Al pie de tus sillares, Salamanca,
de las cosechas del pensar tranquilo
que año tras año maduró tus aulas
      duerme el recuerdo.

Duerme el recuerdo, la esperanza duerme,
y es el tranquilo curso de tu vida
como el crecer de las encinas, lento,
      lento y seguro.

De entre tus piedras seculares, tumba
de remembranzas del ayer glorioso,
de entre tus piedras recogió mi espíritu
      fe, paz y fuerza.

En este patio que se cierra al mundo
y con ruinosa crestería borda
limpio celaje, al pie de la fachada
      que de plateros

ostenta filigranas en la piedra,
en este austero patio, cuando cede
el vocerío estudiantil, susurra
      voz de recuerdos.

En silencio fray Luis quédase solo
meditando de Job los infortunios,
o paladeando en oración los dulces
      nombres de Cristo.

On the other side, by barren Armuña,
ripples the wheat that is gold like thy stone,
and as the evening dies, between the furrows
    is sleeping peace.

Tranquillity sleeps and hope too is sleeping,
of other harvests and sweet afternoons
the hours leave their trace on the earth as
    they hurry by.

At foot of thy blocks of stone, Salamanca,
sleeps the memory of the golden harvests
of tranquil thought that in thy halls grew ripe
    year after year.

Memory sleeps and hope also is sleeping,
while the course of life flows tranquilly on
as slowly as the growing of the trees,
    slowly, securely.

From amongst thy stones, centuries old, tomb
of recollections of glorious yesterday,
from amongst thy stones my spirit received
    faith, peace and fortitude.

In this patio that shuts out the world
and that with its crest in ruins embroiders
delicately the cloudless sky, at foot
    of the façade

that shows jewellers' filigree in stone,
in this austere patio when the voices
of the students have quieted down, whispers
    the voice of memory.

In silence, alone, Fray Luis de León
meditates on the misfortunes of Job,
or in his orisons savors the sweet
    names of our Lord.

Nombres de paz y amor con que en la lucha
buscó conforte, y arrogante luego
a la brega volvióse amor cantando,
    paz y reposo.

La apacibilidad de tu vivienda
gustó andariego soñador, Cervantes,
la voluntad le enechizaste y quiso
    volver a verte.

Volver a verte en el reposo quieta,
soñar contigo el sueño de la vida,
soñar la vida que perdura siempre
    sin morir nunca.

Sueño de no morir es el que infundes
a los que beben de tu dulce calma,
sueño de no morir ese que dicen
    culto a la muerte.

En mi florezcan cual en ti, robustas,
en flor perduradora las entrañas
y en ellas talle con seguro toque
    visión del pueblo.

Levántense cual torres clamorosas
mis pensamientos en robusta fábrica
y asiéntense en mi patria para siempre
    la mi Quimera.

Pedernoso cual tú sea mi nombre
de los tiempos la roña resistiendo,
y por encima al tráfago del mundo
    resuene limpio.

Pregona eternidad tu alma de piedra
y amor de vida en tu regazo arraiga,
amor de vida eterna, y a su sombra
    amor de amores.

Names of peace and of love that in the strife
he sought for his comfort, and bravely then
he returned to the struggle singing love,
        peace and repose.

The sweet peacefulness of thy living tasted
the roving dreamer Cervantes, and drunk
with desire to see thee again he
        wished to return.

To return to see thee in quiet repose,
to dream with thee the dream of life, to dream
of the life that lasts forever, a life
        that never dies.

A dream of not dying thou dost instil
into those who drink thy refreshing calm,
a dream of not dying, that which is called
        worship of death.

In me may there flower as in thee affections
that thrive everlastingly and on them
may I engrave a vision of the people
        with a sure stroke.

Like to strong towers with loud clanging bells
may my thoughts of stout fabric arise and
establish themselves in my land forever,
        my own Chimera.

May my name be strong as flint, as thou art,
resisting the rust of the ages and
above the loud traffic of the world may
        it resound clearly.

Thy soul of stone eternity proclaims
and love of life is rooted in thy lap,
love of life eternal and in its shadow
        the love of loves.

En tus callejas que del sol nos guardan
y son cual surcos de tu campo urbano,
en tus callejas duermen los amores
    más fugitivos.

Amores que nacieron como nace
en los trigales amapola ardiente
para morir antes de la hoz, dejando
    fruto de sueño.

El dejo amargo del Digesto hastioso
junto a las rejas se enjugaron muchos,
volviendo luego, corazón alegre,
    a nuevo estudio.

De doctos labios recibieron ciencia,
mas de otros labios palpitantes, frescos,
bebieron del Amor, fuente sin fondo,
    sabiduría.

Luego en las tristes aulas del Estudio,
frías y oscuras, en sus duros bancos,
aquietaron sus pechos encendidos
    en sed de vida.

Como en los troncos vivos de los árboles,
de las aulas así en los muertos troncos
grabó el Amor por manos juveniles
    su eterna empresa.

Sentencias no hallaréis del Triboniano,
del Peripato no veréis doctrina,
ni aforismos de Hipócrates sutiles,
    jugo de libros.

Allí Teresa, Soledad, Mercedes,
Carmen, Olalla, Concha, Blanca o Pura,
nombres que fueron miel para los labios,
    brasa en el pecho.

In thy narrow streets that shield us from sun,
that seem furrows of the fields in the city,
in thy narrow streets are sleeping the most
        fleeting of loves.

Loves that were born as the passionate poppies
glowing in the fields midst the wheat, born but
to die before the sickle, leaving only
        the fruit of dream.

The bitter taste of tiresome law books
many wiped from their lips at the window's
lattice, returning then, with a light heart,
        again to study.

From the lips of learning they took in knowledge,
but from other lips, trembling with emotion,
fresh lips, they drank at the fathomless fountain
        wisdom of Love.

Then in sad halls of study, cold and dark,
seated on the hard benches, they calmed down
the fire that was burning in their breasts kindled
        by thirst for life.

As upon the living trunks of the trees,
so Love did carve its eternal device
on dead trunks also in the study halls
        with youthful hands.

You shall not find statutes of Roman Law,
you shall not see doctrines of Aristotle,
nor subtle aphorisms of Hippocrates,
        sap of the books.

There are Teresa, Soledad, Mercedes,
Carmen, Olalla, Concha, Blanca, Pura,
names that were like honey on their lips, live
        coal in their breasts.

Así bajo los ojos la divisa
del amor, redentora del estudio,
y cuando el maestro calla, aquellas bancos
         dicen amores.

Oh, Salamanca, entre tus piedras de oro
aprendieron a amar los estudiantes
mientras los campos que te ciñen daban
         jugosos frutos.

Del corazón en las honduras guardo
tu alma robusta; cuando yo me muera
guarda, dorada Salamanca mía,
         tú mi recuerdo.

Y cuando el sol al acostarse encienda
el oro secular que te recama,
con tu lenguaje, de lo eterno heraldo,
         di tú que he sido.

130   *HERMOSURA*

         ¡Aguas dormidas,
         verdura densa,
         piedras de oro,
         cielo de plata!

Del agua surge la verdura densa,
de la verdura
como espigas gigantes las torres
que en el cielo burilan
en plata su oro.
Son cuatro fajas:
la del río, sobre ella la alameda,
la ciudadana torre
y el cielo en que reposa.
Y todo descansando sobre el agua,

Thus under their eyes the emblem of love
redeems them from their dull studies, for when
the master is silent then do those benches
      tell them of love.

Oh Salamanca, midst thy golden stones
the students in their youth did learn of love
whilst the surrounding fields that hem thee in
      gave juicy fruit.

I keep thy vigorous soul in the depths
of my heart, oh my golden Salamanca,
keep thou then, when my last days shall have come,
      keep thou my memory.

And when the sun as it sinks to its rest
kindles the age old gold that adorns thee,
in thy tongue of eternal herald tell
      what I have been.

                    E. L. T.

BEAUTY   130

      Sleeping waters,
      dense verdure,
      stones of gold,
      silver sky!

From the water issues dense verdure,
from the verdure
like giant spears of wheat the towers
that etch their gold against the silver
of the sky.
There are four tiers:
the river, above that the trees,
the city tower
and the sky upon which it rests.
And all reposing on the water,

flúido cimiento,
agua de siglos,
espejo de hemosura.
La ciudad en el cielo pintada
con luz inmoble;
inmoble se halla todo,
el agua inmoble,
inmóviles los álamos,
quietas las torres en el cielo quieto.
y es todo el mundo;
detrás no hay nada.
Con la ciudad en frente me hallo solo,
Y Dios entero
respira entre ella y yo toda su gloria.
A la gloria de Dios se alzan las torres,
a su gloria los álamos,
a su gloria los cielos,
y las aguas descansan a su gloria.
El tiempo se recoge;
desarrolla lo eterno sus entrañas;
se lavan los cuidados y congojas
en las aguas inmobles,
en los inmobles álamos,
en las torres pintadas en el cielo,
mar de altos mundos.
El reposo reposa en la hermosura
del corazón de Dios que así nos abre
tesoros de su gloria.
Nada deseo,
mi volundad descansa,
mi volundad reclina
de Dios en el regazo su cabeza
y duerme y sueña . . .
Sueña en descanso
toda aquesta visión de alta hermosura.
¡Hermosura! ¡Hermosura!
descanso de las almas doloridas
enfermas de querer sin esperanza.
¡Santa hermosura,

a fluid foundation,
water of centuries,
mirror of beauty.
The city painted on the sky
in motionless light;
all is motionless,
motionless water,
motionless poplars,
quiet towers on quiet sky.
And it is all the world;
beyond there is nothing.
I am alone before the city,
and God entire
breathes between it and me all of his glory.
Its towers rise to the glory of God,
to his glory the poplars,
to his glory the heavens,
and the waters rest in his glory.
Time retires;
the eternal unfolds its bowels;
cares and anxieties are washed
in the motionless waters,
in the motionless poplars,
in the towers painted against the sky,
sea of high worlds.
Repose reposes on the beauty
of the heart of God, which thus opens
to us the treasures of his glory.
I desire nothing,
my will reposes,
my will reclines
its head upon the lap of God
and sleeps and dreams . . .
Resting it dreams
of all this vision of deep beauty.
Beauty! Beauty!
The comfort of sorrowing souls,
sick for loving without hope.
Blessed beauty,

solución del enigma!
Tú matarás la Esfinge,
tú reposas en ti sin más cimiento;
gloria de Dios, te bastas.
¿Qué quieren esas torres?
Ese cielo ¿qué quiere?
¿Qué la verdura?
Y ¿qué las aguas?
Nada, no quieren;
su voluntad murióse;
descansan en el seno
de la Hermosura eterna;
son palabras de Dios limpias de todo
querer humano.
Son la oración de Dios que se regala
cantándose a sí mismo,
y así mata las penas.

. . . .

La noche cae, despierto,
me vuelve la congoja,
la espléndida visión se ha derretido,
vuelvo a ser hombre.
Y ahora dime, Señor, dime al oído:
tanta hermosura
¿matará nuestra muerte?

131   *DUERME, ALMA MÍA*

Duerme, alma mía, duerme,
    duerme y descansa,
duerme en la vieja cuna
    de la esperanza;
        ¡duerme!

Mira, el Sol de la noche,
    padre del alba,
por debajo del mundo
    durmiendo pasa;
        ¡duerme!

answer to the riddle!
You shall slay the Sphinx,
you rest on self without other foundation;
glory of God, thou art enough for self.
What do those towers desire?
What desires that sky,
what the verdure
and the waters?
Nothing, they have no desires;
their will has died;
they rest on the bosom
of eternal Beauty;
they are words of God free from all
human desire.
They are the prayer of God that cheers
singing to itself,
thus killing all pain.

. . . .
The night falls; awake,
my anguish returns,
and the splendid vision has melted;
once more I am man.
And now, Lord, tell me, whisper in my ear:
so much beauty,
will it kill our death?

E. L. T.

SLEEP, MY SOUL, SLEEP   131

Sleep, oh my soul, sleep,
   sleep thou and rest,
in the age-old cradle
   of hope; sleep thou,
      sleep!

See the sun of night,
   father of dawn,
'neath the sleeping world
   passes; sleep thou,
      sleep!

Duerme sin sobresaltos,
    duerme, mi alma;
puedes fiarte al sueño,
    que estás en casa;
        ¡duerme!

En su seno sereno,
    fuente de calma,
reclina tu cabeza
    si estás cansada;
        ¡duerme!

Tú que la vida sufres
    acongojada,
a sus pies tu congoja
    deja dejada;
        ¡duerme!

Duerme, que Él con su mano
    que engendra y mata,
cuna tu pobre cuna
    desvencijada;
        ¡duerme!

"Y si de este mi sueño
    no despertara . . ."
Esa congoja sólo
    durmiendo pasa;
        ¡duerme!

" ¡Oh, en el fondo del sueño
    siento a la nada! . . ."
Duerme, que esos sueños
    el sueño sana;
        ¡duerme!

"Tiemblo ante el sueño lúgubre
    que nunca acaba . . ."
Duerme y no te acongojes
    que hay un mañana;
        ¡duerme!

Sleep, be not afraid,
　　sleep thou, my soul;
thou mayst trust in sleep,
　　as in thy home;
　　　　sleep!

On its serene breast,
　　fountain of calm,
recline thy head
　　if worn; sleep thou,
　　　　sleep!

Thou that dost endure
　　this anguished life,
lay thine anguish at
　　its feet; sleep thou,
　　　　sleep!

Sleep, for His hand that
　　gives life and takes,
is rocking thy worn
　　cradle; sleep thou,
　　　　sleep!

"And if from my sleep
　　I should not wake . . ."
That anguish alone
　　passes in sleep;
　　　　sleep!

" In the depths of sleep
　　naught do I feel! . . ."
Sleep that those dreams in
　　sleep may be healed;
　　　　sleep!

" I dread the dark sleep
　　that has no ending . . ."
Sleep and do not grieve,
　　there is a morning;
　　　　sleep!

Duerme, mi alma, duerme,
  rayará el alba,
duerme, mi alma, duerme;
  vendrá mañana . . .
      ¡duerme!

Ya se durmió en la cuna
  de la esperanza . . .
se me durmió la triste . . .
  ¿habrá un mañana?
      ¿Duerme?

132   *¡SIÉMBRATE!*

Sacude la tristeza y tu ánimo recobra,
no quieto mires de la fortuna la rueda
como gira al pasar rozando tu vereda,
que a quién quiere vivir vida es lo que le sobra.

No haces sino nutrir esa mortal zozobra
que así en las redes del morir lento te enreda,
pues vivir es obrar y lo único que queda
la obra es; echa, pues, mano a la obra.

Ve sembrándote al paso y con tu propio arado
sin volver la vista que es volverla a la muerte,
y no a lo por andar sea peso lo andado.

En los surcos lo vivo, en ti deja lo inerte,
pues la vida no pasa al paso de un nublado;
de tus obras podrás un día recojerte.

Sleep, oh my soul, sleep,
   the day will dawn,
sleep, oh my soul, sleep;
   the morn will come . . .
      sleep!

At last in the cradle
   of hope she slept . . .
she slept, my sad soul . . .
   morn, will it come,
      Sleep?

E. L. T.

SOW YOUR SELF!   132

Shake off your sadness and your will regain,
inert you may not look on fortune's wheel
that turns and as it passes rubs your heel,
for who would live, in him life now doth reign.

You only nourish thus that mortal pain
of dying slowly, net whose toils you feel;
to labor is to live, the only weal
is work; set hand to plow and sow the grain!

You, as you pass, your very self must sow,
not looking back, not looking on death's strife,
lest the past weigh upon the path to go.

In you no movement, in the furrows life
whose breathing passes not as clouds but rife
with works, whose reaping is the self you sow.

E. L. T.

EL CRISTO DE VELÁZQUEZ

De la primera parte

Mi amado es blanco . . .

(*Cantares*, v, 10)

¿En qué piensas Tú, muerto, Cristo mío?
¿Por qué ese velo de cerrada noche
de tu abundosa cabellera negra
de nazareno cae sobre tu frente?
Miras dentro de Ti, donde está el reino
de Dios; dentro de Ti, donde alborea
el sol eterno de las almas vivas.
Blanco tu cuerpo está como el espejo
del padre de la luz, del sol vivífico;
blanco tu cuerpo al modo de la luna
que muerta ronda en torno de su madre
nuestra cansada vagabunda tierra;
blanco tu cuerpo está como la hostia
del cielo de la noche soberana,
de ese cielo tan negro como el velo
de tu abundosa cabellera negra
de nazareno.
                    Que eres, Cristo, el único
Hombre que sucumbió de pleno grado,
triunfador de la muerte, que a la vida
por Ti quedó encumbrada. Desde entonces
por Ti nos vivifica esa tu muerte,
por Ti la muerte se ha hecho nuestra madre,
por Ti la muerte es el amparo dulce
que azucara amargores de la vida,
por Ti, el Hombre muerto que no muere,
blanco cual luna de la noche. Es sueño,
Cristo, la vida, y es la muerte vela.
Mientras la tierra sueña solitaria,
vela la blanca luna; vela el Hombre
desde su cruz, mientras los hombres sueñan;
vela el Hombre sin sangre, el Hombre blanco
como la luna de la noche negra;
vela el Hombre que dió toda su sangre
por que las gentes sepan que son hombres.

THE CHRIST OF VELÁZQUEZ   133

From Part One

My beloved is white . . .

(*Song of Songs*, v, 10)

Of what art Thou thinking, oh my dead Christ?
And why does that heavy curtain of night,
the abundant black hair of a Nazarite
fall over thy forehead? Thou look'st within,
there where is the kingdom of God, within
Thyself, there where dawns the eternal sun
of living souls. Thy body is as white
as the mirror of the father of light,
the sun, life-giver; thy body is white
as is the moon, that dead revolves around
its mother, our tired wandering earth;
thy body is white as the host of heaven
of sovereign night, of that heaven as black
as the veil of thine abundant black hair
of a Nazarite.
                    For Thou art the Christ,
the only Man who did willingly die,
the conqueror over death, that to life
through Thee was elevated. And since then
through Thee that death of thine gives to us life,
through Thee death has been made for us a mother,
through Thee death is the welcome, kindly aid
that sweetens the bitterness of our life,
through Thee, the Man dead, He that does not die,
white like the moon of night. Life is a sleep,
Christ, and death is a vigil. While the earth
is sleeping alone, the white moon keeps watch;
from his cross the Man keeps watch while men sleep;
the bloodless Man keeps vigil, the Man white
as is the moon of the black night; He watches,
the Man who gave all of his blood that men
might know that they are men. Thou didst save death,
thine arms open to the night which is black
and most beautiful, for the sun of life
has looked upon it with his eyes of fire:

Tú salvaste a la muerte. Abres tus brazos
a la noche, que es negra y muy hermosa,
porque el sol de la vida la ha mirado
con sus ojos de fuego: que a la noche
morena la hizo el sol y tan hermosa.
Y es hermosa la luna solitaria,
la blanca luna en la estrellada noche
negra cual la abundosa cabellera
negra del nazareno. Blanca luna
como el cuerpo del Hombre en cruz, espejo
del sol de vida, del que nunca muere.

Los rayos, Maestro, de tu suave lumbre
nos guían en la noche de este mundo,
ungiéndonos con la esperanza recia
de un día eterno. Noche cariñosa,
¡oh noche, madre de los blandos sueños,
madre de la esperanza, dulce noche,
noche oscura del alma, eres nodriza
de la esperanza en Cristo salvador!

134   *De la segunda parte*

" ¡Se consumó!," gritaste con rugido
cual de mil cataratas, voz de trueno
como la de un ejército en combate
—Tú a muerte con la muerte—; y tu alarido,
de Alejandría espiritual, la nueva
soberbia Jericó de los paganos,
la de palmeras del saber helénico,
derrocó las murallas, y de Roma
las poternas te abrió. Siguióse místico
silencio sin linderos, cual si el aire
contigo hubiese muerto, y nueva música
surgió, sin son terreno, en las entrañas
del cielo aborrascado por el luto
de tu pasión. Y del madero triste
de tu cruz en el arpa, como cuerdas
con tendones y músculos tendidos
al tormento, tus miembros exhalaban,
al toque del amor—amor sin freno—,
la canción triunfadora de la vida.
¡Se consumó! ¡por fin, murió la Muerte!

for the dark night was made so by the sun,
made so beautiful. And the lonely moon,
the white moon, is beautiful in the star-lit
night that is black as the abundant black
hair of the Nazarite. The moon is white
as the body of the Man on the cross,
that is the mirror of the sun of life,
the sun of life that never, never dies.

Oh Master, the rays of thy quiet light
guide us in the dark night of this our world,
strengthening us with the enduring hope
of an eternal day! Fond night, oh night,
mother of tender dreams, mother of hope,
oh most gentle night, dark night of the soul,
thou art nurse of our hope in Christ the Saviour!

E. L. T.

From Part Two   134

" It is finished! " Thou didst cry like the roar
of a thousand cataracts, voice of thunder,
like the thunder of an army in combat
—Thou, fighting death to the death—; and thine outcry
overthrew the walls of the new proud Jericho
of the pagans, city of the palm trees
of Greek wisdom, the spiritual Alexandria,
and flung wide to Thee the portals of Rome.
There followed a silence, measureless, mystical,
as if the air with Thee had died, and then
new music surged forth of unearthly sound,
made stormy in the recesses of heaven
by the grief of thy passion. With the tendons
and muscles stretched taut, like strings on the harp
of the sad wood of thy cross, in their torture,
thy limbs emitted at the touch of love
—boundless love—, the triumphant song of life.
It is finished! At last, Death has died!

Solo quedaste con tu Padre—solo
de cara a Ti—, mezclasteis las miradas
—del cielo y de tus ojos los azules—,
y al sollozar la inmensidad, su pecho,
tembló el mar sin orillas y sin fondo
del Espíritu, y Dios sintiéndose hombre,
gustó la muerte, soledad divina.
Quiso sentir lo que es morir tu Padre,
y sin la Creación vióse un momento
cuando doblando tu cabeza diste
al resuello de Dios tu aliento humano.
¡A tu postrer gemido respondía
sólo a lo lejos el piadoso mar!

EN GREDOS

135

¡Solo aquí en la montaña,
solo aquí con mi España
—la de mi ensueño—,
cara al rocoso gigantesco Ameal,
aquí, mientras doy huelgo a *Clavileño*,
con mi España inmortal!
Es la mía, la mía, sí, la de granito
que alza al cielo infinito,
ceñido en virgen nieve de los cielos,
su fuerte corazón,
un corazón de roca viva
que arrancaron de tierra los anhelos
de la eterna visión.
Aquí, a la soledad rocosa de la cumbre,
no de tu historia, sino de tu vida,
toca la lumbre;
aquí, a tu corazón, patria querida,
¡oh mi España inmortal!
Las brumas quedan de la falsa gloria
que brota de la historia,
aquí, a mitad de la falda,
ciñéndote en guirnalda,

Thou wast alone with thy Father—and He
face to face with Thee—, glances intermingled
—the blue of heaven and the blue of thine eyes—,
at the sob of immensity, his breast,
the limitless sea of the spirit trembled,
and God, feeling Himself to be a man,
tasted death, solitude divine. Thy Father
desired to feel what it is to die,
He saw Himself for a moment alone
without his Creation, when bowing thy head,
Thou didst give thy human breath to the breathing
of God. To thy last groan responded only
in the far distance the pitying sea!

E. L. T.

ON GREDOS   135

Alone here on the mountain,
alone here with my Spain
—Spain of my dreams—
my face towards rocky, gigantic Ameal,
whilst I give breath to *Clavileño*,* here
with my immortal Spain!
It is mine, it is mine, this pile of granite
that lifts to the infinite sky,
encircled in virgin snow of the heavens,
its steadfast heart,
a heart of living rock,
that yearning for eternal vision drew
from out the earth.
Here the luminous warmth of thy life, not
that of thy history, reaches the rocky
solitude of the summit;
here touches thy heart, my belovèd country,
oh, my immortal Spain!
The mists of the false glories that break forth
from history remain
here, midway of the slope,
girdling thee as a garland,

---

* See *Don Quijote*, Part II, Chap. XIL.

mientras el sol, el de la verdadera,
tu frente escalda
y te da en primavera,
tanto más dulce cuanto que es más breve,
flores de cumbre,
criadas en invierno bajo el manto
protector de la nieve,
manto sin podredumbre,
templo de nuestro Dios, ¡el español!
Este es tu corazón de firme roca
—¡altar del templo santo!—
de nuestra tierra entraña,
¡éste es tu corazón que cielo toca,
tu corazón desnudo,
mi eterna España,
que busca el sol!
No es tu reino, ¡oh mi patria!, de este mundo,
juguete del destino,
tu reino en el profundo
del azul que te cubre has de buscar;
¡esta peña gigante es un camino
de Juan de la Cruz pétrea escala,
la eterna libertad para escalar!
Del piélago de tierra que entre brumas
tiende a tus pies, aquí, sus parameros,
con letras por espumas,
volaron del Dorado a la conquista
buitres aventureros,
mientras hastiado del perenne embuste
de la gloria, enterraba aquí, a tu vista,
su majestad en Yuste
Carlos Emperador.
Aquel vuelo de buitres fué la historia,
tu pesadilla,
y este entierro imperial fué la victoria
sin mancilla,
la que orea la frente a tu Almanzor.
Esta es mi España, un corazón desnudo
de viva roca
del granito más rudo

whilst the sun, sun of truth,
warms thy forehead
and gives to thee in spring,
all the more sweet for being brief,
flowers on the summit,
created in winter beneath protecting
blanket of snow,
pure blanket without spot,
temple of our God, Spanish God!
This is thy heart of solid rock
—the holy temple's altar—
the bowels of our earth,
this is thy heart that touches heaven,
thy very naked heart,
that seeks the sun,
oh my eternal Spain!
Thy kingdom is not of this world, my country,
plaything of destiny,
thou must seek for thy kingdom
in the depths of the blue that covers thee;
this great rock is a way, a stony ladder
of Saint John of the Cross,
the eternal liberty to be scaled!
From the great sea of earth that veiled in mists
stretches out here at thy feet its vast desert,
with letters for its foam
flew adventurous vultures
to the conquest of El Dorado,
whilst disgusted with the perennial fraud
of glory, was buried here, in thy sight,
in the monastery of Yuste,
his majesty, Charles the Fifth, Emperor.
That flight of vultures, thy nightmare,
was history,
and this imperial burial was the spot-
less victory,
that freshens the brow of thy Almanzor.
This is my Spain, a naked heart
of living rock
of most rough granite

que con sus crestas en el cielo toca
buscando al sol en mutua soledad;
ésta es mi España,
patria ermitaña,
que como al nido torna siempre a la verdad.
Tu historia, ¡qué naufragia en mar profundo!
¡Pero no importa,
porque ella es corta,
pasa, y la muerte es larga,
larga como el amor!
Respiras tempestades
y baja a consolar tus soledades
el rayo del Señor,
mientras, en transverberación tempestuosa,
tu corazón, sobre que el cielo posa,
hieren flechas del fuego de su amor.
De los sudarios que a tu frente envuelven
y en agua se revuelven
bajan cantando ríos de frescor
y visten luego
la zahorra, escurraja que a tu cumbre
royó la herrumbre,
con capa de verdor.
De noche temblorosas las estrellas
te ciñen con su ensueño,
y edades ha que en ellas
señas cual vuelve siempre igual mudanza
trayendo un mismo sino,
y este volver es causa de esperanza,
que no muda,
de un reposo final;
para mi corazón, que angustia suda
bajo el yugo sin fin del infinito,
eres tú solo propio pedestal.
Que es en tu cima, donde al fin me encuentro,
siéntome soberano,
y en mi España me adentro,
tocándome persona,
hijo de siglos de pasión, cristiano,
y cristiano español;
aquí, en la vasta soledad serrana,

that with its crests touching the sky
in mutual solitude seeks the sun;
this is my Spain,
a hermit country,
that as to its nest turns always to truth.
Thy history, what shipwreck in deep sea!
But 'tis no matter,
for history is short,
passes, and death is long,
long as is love!
Thou dost breathe tempests,
and to console thy solitude comes down
the lightning of the Lord,
whilst in tempestuous cross-reverberation
arrows of the fire of his love wound
thy heart upon which is resting the sky.
From the winding sheets that wrap round thy brow
and in water return
come down singing rivers of freshness
and they clothe then
the gravel with a covering of green,
this trickle that upon thy summit
rusted the rocks.
At night the trembling stars
hem thee in with their dream,
and through the centuries in them
thou dost show that like change always recurs
carrying the same fate,
and this return is cause for hope,
that changes not,
of a final repose;
for my heart that sweats anguish
beneath the unending yoke of the infinite,
thou alone art the proper pedestal.
On thy summit at last I find myself,
I feel myself supreme,
I penetrate into my Spain,
at last a person,
son of centuries of passion, a Christian,
and Spanish Christian;
here, in this vast solitude of the mountains,

renaciendo al romper de la mañana
cuando renace solitario el sol.
Aquí me trago a Dios, soy Dios, mi roca;
sorbo aquí de su boca con mi boca
la sangre de este sol, su corazón,
de rodillas aquí, sobre la cima,
¡mientras mi frente con su lumbre anima,
al cielo abierto, en santa comunión!
Aquí le siento palpitar a mi alma
de noche frente a Sirio,
que palpita en la negra inmensidad,
y aquí, al tocarme así, siento la palma
de este largo martirio
de no morir de sed de eternidad.
¡Alma de mi carne, sol de mi tierra,
Dios de mi España,
que sois lo único que hay, lo que pasó,
no la eterna mentira del mañana,
aquí, en el regazo de la sierra,
aquí entre vosotros, aquí me siento yo!

being reborn at break of day
when is reborn the solitary sun.
Here I devour God, I am God, my rock;
I drink from his lips with my lips the blood
of this sun, his heart, here,
on my knees, on the summit,
whilst my forehead with his splendor is lit
open to heaven, in holy communion!
Here I feel my soul trembling
at night at sight of Sirius,
that palpitates within the black immensity,
and here, touching me thus, I feel the palm
of this long martyrdom
of not dying of the thirst for eternity.
Soul of my flesh, sun of my earth,
God of my Spain,
ye are all that there ever was,
not the eternal falsehood of tomorrow,
here on the bosom of the mountain range,
here in your midst, here I feel myself mine.

E. L. T.

Antonio Machado

Antonio Machado was born in Seville in 1875; he received his education in Madrid. In 1907 he was called to a professorship of French in Soria. While there he was married, and three months later he lost his wife, "whose memory is with me always" he wrote. In 1917 he was transferred to a position at the Institute of Segovia, and in 1932 to the Institute Calderón in Madrid.

In figure he was like a great mountain. In his life he was noble and simple. His poetry was a colloquy with his inner man; he said: "kill your words and listen to your soul."

His books of poetry are *Soledades*, 1903; *Soledades, galerías y otros poemas*, 1907; *Campos de Castilla*, 1912; and *Nuevas canciones*, 1924. They are books of the inner life exclusively. The first, *Soledades* and *Galerías*, are full of tenderness and introspective melancholy. The poet lives in a kind of monastery and his poems are notes of dream and mystery.

In *Campos de Castilla*, the poet has changed. This book is the key to the spirit of 1898; it is the discovery of Castile. The poet passes from the contemplation of its exterior to its inner world, for Castile is a landscape of the soul and of the mystics. It is the most impressive landscape in Spain, a land of great, barren plains, an imposing, tragic sight. This is not a book of description; it shows a preoccupation with serious and profound things.

1875 - 1939

In his last period Machado passes from his phase of poetry of the inner man, now it is humorous philosophy. He writes of the inner world, but his poetry has fewer elements of sentiment. The poems are very short, of great intensity and epigrammatic in form. They are like the popular songs of three, four or five lines, meant to be sung; the kind of humorous philosophy that constitutes folk poetry. The impression they give is of great simplicity, but of great depth. They have the concise grace born in Andalusia and the profundity and simplicity of Castile. They are never frivolous. They remind one in a certain way of the poems of China and Japan.

Antonio Machado says: "I adore beauty," but he does not like adornment, or as he says, "the birds that sing just to sing." He does not belong to the artificial school, he distinguishes between voice and echo, he finds his poetry not in the flowing river, but in the source of the river, springing from the rock of his heart. He asks in his autobiography: "Am I a classicist or a romanticist? I do not know." He aspires to the true, the natural with the most pure, most profound expression. He says: "Let echoes cease, let voices begin!"

Like Unamuno, his activity is of the spirit, he is a mystic poet, he looks within. Reading Machado, there come to mind the great ones of antiquity. He has the dignity, the seriousness of the great painter of Spain, Velázquez.

From notes

136   *Daba el reloj las doce . . .*

Daba el reloj las doce . . . y eran doce
golpes de azada en tierra . . .
¡Mi hora!—grité— . . . El silencio
me respondió:—No temas;
tú no verás caer la última gota
que en la clepsidra· tiembla.

Dormirás muchas horas todavía
sobre la orilla vieja,
y encontrarás una mañana pura
amarrada tu barca a otra ribera.

137   *¡Tenue rumor de túnicas que pasan*

¡Tenue rumor de túnicas que pasan
sobre la infértil tierra! . . .
¡Y lágrimas sonoras
de las campanas viejas!

Las ascuas mortecinas
del horizonte humean . . .
Blancos fantasmas lares
van encendiendo estrellas.

—Abre el balcón. La hora
de una ilusión se acerca . . .
La tarde se ha dormido,
y las campanas sueñan.

138   *Desde el umbral de un sueño*

Desde el umbral de un sueño me llamaron . . .
Era la buena voz, la voz querida.

—Dime: ¿vendrás conmigo a ver el alma? . . .
Llegó a mi corazón un caricia.

The clock struck twelve   136

The clock struck twelve . . . and twelve blows of a spade
on the hard earth they were . . .
. . .—My hour!—I cried . . . and silence
answered me:—Do not fear;
you shall not see the last drop of the water clock,
trembling, fall as a tear.

On the old familiar bank you shall sleep
for many hours more,
and one fair morning you shall find your barque
moored to the other shore.

                                        E. L. T.

A frail sound of a tunic trailing   137

A frail sound of a tunic trailing
across the infertile earth,
and the sonorous weeping
of the old bells.

The dying embers
of the horizon smoke.
White ancestral ghosts
go lighting the stars.

—Open the balcony-window. The hour
of illusion draws near . . .
The afternoon has gone to sleep
and the bells dream.

                                   John Dos Passos

From the threshold of a dream   138

From the threshold of a dream I was called . . .
It was the dear voice, the loved voice.

—Tell me: wilt come with me to see the soul? . . .
There came to my heart a caress.

—Contigo siempre . . . Y avancé en mi sueño
por una larga, escueta galería,
sintiendo el roce de la veste pura
y el palpitar suave de la mano amiga.

139   *La casa tan querida*

    La casa tan querida
donde habitaba ella,
sobre un montón de escombros arruinada
o derruída, enseña
el negro y carcomido
mal trabado esqueleto de madera.

    La luna está vertiendo
su clara luz en sueños que platea
en las ventanas. Mal vestido y triste,
voy caminando por la calle vieja.

140   *Desnuda está la tierra,*

    Desnuda está la tierra,
y el alma aúlla al horizonte pálido
como loba famélica. ¿Qué buscas,
poeta, en el ocaso?

    Amargo caminar, porque el camino
pesa en el corazón. ¡El viento helado,
y la noche que llega, y la amargura
de la distancia! . . . En el camino blanco

    algunos yertos árboles negrean;
en los montes lejanos
hay oro y sangre . . . El sol murió . . . ¿Qué buscas,
poeta, en el ocaso?

—With thee always . . . And in my dream I went
through a long, solitary gallery,
feeling the touch of the pure garments,
and the gentle throb of the friendly hand.

E. L. T.

The well belovèd house   139

The well belovèd house
in which she used to live,
ruined and wrecked above a pile
of rubble, shows
its black worm-eaten,
disintegrating skeleton of wood.

In dreams the moon
is shedding its clear light that gleams as silver
upon the windows. Poorly dressed and sad
along the old street I am walking.

E. L. T.

Denuded is the land,   140

Denuded is the land,
and the soul howls towards the pale horizon
like a ravening she-wolf. What seek you,
poet, in the waning west?

Bitter to walk along, because the pathway
weighs upon the heart. The icy wind,
and the night coming in, and the bitterness
of the distance! . . . Along the white pathway

some of the stiffened trees show black;
in the mountains far off
are gold and blood . . . The sun has died . . . What seek you,
poet, in the waning west?

Philip Warnock Silver

141   *Tal vez la mano, en sueños,*

Tal vez la mano, en sueños,
del sembrador de estrellas,
hizo sonar la música olvidada

como una nota de la lira inmensa,
y la ola humilde a nuestros labios vino
de unas pocas palabras verdaderas.

142   *EL DIOS IBERO*

Igual que el ballestero
tahur de la cantiga,
tuviera una saeta el hombre ibero
para el Señor que apedreó la espiga
y malogró los frutos otoñales,
y un "gloria a ti" para el Señor que grana
centenos y trigales·
que el pan bendito le darán mañana.

"Señor de la ruina,
adoro porque aguardo y porque temo:
con mi oración se inclina
hacia la tierra un corazón blasfemo.

¡Señor, por quien arranco el pan con pena,
sé tu poder, conozco mi cadena!
¡Oh dueño de la nube del estío
que la campiña arrasa,
del seco otoño, del helar tardío,
y del bochorno que la mies abrasa!

¡Señor del iris, sobre el campo verde
donde la oveja pace,
Señor del fruto que el gusano muerde
y de la choza que el turbión deshace,

Perchance in dreams   141

Perchance, in dreams, the hand
of the sower of stars
struck the chords of some forgotten music

as a note of the immense lyre,
and the humble wave reached our lips
as a few simple words of truth.

E. L. T.

IBERIAN GOD   142

As the gambler drew his bow
For vengeance in the song,
So the Iberian recklessly let go
A sharp shaft to the Lord of blighting wrong
Who felled his wheat with hail and killed his fruit;
But he praised the Lord who brought his crops to head
Full eared, gold to the root,
The rye and wheat that tomorrow would be his bread.

"Lord of ruin and loss,
I adore because I fear, because I wait,
But my heart is blasphemous:
Bowing to earth, I pray in pride and hate.

"I know Thy power, my chain I recognize,
Lord, for Thee I dig my bread in sweat and sighs;
O master of the flooding clouds that cost
So dear to summer yield,
Of the autumn drought and spring's belated frost,
Of the scorching heat that sears the harvest field.

"Lord of the bow above the tender grass
Where the white ewe grazes,
Lord of the hut undone when tempests pass
And of the fruit where the worm carves its mazes,

tu soplo el fuego del hogar aviva,
tu lumbre da sazón al rubio grano,
y cuaja el hueso de la verde oliva,
la noche de San Juan, tu santa mano!

¡Oh dueño de fortuna y de pobreza,
ventura y malandanza,
que al rico das favores y pereza
y al pobre su fatiga y su esperanza!

¡Señor, Señor: en la voltaria rueda
del año he visto mi simiente echada,
corriendo igual albur que la moneda
del jugador en el azar sembrada!

¡Señor, hoy paternal, ayer cruento,
con doble faz de amor y de venganza,
a ti, en un dado de tahur al viento
va mi oración blasfemia y alabanza!"

Este que insulta a Dios en los altares,
no más atento al ceño del destino,
también soñó caminos en los mares
y dijo: es Dios sobre la mar camino.

¿No es él quien puso a Dios sobre la guerra,
más allá de la suerte,
más allá de la tierra,
más allá de la mar y de la muerte?

¿No dió la encina ibera
para el fuego de Dios la buena rama,
que fué en la santa hoguera
de amor una con Dios en pura llama?

Mas hoy . . . ¡Qué importa un día!
Para los nuevos lares
estepas hay en la floresta umbría,
leña verde en los viejos encinares.

"Thy breathing quickens the hearth fire when it
Is low, Thy splendor ripens ruddy grain,
And on Midsummer Eve the olive pit
Forms and hardens where Thy hand has lain.

"O master of fortunes and of poverties,
Good luck and bad, who yet
Giv'st to the rich man favors and soft ease
And to the poor, his hope and bitter sweat,

"Lord, Lord, in the twelve months' whirling round
I have watched my seed with patient labor sown
Run the same risk in the hard and faithless ground
As a gambler's cash on the losing hazard thrown.

"Lord, paternal now, who wert before a God
Cruel, two-faced, Thy love with vengeance dimmed,
To Thee my prayer of blasphemy and laud
Ascends, a gambler's die cast on the wind."

This man who, insulting God, at His altar prayed,
Defiant of all fate's frowning might forbode,
With dreaming tamed the seas and highways laid
Across them, saying, He is the ocean road.

Is it not this man who raised his God to be
Above all war? Beyond
Fate, beyond earth and sea,
Beyond death and dying, free of every bond?

Did not the Iberian tree,
The encina, yield her branch for holy fire
And, burning, find unity
With God in love's pure flame on the sacred pyre?

But now, so quickly day grows into day!
There are new hearths; for these
New roses thrive in field and wooded bay
And fresh green branches on the ancient trees.

Aun larga patria espera
abrir al corvo arado sus besanas;
para el grano de Dios hay sementera
bajo cardos y abrojos y bardanas.

¡Qué importa un día! Está el ayer alerto
al mañana, mañana al infinito,
hombre de España, ni el pasado ha muerto,
ni está el mañana—ni el ayer—escrito.

¿Quién ha visto la faz al Dios hispano?
Mi corazón aguarda
al hombre ibero de la recia mano,
que tallará en el roble castellano
el Dios adusto de la tierra parda.

143   *AMANECER DE OTOÑO*

Una larga carretera
entre grises peñascales,
y alguna humilde pradera
donde pacen negros toros. Zarzas, malezas, jarales.

Está la tierra mojada
por las gotas del rocío,
y la alameda dorada,
hacia la curva del río.

Tras los montes de violeta
quebrado el primer albor;
a la espalda la escopeta
entre sus galgos agudos, caminando un cazador.

The fatherland is still
Waiting to open furrows to the plow;
For the seed of God there is a field to till
Overgrown with burdocks, thorns, and thistles now.

Day merges into day; the past is wide
To the morrow, the morrow to the infinite;
Men of Spain, no yesterday has died,
Future and past have yet no holy writ.

Did ever the Spanish God His face reveal?
My heart awaits the hand
Of an Iberian, vigorous and leal,
To carve in oaken timbers of Castile
The God austere who reigns in this brown land.

Ruth Matilda Anderson

AUTUMN DAWN   143

A highroad's barren scar
Among the grey rock-spires
And humble pastures far
Where strong black bulls are grazing. Brambles, thickets, briars.

The dew has drenched with cold
The landscape in the dark
And the poplars' frieze of gold,
Toward the river's arc.

A hint of dawn half seen
With purple crags for frame.
Beside his greyhounds keen,
His eager gun at rest, a hunter stalking game.

Jean Rogers Longland

CAMPOS DE SORIA

144   III

Es el campo undulado, y los caminos
ya ocultan los viajeros que cabalgan
en pardos borriquillos,
ya al fondo de la tarde arrebolada
elevan las plebeyas figurillas,
que el lienzo de oro del ocaso manchan.
Mas si trepáis a un cerro y veis el campo
desde los picos donde habita el águila,
son tornasoles de carmín y acero,
llanos plomizos, lomas plateadas,
circuídos por montes de violeta,
con las cumbres de nieve sonrosada.

145   IV

¡Las figuras del campo sobre el cielo!
Dos lentos bueyes aran
en un alcor, cuando el otoño empieza,
y entre las negras testas doblegadas
bajo el pesado yugo,
pende un cesto de juncos y retama,
que es la cuna de un niño;
y tras la yunta marcha
un hombre que se inclina hacia la tierra,
y una mujer que en las abiertas zanjas
arroja la semilla.
Bajo una nube de carmín y llama,
en el oro flúido y verdinoso
del poniente, las sombras se agigantan.

FIELDS OF SORIA

III   144

   An undulating country, where the roads
Do now conceal the travellers, astride
Their dusky-coated asses,
Now, in the crimson light of dying day,
Uplift in full relief their rustic forms,
Darkening the golden canvas of the West.
Climb now yon mount, and from those jagged peaks
Where dwells the eagle, gaze upon the scene;
And see the leaden plains and silvery slopes
All bathed in carmine, shot with steely grey,
Circled by mountains of deep violet,
With snowy summits blushing like the rose.

Ida Farnell

IV   145

   Lo, these are they that move 'twixt land and sky:
Two oxen slowly ploughing
Upon a hillside, touched by Autumn's breath,
The while between their sturdy heads, low bent
Beneath the heavy yoke,
A basket hangs woven of reeds and broom—
An infant's rustic cradle;
And following the team,
A man, who bows him down towards the earth,
Likewise a woman, who in the gaping furrows
Scatters the precious seed.
Beneath a cloud of crimson and of flame
See in the West, all liquid gold and green,
Their shadows slowly lengthen as they pass.

Ida Farnell

VII

¡Colinas plateadas,
grises alcores, cárdenas roquedas
por donde traza el Duero
su curva de ballesta
en torno a Soria, obscuros encinares,
ariscos pedregales, calvas sierras,
caminos blancos y álamos del río,
tardes de Soria, mística y guerrera,
hoy siento por vosotros, en el fondo
del corazón, tristeza,
tristeza que es amor! ¡Campos de Soria
donde parece que las rocas sueñan,
conmigo vais! ¡Colinas plateadas,
grises alcores, cárdenas roquedas! . . .

147

Señor, ya me arrancaste

Señor, ya me arrancaste lo que yo más quería.
Oye otra vez, Dios mío, mi corazón clamar.
Tu voluntad se hizo, Señor, contra la mía,
Señor, ya estamos solos mi corazón y el mar.

148

A JOSÉ MARÍA PALACIO

Palacio, buen amigo,
¿está la primavera
vistiendo ya las ramas de los chopos
del río y los caminos? En la estepa
del alto Duero, Primavera tarda,
¡pero es tan bella y dulce cuando llega! . . .
¿Tienen los viejos olmos
algunas hojas nuevas?
Aun las acacias estarán desnudas
y nevados los montes de las sierras.
¡Oh, mole del Moncayo blanca y rosa,

Silvered hills,
grey downs and sombre rocky spaces
there where the river Duero
winds its curve of a bow round about Soria,
dusky groves of evergreen oaks,
rough stony ground, bare mountain ridges,
white roadways and poplars beside the river,
afternoons of Soria, mystic, warlike,
today, in the depths of my heart,
I feel for you a sadness,
sadness that is love! Fields of Soria
where the rock seems to dream,
I carry you with me! You silvered hills,
grey downs and sombre rocky spaces!

E. L. T.

Behold, Lord, Thou didst tear from me   147

Behold, Lord, Thou didst tear from me what I most did love.
Hear, Thou, once more my heart cry out, oh, my God above!
Thy will was done, dear Lord, it was counter to mine own.
And now, Lord, are we, my heart and the sea all alone.

E. L. T.

TO JOSÉ MARÍA PALACIO   148

Palacio, dear friend,
is spring now decking
the branches of the poplars
beside the river and along the highways?
On the plain of deep Duero, Spring tarries,
but when it comes, how sweet it is, how beautiful! . . .
Have the ancient elm trees
put forth tender green leaves?
The branches of the acacias will still
be bare, and snow upon the mountain ridges.
Oh, massive Moncayo all white and rose,

allá, en el cielo de Aragón, tan bella!
¿Hay zarzas florecidas
entre las grises peñas,
y blancas margaritas
entre la fina hierba?
Por esos campanarios
ya habrán ido llegando las cigüeñas.
Habrá trigales verdes,
y mulas pardas en las sementeras,
y labriegos que siembran los tardíos
con las lluvias de abril. Ya las abejas
libarán del tomillo y del romero.
¿Hay ciruelos en flor? ¿Quedan violetas?
Furtivos cazadores, los reclamos
de la perdiz bajo las capas luengas,
no faltarán. Palacio, buen amigo,
¿tienen ya ruiseñores las riberas?
Con los primeros lirios
y las primeras rosas de las huertas,
en una tarde azul, sube al Espino,
al alto Espino donde está su tierra . . .

149 *A DON FRANCISCO GINER DE LOS RÍOS*

Como se fué el maestro,
la luz de esta mañana
me dijo: Van tres días
que mi hermano Francisco no trabaja.
¿Murió? . . . Sólo sabemos
que se nos fué por una senda clara,
diciéndonos: Hacedme
un duelo de labores y esperanzas.
Sed buenos y no más, sed lo que he sido
entre vosotros: alma.

there, in the sky of Aragon, so radiant!
Are there blossoming blackberries
among the sombre rocks,
and delicate white daisies
sown there midst the fine grass?
The storks will have been coming
to build their nests on the roofs of the belfries.
Fields will be green with wheat,
brown mules will be plowing between the furrows,
and peasants sowing the late grain
with the soft rains of April. Now the bees
will sip honey from thyme and rosemary.
Are the plum trees in flower? Linger the violets?
Furtive huntsmen that under their long cloaks
decoy the poor partridge, will not be lacking.
Palacio, dear friend,
are nightingales now on the river banks?
On a blue afternoon,
go up with the first lilies and first roses
of the gardens, to the quiet Espino,
high Espino where is her plot of earth . . .

E. L. T.

TO DON FRANCISCO GINER DE LOS RÍOS   149

Now, when the Master left us,
There came that morning's light,
Whispering: 'Three days have fled,
And lo, my brother Francis worketh not!
Died he?' We only know
That he went hence upon a shining path,
And spake: 'Mourn me with works,
Mourn me with hopes, I would no dole of tears;
Only be good. Be, as I strove to be
While in this life—a soul.
Live on, life hath no end;
The dead alone shall die, and shadows pass;
Who sowed is reaping now, who lived yet liveth;

Vivid, la vida sigue,
los muertos mueren y las sombras pasan;
lleva quien deja y vive el que ha vivido.
¡Yunques, sonad; enmudeced, campanas!

Y hacia otra luz más pura
partió el hermano de la luz del alba,
del sol de los talleres,
el viejo alegre de la vida santa.
. . . Oh, sí, llevad, amigos,
su cuerpo a la montaña,
a los azules montes
del ancho Guadarrama.
Allí hay barrancos hondos
de pinos verdes donde el viento canta.
Su corazón repose
bajo una encina casta,
en tierra de tomillos, donde juegan
mariposas doradas . . .
Allí el maestro un día
soñaba un neuvo florecer de España.

Let the good anvils sound, let bells be dumb! '
Then to a purer light
The brother of the light of dawn went forth,
Forth from the scene of toils
That bright and glad old man of saintly life.

. . . Yea, comrades, let us bring
His body to the mountains,
Up to those azure heights
Where Guadarrama towers.
Yonder are shadowy gorges
With pine-trees, where the winds make melody.
Let his great heart repose
Beneath this sacred oak,
Where beds of thyme scatter their fragrance sweet,
And golden butterflies play.
'Tis there of old our Master
Dreamt his sweet dream of Spain's new blossoming.

Ida Farnell

[Francisco Giner, who died in 1915, was the founder of the 'Institución
libre de la Enseñanza,' and it is largely to him that Spain owes a reform in
education accepted by her most enlightened men.]

Juan Ramón Jiménez

The great expression of the xxth century is lyric poetry, and one of its greatest exponents is Juan Ramón Jiménez. He was born in 1881 in Moguer, a province of Andalusia. It is a land of sun, of vineyards and of villages close to the sea. Here in this sunny little town Jiménez lived, the petted son of a wealthy family, a child different from others, apart and individual.

In 1895, at the age of fourteen, he began to write and publish in reviews of Andalusia and Madrid; therefore before going to Madrid in 1900, his poetry was known to the literati who were very curious to meet this gifted young writer. But Jiménez was not a man for "tertulias"—literary circles—and in Madrid he lived a life apart.

In 1916 he went to New York, where he married Zenobia Camprubi Aymar. This period is recorded in his poems, *Diario de un poeta recién-casado*. With his wife he has collaborated in the translation of the works of Rabindranath Tagore.

Arias tristes, 1903, *Jardines lejanos*, 1904, and *Pastorales*, 1911, are

Born 1881

books that show exquisite sensibility. His quality of simplicity is seen in its perfect form and naturalness.

In 1907 Jiménez passes into another phase, he uses the Alexandrine line, his style becomes more complicated, but the keynote persists: "a sigh for some distant enchantment." *Elejías puras, Elejías intermedias* and *Elejías lamentables,* 1907-1908, belong to this epoch.

In his third period, about 1917, the poet is stronger, more profound, his form is free, pure and brief. He employs the exact word. His book *Poesías escojidas,* 1899-1917, was published by the Hispanic Society of New York.

Jiménez lives only for his work. He is constantly changing and revising his poems, bringing out more and more beauties, thus indicating a desire for literary perfection.

His latest books are *La estación total con las Canciones de la nueva luz,* 1923-1936, and *Animal de fondo,* 1949. Jiménez's poetry is growing more and more in importance, making him the most universal of modern Spanish poets.

From notes

150   *No era nadie*

    —No era nadie. El agua.—¿Nadie?
¿Que no es nadie el agua?—No
hay nadie. Es la flor. ¿No hay nadie?
Pero, ¿no es nadie la flor?
    —No hay nadie. Era el viento.—¿Nadie?
¿No es el viento nadie?—No
hay nadie. Ilusión.—¿No hay nadie?
¿Y no es nadie la ilusión?

151   *PRIMAVERA AMARILLA*

    Abril venía, lleno
todo de flores amarillas:
amarillo el arroyo,
amarillo el vallado, la colina,
el cementerio de los niños,
el huerto aquel donde el amor vivía.
    El sol unjía de amarillo el mundo,
con sus luces caídas;
¡ay, por los lirios áureos,
el agua de oro, tibia;
las amarillas mariposas
sobre las rosas amarillas!
    Guirnaldas amarillas escalaban
los árboles; el día
era una gracia perfumada de oro,
en un dorado despertar de vida.
Entre los huesos de los muertos,
abría Dios sus manos amarillas.

There was no one   150

—There was no one. Water.—No one?
And is the water no one?—There
is no one. The flower. Is there no one?
But, the flower, is it no one?
   —There is no one. It was the wind.—No one?
But, the wind, is it no one?—There
is no one. Illusion.—Is there no one?
And is illusion no one?

E. L. T.

YELLOW SPRING   151

April had come, brimful
of yellow flowers:
the rivulet ran yellow
and yellow were the hedgerow and hillside,
the cemetery of the children,
that garden where love used to dwell.
   The sun was anointing the world with yellow
from its dripping sunbeams;
alas, for the golden lilies,
the warm water of gold,
the yellow butterflies fluttering
over the yellow roses!
   Garlands of yellow were entwined
in the trees, and the day
was a blessing perfumed with gold,
in a golden awakening of life.
Midst the bones of the dead,
God was opening his hand full of yellow.

E. L. T.

152   *EL VIAJE DEFINITIVO*

  . . . Y yo me iré. Y se quedarán los pájaros
cantando;
y se quedará mi huerto, con su verde árbol,
y con su pozo blanco.
  Todas las tardes, el cielo será azul y plácido;
y tocarán, como esta tarde están tocando,
las campanas del campanario.
  Se morirán aquellos que me amaron;
y el pueblo se hará nuevo cada año;
y en el rincón aquel de mi huerto florido y encalado,
mi espíritu errará, nostáljico . . .
  Y yo me iré; y estaré solo, sin hogar, sin árbol
verde, sin pozo blanco,
sin cielo azul y plácido . . .
Y se quedarán los pájaros cantando.

153   *AMOR*

  No has muerto, no.
        Renaces,
con las rosas, en cada primavera.
  Como la vida, tienes
tus hojas secas;
tienes tu nieve, como
la vida . . .
      Mas tu tierra,
amor, está sembrada
de profundas promesas,
que han de cumplirse aun en el mismo
olvido.
    ¡En vano es que no quieras!
La brisa dulce torna, un día, al alma;

THE LAST JOURNEY   152

. . . I shall go away. And the birds will stay
still singing;
and my garden will remain, with its tree of green,
and its white well of water.
    Every afternoon the sky will be blue and placid;
and the bells will chime as this afternoon
they are chiming,
the bells of the old belfry.
    And those will die who once did love me;
the town will be made over new each year;
and in that corner of my whitewashed, blossoming garden,
my nostalgic spirit will wander . . .
    I shall go away; I shall be lonely without hearth
            and green tree,
without well of clear water,
without the sky so blue and placid . . .
and the birds will remain still singing.

                                        E. L. T.

LOVE   153

    You have not died, no.
                        You are reborn,
with the roses, each spring.
    Even as life, you have
your withered petals;
you have your snow,
even as life . . .
                    But your soil,
love, is sown with
profound promises,
which shall be redeemed even though
in oblivion.
                    In vain is your not loving.
    The fresh breeze, one day, returns to your soul;

431

una noche de estrellas,
bajas, amor, a los sentidos,
casto como la vez primera.
    ¡Pues eres puro, eres
eterno! A tu prescencia,
vuelven por el azul, en blanco bando,
tiernas palomas que creímos muertas . . .
Abres la sola flor con nuevas hojas . . .
Doras la inmortal luz con lenguas nuevas . . .
    ¡Eres eterno, amor,
como la primavera!

154   *RETORNO FUGAZ*

    ¿Cómo era, Dios mío, cómo era?
—¡Oh corazón falaz, mente indecisa!—
¿Era como el pasaje de la brisa?
¿Como la huída de la primavera?
    Tan leve, tan voluble, tan lijera
cual estival vilano . . . ¡Sí! Imprecisa
como sonrisa que se pierde en risa . . .
¡Vana en el aire, igual que una bandera!
    ¡Bandera, sonreír, vilano, alada
primavera de junio, brisa pura . . .
¡Qué loco fué tu carnaval, qué triste!
    Todo tu cambiar trocóse en nada
—¡memoria, ciega, abeja de amargura!—
¡No sé cómo eras, yo que sé que fuiste!

upon a night of stars,
love, you descend upon the senses,
as chaste as the very first time.
   Since you are pure, you are
eternal! Through the blue,
the tender doves we thought were dead
return to your presence, in flock of white . . .
Your single flower opens with new petals . . .
You gild with new tongues the immortal light . . .
   You are eternal, love,
even as is the spring!

E. L. T.

FLEETING RETURN   154

   What did she resemble, my God, tell me?
—Oh treacherous heart, oh irresolute mind!—
Was she most like the passing of the wind,
or like the flight of spring, my God, tell me?
   As light, as fickle, as fleeting was she
as thistledown of summer . . . Yes, I find
her vague smile within a laugh entwined . . .
a banner waving in air futilely.
   Oh banner, airy thistledown, caress
of smile and breeze, and wingèd flight of spring,
how mad, how sad your carnival, for lo,
   your change was bartered for nothing—oh sting
of memory, blind bee of bitterness!
I know not how you were, but that you were I know.

E. L. T.

VÍSPERA

Ya, en el sol rojo y ópalo del muelle,
entre el viento lloroso de esta tarde
caliente y fresca de entretiempo,
el barco, negro, espera.
　　Aún, esta noche, tornaremos
a lo que ya casi no es nada
—adonde todo va a quedarse
sin nosotros—,
infieles a lo nuestro.
Y el barco, negro, espera.—
　　Decimos: ¡Ya está todo!
Y los ojos se vuelven, tristemente,
buscando no sé qué, que no está con nosotros,
algo que no hemos visto
y que no ha sido nuestro,
¡pero que es nuestro porque pudo serlo! . . . ¡Adiós!
　　¡Adiós! ¡Adiós! ¡Adiós a todas partes, aún sin irnos.
y sin querernos ir y casi yéndonos!
　　. . . Todo se queda con su vida,
que ya se queda sin la nuestra.
¡Adiós, desde mañana!—y ya sin casa—
a ti, y en ti, ignorada tú, a mí mismo,
a ti, que no llegaste a mí, aun cuando corriste,
y a quien no llegué yo, aunque fuí de prisa
—¡qué triste espacio enmedio!—
　　. . . Y lloramos, sentados y sin irnos,
y lloramos, ya lejos, con los ojos mares,
contra el viento y el sol, que luchan, locos.

ON THE EVE OF DEPARTURE *   155

Now in the red and opalescent sun
is waiting the black ship, there at the wharf,
this afternoon between seasons, both warm
and cool, in the sighing wind.
    Tonight we shall return once more
to what is already almost nothing
—where everything is going to remain
without us—
faithless to what is ours.
And the black ship is waiting.
    We say: Now all is ready!
And we turn our eyes sadly,
seeking for something that is not with us,
something we have not seen
and that has not been ours,
but that is ours because it might have been! Farewell!
    Farewell, farewell, to all places, we still not going,
without wishing to go and almost going!
    . . . All remains with its life
that now is without ours.
Farewell, from tomorrow—we already homeless,
to you, and in you, you unknowing, to myself,
to you, who did not reach me even when you were running,
and to whom I did not reach, although I went in haste
—how sad the space between!—
    . . . And we weep, seated there without going,
we weep, already distant, with our eyes like seas,
against the wind and sun that struggle, madly.

                                             E. L. T.

* From New York.

MARES

    Siento que el barco mío
ha tropezado, allá en el fondo,
con algo grande.
                  ¡Y nada
sucede! Nada . . . Quietud . . . Olas . . .
    —¿Nada sucede; o es que ha sucedido todo,
y estamos ya, tranquilos, en lo nuevo?—

NOCTURNO SOÑADO

    La tierra lleva por la tierra;
mas tú, mar,
llevas por el cielo.
    ¡Con qué seguridad de luz de plata y oro,
nos marcan las estrellas
la ruta!—Se diría
que es la tierra el camino
del cuerpo,
que el mar es el camino
del alma—.
    Sí, parece
que es el alma la sola viajera
del mar, que el cuerpo, solo,
se quedó allá en las playas,
sin ella, despidiéndola,
pesado, frío, igual que muerto.
    ¡Qué semejante
el viaje del mar al de la muerte,
al de la eterna vida!

SEAS   156

I feel this barque of mine
has struck against something there in the depths,
something vast.
              And yet nothing
happens! Nothing . . . Quietude . . . Waves . . .
    —Nothing happens; or has all come to pass
and are we now, tranquil, within the new?

E. L. T.

DREAM NOCTURNE   157

The earth leads through the earth;
but you, sea,
lead through heaven.
    With what a steady light of gold and silver
do the stars show us
the way!—One would say
that the earth is the way
of the flesh,
that the sea is the way
of the soul—.
    Yes, it seems
that the soul is the only traveler
of the sea, that the flesh, alone,
remained there on the shore
without her, saying farewell,
heavy and cold, like unto death.
    A voyage on the ocean,
how it resembles the voyage to death,
voyage to life eternal!

E. L. T.

LAS FLORES BAJO EL RAYO

Las flores se dan la mano
y vuelan como los pájaros.
No se van.
(Mas vuelan como los pájaros.)

Tiran, se alzan allá abajo,
bajo el nubarrón del rayo.
No se van.
(Bajo el nubarrón del rayo.)

Llaman con pena y con blanco,
con amarillo y con llanto.
No se van.
(Con amarillo y con llanto.)

Cada trueno con su dardo
les saca un ay, al relámpago.
No se van.
(Les saca un ay, al relámpago.)

Mordido su olor, es tanto
que sangra el olor mojado.
No se van.
(Que sangra su olor mojado.)

Vuelan, pues huyen los pájaros,
por no secarse de espanto.
No se van.
(Por no secarse de espanto.)

Las flores se dan la mano
y gritan como los pájaros.
No se van.
(Mas gritan como los pájaros.)

FLOWERS UNDER THE LIGHTNING 158

The flowers take hold of hands,
they fly as the birds are flying.
They do not go.
(They fly as the birds are flying.)

They pull back, forth, up, down, there,
under the dark cloud of lightning.
They do not go.
(Under the dark cloud of lightning.)

They call with sorrow and whiteness,
they call with yellow and weeping.
They do not go.
(They call with yellow and weeping.)

Each thunder clap with its dart
draws from them a cry with the lightning.
They do not go.
(Comes from them a cry with the lightning.)

Their fragrance is so much bitten,
that the wet perfume is bleeding.
They do not go.
(But their wet perfume is bleeding.)

They fly as the birds are flying,
lest they should wither for fear.
They do not go.
(Lest they should wither for fear.)

The flowers take hold of hands
and cry as the birds are crying.
They do not go.
(But cry as the birds are crying.)

E. L. T.

159   *RENACERÉ YO*

Renaceré yo piedra,
y aún te amaré mujer a ti.

Renaceré yo viento,
y aún te amaré mujer a ti.

Renaceré yo ola,
y aún te amaré mujer a ti.

Renaceré yo fuego,
y aún te amaré mujer a ti.

Renaceré yo hombre,
y aún te amaré mujer a ti.

160   *LUZ TÚ*

Luz vertical,
luz tú;
alta luz tú,
luz oro;
luz vibrante,
luz tú.

Y yo la negra, ciega, sorda, muda sombra horizontal.

WERE I REBORN   159

Were I reborn a stone,
even so I should love you, woman.

Were I reborn as wind,
even so I should love you, woman.

Were I reborn a wave,
even so I should love you, woman.

Were I reborn as fire,
even so I should love you, woman.

Were I reborn a man,
even so I should love you, woman.

E. L. T.

YOU LIGHT   160

Vertical light,
you, light;
golden light, you,
tall light;
vibrating light,
you, light.

And I, the black, the blind, the deaf, the dumb horizontal shadow.

E. L. T.

161   *CRIATURA AFORTUNADA*

Cantando vas, riendo por el agua,
por el aire silbando vas, riendo,
en ronda azul y oro, plata y verde,
dichoso de pasar y repasar
entre el rojo primer brotar de abril,
¡forma distinta, de instantáneas
igualdades de luz, vida, color,
con nosotros, orillas inflamadas!

    ¡Qué alegre eres tú, ser,
con qué alegría universal eterna!
¡Rompes feliz el ondear del aire,
bogas contrario el ondular del agua!
¿No tienes que comer ni que dormir?
¿Toda la primavera es tu lugar?
¿Lo verde todo, lo azul todo,
lo floreciente todo es tuyo?
¡No hay temor en tu gloria:
tu destino es volver, volver, volver,
en ronda plata y verde, azul y oro,
por una eternidad de eternidades!

    Nos das la mano, en un momento
de afinidad posible, de amor súbito,
de concesión radiante;
y, a tu contacto cálido,
en loca vibración de carne y alma,
nos encendemos de armonía,
nos olvidamos, nuevos, de lo mismo,
lucimos, un instante, alegres de oro.
¡Parece que también vamos a ser
perenes como tú,
que vamos a volar del mar al monte,
que vamos a saltar del cielo al mar,
que vamos a volver, volver, volver
por una eternidad de eternidades!
¡Y cantamos, reímos por el aire,
por el agua reímos y silbamos!

FORTUNATE BEING

Singing you go, and laughing through the water,
and through the air you go whistling and laughing,
a round of blue and gold, of green and silver,
so happy passing and repassing ever
amidst the first red blossoming of April,
the distinct form of instantaneous
equalities of light, of life, of color,
with us, kindled like river banks aflame!

What a happy being you are,
with universal and eternal happiness!
Happy, you break through the waves of the air,
you swim contrary to the waves of water!
Do you not have to eat, neither to sleep?
All the springtime, is it yours to enjoy?
All of the green, all of the blue,
the flowering all, is it yours?
There is no fear in your glory;
your fate is to return, return, return,
in rounds of green and silver, blue and gold,
through an eternity of eternities!

You give your hand to us in a moment
of possible affinity, of sudden love,
of radiant concession;
and with your warm contact,
in wild vibration of flesh and of soul,
we are enkindled with sweet harmony,
and we, made new, forget the usual,
we shine for an instant, happy with gold.
It seems that we too are going to be
perennial as you,
that we shall fly from ocean to the mountain,
that we shall leap from heaven to the sea,
and that we shall return, return, return
for an eternity of eternities.
We sing and we laugh through the air,
through the water we laugh and whistle.

¡Pero tú no te tienes que olvidar,
tú eres presencia casual perpetua,
eres la criatura afortunada,
el májico ser solo, el ser insombre,
el adorado por calor y gracia,
el libre, el embriagante robador,
que, en ronda azul y oro, plata y verde,
riendo vas, silbando por el aire,
por el agua cantando vas, riendo!

162   *EN LO MEJOR QUE TENGO*

Mar verde y cielo gris y cielo azul
y albatros amorosos en la ola,
y en todo, el sol, y tú en el sol, mirante
dios deseado y deseante,
alumbrando de oros distintos mi llegada;
la llegada de éste que soy ahora yo,
de éste que ayer mismo yo dudaba
de que pudiera ser en ti como lo soy.

¡Qué trueque de hombre en mí, dios deseante,
de ser dudón en la leyenda
del dios de tantos decidores,
a ser creyente firme
en la historia que yo mismo he creado
desde toda mi vida para ti!

Ahora llego yo a este término
de un año de mi vida natural,
en mi fondo de aire en que te tengo,
encima de este mar, fondo de agua;
este término hermoso cegador
al que me vas entrando tú,
contento de ser tuyo y de ser mío
en lo mejor que tengo, mi espresión.

But you must not forget yourself,
you are the casual, perpetual presence,
you are the fortunate creature,
the only magic being without shadow,
the one adored for warmth and grace,
the free, enraptured robber
that, in rounds of blue and gold, green and silver,
goes laughing, whistling through the air,
through the water singing and laughing!

E. L. T.

THE BEST THAT I HAVE   162

Green sea and grey sky and blue sky
and loving albatross upon the waves,
and in all, the sun, and thou in the sun,
observing desired and desiring god,
lighting with distinct golden rays my arrival;
the arrival of him that I am today,
of him that even yesterday I doubted
he could be in thee as I am.

What a changed man in me, desiring god,
from the being doubting the legend
of the god of the many glib speakers,
to be the firm believer
in the story I myself have created
all through my life for thee.

Now I come to this termination
of a year of my natural life,
in the depths of the air where I keep thee,
above this sea, these depths of water,
to this beautiful, blinding termination,
where thou art gradually entering me,
content to be thine, to be mine,
through the best that I have, my own expression.

E. L. T.

SOBRE UNA NIEVE

(entre un sol y la eternidad)

Ni su esbeltez de peso exacto, tendida aquí, mi mundo,
y como para siempre ya; ni su a veces verde mirar de fuente
ya con agua de sol sólo; ni el descenso sutil de su mejilla
a la callada cavidad oscura de la boca; ni su hombro pulido,
tan rozado ahora de camelia diferente; ni su pelo, de oro
gris un día, luego negro, ya absorbido en valor único; ni
sus manos menudas que tanto trajinaron en todo lo del día y
de la noche, y sobre todo en máquina y en lápiz y en pluma
para mí; ni . . . , me dijeron, por suerte mía:

"Mi encanto decisivo residía, ¡acuérdate tú bien! ¡acuér-
date tú bien!, en algo negativo que yo de mí tenía; como un
aura de sombra que exhalara luces de un gris, sonidos de un
silencio (y que ahora será de la armonía eterna), incógnita
fatal de una belleza libertada; residente, sin duda, mas vi-
sible, quizás, en los eclipses."

Por mi suerte, quedó la eternidad para más tarde; y ella
salió, como depués me dijo, por la otra boca del pensado túnel:
y vió salir también el rojo sol sobre la nieve.

ABOVE A SNOW   163

(between a sun and eternity)

Not even her slenderness of perfect weight, lying here,
my world, and as forever now; not even her sometimes green
glance, a fountain all water of sun; not even the subtle tilt of
her cheek down to the still, dark cavity of her mouth; not
even her polished shoulder now so lightly touched by the
unlike camelia; not even her hair, grey gold one day, then
black, now absorbed into unmatched color; not even her small
hands that busied themselves with all the things of the day
and night, above all on the typewriter and with pencil and pen
for me; not even . . . , they told me, for my good fortune:

" My final fascination, oh, remember, remember well! was
lodged in something negative of myself, that I had; as an
air of shadow that would exhale light out of a grey, sounds
out of a silence (and that now will be part of the eternal
harmony), the fatal unknown of a liberated beauty; tenant,
without doubt, more visible, perhaps, in eclipses."

For my good fortune, eternity was left for later; and she
came out, as she told me afterwards, by the other mouth of
the imagined tunnel; and she also saw the red sun rise above the snow.

E. L. T.

SPANISH TEXTS

Mozarabic Songs—Nos. 1, 2, 3, 4, Dámaso Alonso in *Revista de Filología española*, 1949, vol. 33; no. 5, Gerald Brenan, *The Literature of the Spanish People*, Cambridge, 1951.

The Lay of the Cid—*Poema de mio Cid*, R. Menéndez Pidal, ed., *Clásicos castellanos*, 1951.

Gonzalo de Berceo—Nos. 12, 13, A. G. Solalinde, ed., *Clásicos castellanos*; no. 14, *Biblioteca de Autores Españolas*, vol. 57.

Juan Ruiz, Arcipreste de Hita—*Libro de buen amor*, J. Ducamin, ed. Toulouse, 1901.

Marqués de Santillana—*Poesía de la Edad Media*, D. Alonso, ed., Losada, Buenos Aires, 1942.

Jorge Manrique—*ibid*.

Ancient Ballads—Nos. 24, 25, 27, 28, 29, 30, 32, 33, 34, *Flor nueva de romances viejos*, R. Menéndez Pidal, ed.; nos. 26, 31, 35, 36, *Romancero general*, A. Durán, ed., B A E, vols. 10 and 16.

Songs of Traditional Type—All from *Poesía de la Edad Media*, D. Alonso, ed., Losada, Buenos Aires, 1942, except no. 47, *Romancero general*, A. Durán, ed., B A E, vol. 16, and nos. 48 and 49, *Cancionero musical de los siglos XV y XVI*, F. A. Barbiere, ed.

Gil Vicente—*Poesía de la Edad Media*, D. Alonso, ed., Losada, Buenos Aires, 1942.

Garcilaso de la Vega—Tomás Navarro, ed., *Clásicos castellanos*.

Fray Luis de León—*The Oxford Book of Spanish Verse*, J. Fitzmaurice-Kelly, ed., 1932.

San Juan de la Cruz—*Obras de San Juan de la Cruz*, P. Silverio de Santa Teresa, C. D., ed., Burgos, 1929-1931.

Fernando de Herrera—Nos. 73, 76, 78, Vicente García de Diego, ed., *Clásicos castellanos*; nos. 74, 75, 77, *Versos de Fernando de Herrera*, Sevilla, 1619.

Anonymous Sonnet, To Christ Crucified—*The Oxford Book of Spanish Verse*, J. Fitzmaurice-Kelly, ed., 1932.

Later Poems from the Cancioneros—Nos. 80, 81, 82, 83, *Cancionero y Romancero*, A. Durán, ed.; no. 84, *Primavera y flor de los mejores romances*, Juan de la Cuesta, ed., Madrid, 1623, fol. 138 Vº.

Andrés Fernández de Andrada—*Las cien mejores poesías*, M. Menéndez y Pelayo, ed., 1919.

Luis de Góngora—Nos. 86, 87, 88, 89, *Las Soledades*, D. Alonso, ed., Cruz y Raya, Madrid, 1936; nos. 90, 91, 92, 93, 94, *Obras completas*, Juan y Isabel Giménez, eds., M. Aguilar, Madrid.

Lope de Vega—Nos. 95, 96, 97, 98, 99, *Poesías liricas*, J. F. Montesinos, ed., *Clásicos castellanos*; no. 100, B A E, vol. 38.

Francisco de Quevedo—*Obras completas, verso*, Luis Astrana Marín, ed., Madrid, 1932.

Calderón de la Barca—Nos. 107, 109, 110, 111, B A E, vol. 17; no. 108, Gerald Brenan, *The Literature of the Spanish People*, Cambridge, 1951.

Juan Meléndez Valdés—No. 112, P. Salinas, ed., *Clásicos castellanos*; nos. 113, 114, 115, L. A. Cueto, ed., B A E, vol. 66.

José de Espronceda—J. Moreno Villa, ed., *Clásicos castellanos*.
Gustavo Adolfo Bécquer—*Rimas*, first edition, 1870.
Miguel de Unamuno—*Antología poética*, L. F. Vivanco, ed., Madrid, 1942.
Antonio Machado—*Poesías completas* (1899-1936), Buenos Aires, 1946.
Juan Ramón Jiménez—Nos. 150, 151, 152, 153, 154, 155, 156, 157, *Segunda antolojía poética*, Madrid, 1952; nos. 158, 159, 160, 161, *Estación total con las canciones de la nueva luz* (1923-1936), Losada, Buenos Aires, 1946; no. 162, *Animal de fondo*, Pleamar, Buenos Aires, 1949; no. 163, *Insula*, Jan. 15, 1953.

In the transcription of the Spanish texts, the following criterion has been used: for those texts dating from 1500 the modern spelling has been employed. What would be most important, namely the distinction between *c* and *z*, between *x* and *j*, between *s* and *ss*, was soon to fall into disuse; the process must have been already far advanced, at least in some regions, in the sixteenth century and complete in the seventeenth century. On the other hand, nothing would be gained by immortalizing the spelling of mere copyists or printers.

In the case of Herrera, it has seemed fitting not to oppose the definite wish of the writer. We have used the texts taken from *Obras de Fernando de Herrera* printed in 1582 in Seville, during the poet's life, and the posthumous edition, *Versos de Fernando de Herrera*, Seville, 1619. The spelling is basically the same as that used by Herrera, except for slight differences.

In the mediaeval texts, the spelling of sources cited has been kept, save for the following exceptions, universally accepted today, when works are not intended to be strictly scientific: every *v* with the value of a vowel is written *u*; every *u* with the value of a consonant is written *v*; every *y* and *j* with value of *i* is written *i*. For the accents and punctuation, modern usage is followed.

INDEX OF TRANSLATORS

451